CONTEMPORARY ABORIGINAL & TORRES STRAIT ISLANDER ART

Now Days - Early Days

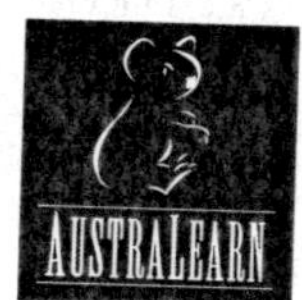

CONTEMPORARY ABORIGINAL & TORRES STRAIT ISLANDER ART

Now Days - Early Days

Art Works and Legends

Editor

Anna Eglitis

Associate Editors

Arone Meeks & Ken Thaiday

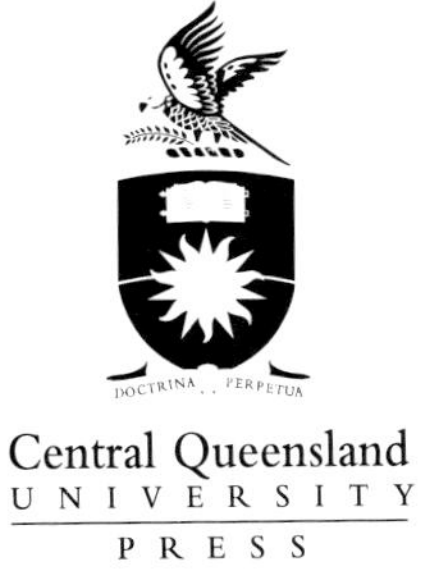

Central Queensland
UNIVERSITY
PRESS

First published in 2000 by
Central Queensland University Press
PO Box 1615
Rockhampton
Queensland 4700

Phone: 07 4922 8144
Fax: 07 4922 8151
email: d.myers@cqu.edu.au
web: www.outbackbooks.com

National Library of Australia
Cataloguing-in-Publication entry:

Contemporary Aboriginal and Torres Strait Islander Art
Now Days - Early Days
Art Works and Legends

1. Aborigines, Australian - Queensland, Northern - Painting.
2. Painting, Torres Strait Islander - Queensland, Northern
3. Painting, Australian - Queensland, Northern - Aboriginal artists
4. Aborigines, Australian - Queensland, Northern - Legends
   I. Eglitis, Anna. II. Meeks, Arone Raymond. III. Thaiday, Ken

759.9943

ISBN: 1 875998 72 1 (h/cover)
ISBN: 1 875998 33 0 (pbk)

CQU Press Client Liaison, Sheila McCarthy.

Typeset in Minion by Ampersand Design

Printed and bound by Watson Ferguson & Co, Moorooka, Brisbane.

Front cover painting *Shark Dancer* by Anne Abednego Gela.

Back cover painting *In Search of...* by Zane Saunders.

ACKNOWLEDGEMENTS

This project, to celebrate the work of our artists, has been made possible by the support and friendship of many people over the last seventeen years. During this period of time the Aboriginal and Torres Strait Islander Arts Course has grown from humble beginnings to a nationally recognised course of excellence at the Tropical North Queensland Institute of TAFE. The publication of the book has been made possible through generous funding from Arts Queensland through the Commonwealth Regional Arts Fund, the Cairns City Council, the Cairns TAFE and Central Queensland University Press.

I would like to thank all the artists whose works appear in *Now Days - Early Days*, for their interest and co-operation in providing artworks to be photographed for the book, for biographical material and also the background stories that inspired their chosen artwork.

In several instances the artworks chosen for the book were in touring exhibitions or state collections. Thanks go to the following lending institutions for supplying photographs of these artworks:

National Museum of Australia, Canberra, National Gallery of Victoria, Melbourne, Perc Tucker Regional Gallery, Townsville, Cairns Regional Gallery, Cairns, Centre Culturel Jean-Marie Tjibaou, Noumea.

From the "Early Days", the list of people who supported and helped the course to grow is too numerous to mention everybody here. They know who they are. Special recognition must go to Joe and Betty Morgan, Enoch Tranby, Jenny Martens, Thancoupie, James Last, Tom Vudrag, Garry Andrews, Rod Delaforce, Don and Judy Freeman, Merv Ahkee, Dulcie Watling, John Conroy, the late Mick Miller, Terry O'Shane, Fr. Jim Leftwich, Sue and Ed Barstow, David and Cindy Hudson, Colin Skerrit, Des Egan, Ruth Lipscombe, Val Schier, Pat Mortensen, Robert Reid, Percy Trezise, A.M., Matt and Stephen Trezise, Darryl & Diane Hook.

The first graduates who gained what was then an Associate Diploma after two years of study were Lillian Christian, Shirley Chistian, Ursula Morgan, Peter Dabah, Tina Klaus, Elaine Lampton Burroughs and Francis Newbury. Thanks go to not only these successful students but also to the many others who joined the course from the beginning but had to leave for many different reasons, such as family or health problems, but who shared the workload of those early days. The ongoing success of the course rests firmly on their shoulders.

Through the exhibition held at the Ben Grady Gallery , Canberra in 1986 came the first important recognition of what was happening in Cairns. James Mollison, then Director of the Australian National Gallery, authorised the purchase of prints and paintings for the national collection. Wally Caruana , Senior Curator Aboriginal and Torres Strait Islander Art and Roger Butler, Senior Curator Prints, Posters and Illustrated Books - Australian Art have consistently continued to purchase from our artists since that time. We greatly value their friendship and support.

Thanks to Judith Ryan, Senior Curator in the Department of Aboriginal and Torres Strait Islander Art at the National Gallery of Victoria for her acquisitions for the Gallery over the years, including the eight batiks which form part of the important "Raiki Wara Long Cloth from Aboriginal Australia and the Torres Strait" exhibition which is at present touring nationally. Thanks to Doug Hall, Director, Queensland Art Gallery, Brisbane for support and encouragement when visiting Cairns and for purchases made from our artists for the state collection. Thanks to the organisers of the "Ageless Art" exhibition curated by Judith Bartlett at the Queensland Museum in 1988 for the invitation for our artists to be represented, and a further invitation to exhibit in "You Came to my Country and You Didn't Turn Black" in 1990.

Thanks to Cameron and Linda McTavish for presenting our artists works at the Gallery of the Australian Landscape, Brisbane and for welcoming all the group to stay in their home.

Thanks to Jennifer Isaac for recognising the strength of the artist's images so early on and including eight of our students in her book "Aboriginality - Contemporary Aboriginal Paintings and Prints" published in 1989. Further thanks to Jennifer and Dr. Jean Battersby who secured a commission for our artists at the Brisbane International Airport and purchased work for the Telstra collection several years later.

Thanks to the Kamsler Family, the Pacific International Hotel, Cairns who hosted the annual art exhibition at the end of those early years, providing a high profile venue in the huge ballroom on the first floor.

Thanks to Gabrielle Pizzi, Gallery Gabrielle Pizzi, Melbourne; Ace Bourke at the Hogarth Galleries, Sydney; Ruth Evatt at the Aboriginal and Tribal Art Centre, Sydney; Adrian Newstead at Coo-ee Aboriginal Art Gallery, Sydney; The Director and Staff, Studio One, Canberra; Michael Eather, Fireworks Gallery, Brisbane.

Thanks also to former Prime Minister of Australia, Bob Hawke, who met with a group of students and myself from the TAFE college. Following discussions and after seeing the work that the students had completed, Mr Hawke promised to allocate funding towards the building of the new facility for the Arts course.

From the "Now Days" there are many people to mention.

Thanks to Wendy Ludwig, Head of the Faculty of Aboriginal and Torres Strait Islander Studies at the Cairns TAFE, Elinor Boyd the course Program Manager, Keith Tardent our Administrative Officer and to all the dedicated staff at the ATSI unit. Thanks to the Elders Thancoupie, Tommy George, Henry Fourmile, Enoch Tranby and Barclay Miller, the late George Moynahan and to the Yidinji Peoples and Yirrganydji Peoples, the Traditional Owners of the region.

Thanks to Jenuarrie, Far North Queensland Industry Development Consultant for Aboriginal and Torres Strait Islander Art: Bama Ngappi Ngappi Association, Yarrabah; Tom Mosby, Conservator of Aboriginal and Ethnographic Art, National Gallery of Victoria; Peter Kartsounis, RMIT, Melbourne; Ernest Kinsey, Indigenous Education Officer, Swinburne University, Melbourne; Avril Quail, National Gallery of Australia, Canberra; Mary Bani, National Museum of Australia, Canberra; The Director, Alice-Anne Boylan and Staff, Cairns Regional Gallery: Ellen Jose, Ray Crook, Eve Stafford, Jorg Smeisser, Theo Tremblay, Basil Hall, Michael and Jane Tuffery, Sheila Sparks: Janelle Trezise, Ray Sambo: Billy Gordon, Jeannie Bell, Sharon Pacey, Eric Oates, Alan Oldfield, Chris Watson, Margie West, Barbara Adams, Lionel and Val Daniels, Nancy Bamaga, Susan Cochrane, Brenda Croft, Kerry Grierson, Lesley Everley, Yvonne Duncan, Esther Bong (31/07/51-06/01/00) and family, Ian and Ann Horn, Ursula Frederick, Bishop James Foley and Lotus Glen Correctional Center Education Officer Rowan Partridge.

Thanks to the local Cairns media: *The Cairns Post; Barfly, Bama Bippera. ABC Radio* and Local Television stations.

Thanks to Doug Drummond for the superb photographs of the artworks, and to my Associate Editors, Arone Meeks and Ken Thaiday Snr, for their care to ensure the cultural integrity of the images and text.

FOREWORD

Here, in vibrant colour, are the works of seventy Aboriginal and Torres Strait Islander artists. All are graduates of the Visual Arts program at the Tropical North Queensland Institute of TAFE in Cairns. The Principal Teacher of the program, Anna Eglitis, has been instrumental in putting together this important collection of images and legends to showcase contemporary Queensland Aboriginal and Torres Strait Islander culture.

The book is titled *Now Days - Early Days* evoking a sense of the past and the present, ancient custom and contemporary practice, traditional materials and urban artefacts. Here lie sedimentary layers of stories; rituals and memories interspersed with twenty-first century commerce and technologies. Here, Aboriginal Torres Strait Islander artists express their culture and traditions in terms of their own daily experiences.

However, the title also prompts another reading. It suggests that the *Now Days* are the *Early Days* in a revival of Aboriginal and Torres Strait Islander Arts practice. For too long, Indigenous art has been stereotyped as ochre dots on bark panels. These artists show us the vivid colours of North Queensland with dugong, jabiru, sea turtles and fish. Strong, confident and boldly forging a new tradition in Aboriginal and Torres Strait Islander art, these paintings, batiks and sculptures are inventive and pioneering. It is, indeed, *Early Days* in this economic and social genesis of Aboriginal and Torres Strait Islander arts.

I offer my congratulations to all involved in this project. The book was published by Central Queensland University Press with funding from Arts Queensland and the Commonwealth Government's Regional Arts Fund. It is a significant marker of the growing vigour and prosperity of the Aboriginal and Torres Strait Islander arts industry in Queensland.

Matt Foley

The Honourable Matt Foley

ATTORNEY-GENERAL AND MINISTER FOR JUSTICE AND MINISTER FOR THE ARTS

Contemporary Aboriginal and Torres Strait Islander Art

Editor: Anna Eglitis

Associate Editors: Arone Meeks, Ken Thaiday

Central Queensland University Press acknowledges the generous support of Arts Queensland and the Regional Arts Fund. The Regional Arts Fund is a Commonwealth Government Initiative through the Australia Council, its arts funding and advisory body.

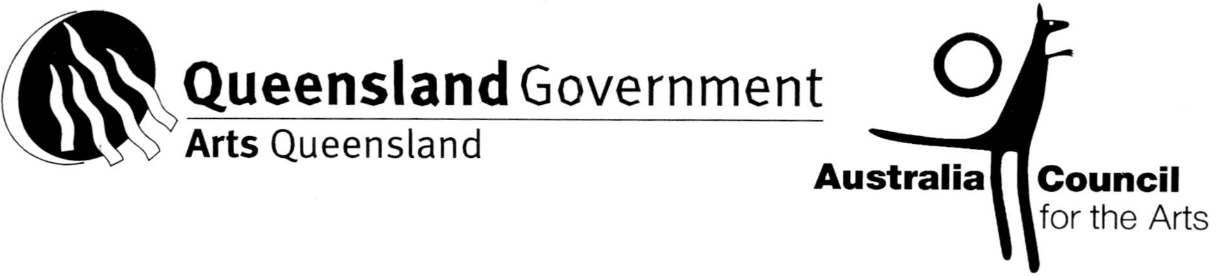

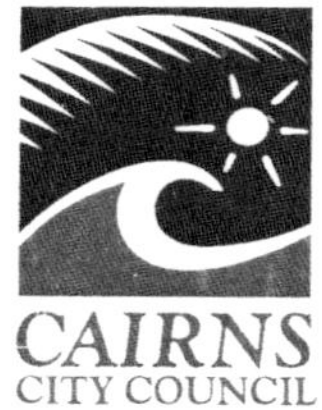

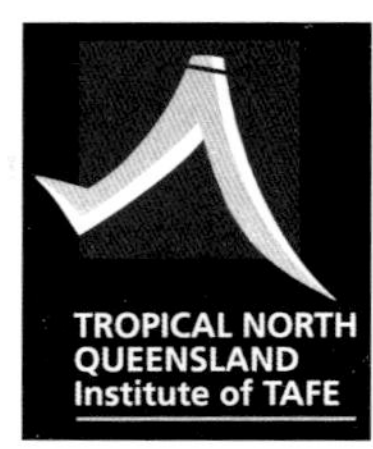

INTRODUCTION

Now Days - Early Days celebrates the achievements of Aboriginal and Torres Strait Islander artists who have studied visual art at the Tropical North Queensland Institute of TAFE since 1984.

Today the Visual Arts Course classes are conducted in a dedicated building which was officially opened on November 9th, 1998. The building is called the Banggu Minjaany Arts and Cultural Centre, and boasts a small art gallery, air-conditioned lecture rooms, studios, and spacious staff and student work areas. Banggu Minjaany in the Yidinji language means "The place which keeps and shares knowledge". Also incorporated in this new building is a performing arts theatre and amphitheatre, where the first music course offered in Cairns to Aboriginal and Torres Strait Islander students is now in its fourth successful year.

It was not always so comfortable for the Visual Arts students.

Early art classes in 1983 were held in a Cairns Aboriginal artefacts and craft shop run by Betty and Joe Morgan. They were first conducted by Aboriginal Elder Enoch Tranby.

Funding was received through Australia Catholic Relief, and with the money to purchase art material classes began under the old Cathedral at St. Monica's in Cairns. In this first group of students were Shirley and Lillian Christian, Tina Williams, Jenny Martens, Betty Morgan, and Mr and Mrs Ray Tooth.

At this time Betty Morgan and Jenny Martens met Tom Vudrag, a batik artist who had been studying in Indonesia with the internationally renowned Saad Suyachmir. They immediately realised how their group would benefit by learning this new technique and Tom was invited to teach with them. From this invitation came the first move to gain the support of the Cairns TAFE College when Tom met the (then) Senior Technical Teacher of Aboriginal Studies, James Last. When ongoing funding applied for by the Morgans was not granted, Tom approached James Last, who advised Tom to set up a course which could be funded under the college extensions program. This led to a small group of students being enrolled at TAFE, and a working space on campus was allocated.

Here I quote Mabel Edmund, A.M. from an article in *Artlink*, Vol 10, Nos 1 & 2.

"The first year classes began(in 1984)they were held in a small shed in the TAFE College grounds. Most of the classes were held outside on the grass, they had no reticulated water supply and had to carry all the water in buckets to do their batiks and wash their screens after doing screenprinting. Eventually they were given a long hose and there was no more need to carry water.

During the wet season, and it gets wet in Cairns, the old shed used to flood and everything would be wet, mouldy and smelly. Enough to turn any artist off their work!

If they weren't working in ankle deep mud, they were working in the blistering sun. With their determination to make a success of their Art Centre, and with the support of their teachers Tom Vudrag, Garry Andrews, Anna Eglitis and Thancoupie, they put up with all the inconveniences and frustrations and laid the foundation for what is today a very successful Arts College for Aboriginal and Torres Strait Islander students."

In reaction to these conditions the students mounted an exhibition in April of the first year, seeking funding for better facilities. Representatives from the Department of Employment and Industrial Relations were so impressed by the work achieved in such a short time that funding was granted to buy equipment, assist a new and more ambitious course to be planned and, as there was no space available on the TAFE Campus at that time, to pay rent on an off campus venue. Such a venue was found - the old Hanush Cordial Factory in Draper Street, in the middle of Cairns.

To continue Mabel Edmund's story from the *Artlink* article:

"In 1985, the year that I began classes at the Art Centre, they had moved from the shed to the top floor of an ex-soft drink factory, a rambling amalgamation of converted classrooms, studios, open-air patios, leaking plumbing and makeshift conveniences.

It had an environment of space, light and friendly confidence. The students were more relaxed and casual and it seemed to have an air of positive achievement.

Prior to classes starting that year, the original group of students (seven continued into the second year) gave up a lot of their vacation time to build benches and tables from old scrap timber that was stored in the building. They also painted some of the rooms and made the place more habitable."

In 1989, the Visual Arts Course, now accredited to Associate Diploma level, was re-located back to the Cairns TAFE campus. We moved into three demountables and a large machinery shed was erected in which to hold the batik and silkscreen classes. These techniques required room for dye tanks, hot waxing areas and long tables for silkscreen fabric printing.

By this time the artwork being produced by the Cairns group was gaining national recognition. Locally the annual exhibition was held at the end of each year at the Pacific International Hotel, and well received by both the local community and the growing numbers of tourists coming into Cairns.

Exhibitions at the Ben Grady Gallery in Canberra, the Gallery Gabrielle Pizzi in Melbourne, the Hogarth Galleries in Sydney, and the Fireworks Gallery, and Queensland Aboriginal Creations Gallery in Brisbane exposed the new contemporary school of art that was emerging in Cairns, to an ever-widening audience.

Paintings, prints, fabrics and ceramic pieces were being purchased for important collections and State Galleries, commissions were being offered to graduates. Murals, such as the ones featured in this book were being painted every year in the local State Schools during the NAIDOC Week celebrations by the students and the reputation of the artists continued to grow. Graduates were going on to further study in the arts and education. A third year was added to the existing Cairns Visual Arts Course offering an Advanced Diploma at the end of three years study.

Cairns Regional Gallery became a reality for the city at last in July 1995. In September that year the exhibition which inspired the name for this volume *Now Days - Early Days* opened in the Loft Gallery. This show featured four graduate artists from the TAFE Arts course and the sell-out exhibition saw their paintings and prints going all over the world through the exposure offered to overseas visitors in the prestigious Regional Gallery.

Each year since then an annual exhibition has been presented by the graduating group at the Regional Gallery. The gallery in the new Art and Cultural Centre is now used to present the final 1st year students work. Through these avenues the diverse and exciting ideas of the artists can be seen each year by the art lovers of the region and visitors from interstate and overseas.

Now Days - Early Days, the book, will find an even larger audience and it will become apparent that individual vision is encouraged for all artists who study with the course in Cairns while at all times they are encouraged to retain their links with their own heritage.

We sadly missed Tom Vudrag when he left Cairns in 1986. I became course coordinator, inheriting all the nightmares of bureaucracy and mountains of paperwork, when all I wanted to do was teach drawing and painting. Every day, every year, was filled with excitement and wonder as the students explored new ideas and new art techniques with which to express those ideas.

For myself and all the different staff who have worked over the years with the Visual Arts Course, it has been a privilege to watch each student experiencing life, growing in years, searching for a place in this contemporary world through their art, telling their stories.

Anna Eglitis

THE EDITORS
OF
CONTEMPORARY ABORIGINAL & TORRES STRAIT ISLANDER ART

Now Days - Early Days

Anna Eglitis
has been a Lecturer in art with the Aboriginal and Torres Strait Islander Visual Arts Course since 1984. Over the last sixteen years with the students at the Tropical North Queensland Institute of TAFE she has seen the artists seeking to rediscover their culture through their art, talking with the elders to find links with the old days, writing books, making important art statements, slowly gaining recognition for what they had to offer to the contemporary art world. This book is her tribute to these very fine young and not so young artists.

Arone Meeks,
an artist whose images have so enriched Aboriginal contemporary art, has worked as Associate Editor to ensure the cultural integrity of the artworks reproduced in Now Days - Early Days by the Aboriginal students and graduates. Arone is a founding member of the Boomalli Artists Co-operative, which was started in Sydney to provide a marketing outlet for urban Aboriginal artists. He has travelled widely in New Zealand and North America to study indigenous cultures, and also to New York, London, Paris and India. He now resides in Cairns. Arone's works are in important collections in Australia and overseas.

Ken Thaiday, Senior
grew up on Darnley Island in the Torres Strait where the living skills of art and dance formed part of everyday life. He states: "During my period as a dancer I also took on the role of designer of dancing equipment. Each piece of work I do is related to my culture and has cultural significance." Ken's father, Tat Thaiday, was a composer of song and dance and was Chairman of Darnley Island Community for many years. Ken has acted as cultural adviser for the artworks by the Torres Strait Islander students and graduates that are reproduced in Now Days - Early Days. Ken's Islander dance artefacts are in museum and gallery collections worldwide.

Central Queensland University Press
PO Box 1615
Rockhampton

CONTENTS

This book is dedicated to the memory of Jacob Mene, Mundabaree (Jennifer Green), Derwent Riley, Gavin Patterson, Albie Geia, Bonny-Jo Tait, Dennis Coburn, and Shirley Christian, students who generously shared their history, their stories, their talents.
Always remembered.

THE BROLGAS AND THE ANIMALS

CAIRNS NORTH STATE PRIMARY SCHOOL MURAL

BRIAN ROBINSON, SHAUN KALK EDWARDS, THOMAS BOSEN

Long ago, in the Dreamtime, a group of tribal Aboriginal people lived next to the sea on Cape York. These people were not only the best dancers, and hunters and gatherers in the Dreamtime, but they also possessed special powers. These powers were handed down to them from their tribal Chief, the most powerful of all.

The Chief and his wife had a son and a daughter. These two children grew to become skilful hunters and two of the best dancers of the Dreamtime. They danced all the time with the tribal clan, joining them in all the ceremonies (Men's business, and Women's business). The tribe were trade partners with different Clan groups, and sometimes traded items with Torres Strait Islanders. The Islanders were extremely impressed by the talents of the Chief's son and daughter, and gave the Chief a great canoe as a present for his tribe.

When the children reached adulthood, the Chief decreed that they would marry another couple from a distant tribe. However, the son and daughter were not at all happy with this arrangement and decided to run away. They waited until night when all of their people would be at a corroboree. They then put on their tribal body paint and joined in the corroboree. During the night ,when no one was watching, they stole away into the distant darkness.

In the morning, the Chief and his wife found that the couple were missing and sent out a large search party to look for them. The son and daughter knew that if they were still in human form the tribe would quickly track them down, so using their special powers they changed into two beautiful dancing brolgas still wearing tribal body paint. When the search party could find no human tracks, the tribe realised that the couple had changed into some animal form. The Chief and his wife were very sad. They held a big meeting with the tribe where they told the tribe that in their human forms they had no chance of finding their children.

The mother said "I will change into a sea eagle so that I can fly high above and look for our beloved children." Having said that, she changed into a great white-headed eagle.

The Chief then took on the form of a powerful sand goanna, and said to his wife " I too will be by the seaside, and I will climb the tall trees looking for our beloved children."

So the people of the tribe, having seen and heard this, decided to change into many different animal forms, to help continue the search. They were also still wearing their tribal body paint.

Today, whenever you see the beautiful dancing brolgas, you can see the body paint on them. The sand goanna still has his yellow body paint, and the sea eagle is distinguished by its white head and brown body paint. All the different animals who were originally tribal people have their special markings. They eventually went their different ways, some staying by the seaside, and others going inland to live in the swamps and scrubland.

The beautiful dancing brolgas can be seen to this day dancing their Dreamtime dance on the salt pans or swamp edges.

Text supplied by Thomas Bosen

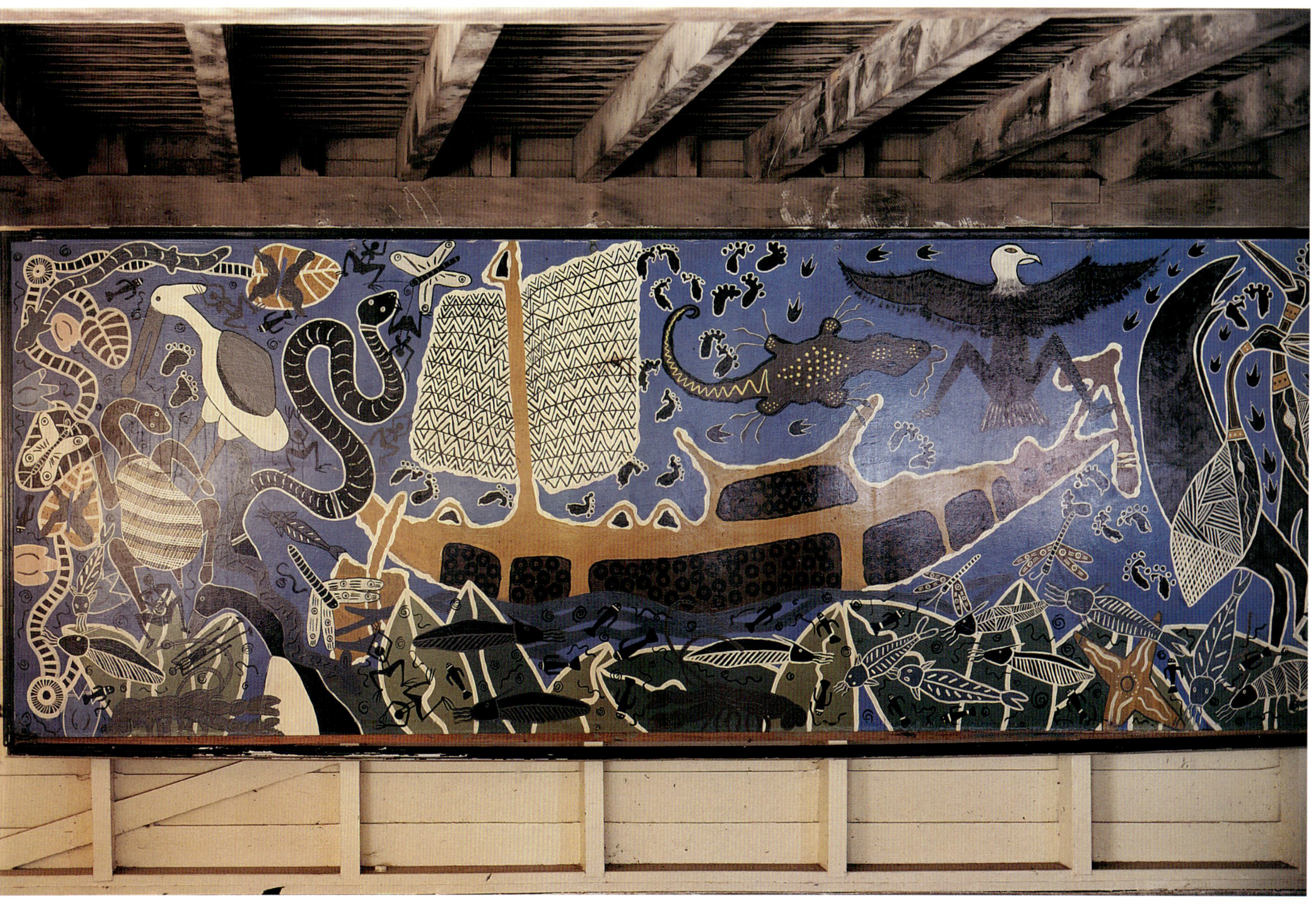

Brian Robinson, Shaun Kalk Edwards, Thomas Bosen
THE BROLGAS AND THE ANIMALS
CAIRNS NORTH STATE PRIMARY SCHOOL MURAL

ARTEFACTS OF THE TORRES STRAIT
BEFORE THE LONDON MISSIONARY SOCIETY'S ARRIVAL

RICARDO IDAGI

1998
Acrylic, Crayon, and gouache on Paper
56 x 76cm
Collection of the Cairns Regional Gallery

The objects depicted in the painting are artefacts of the Torres Strait people which were in use before contact with the missionaries. These are reproduced by Lindsay Wilson in *Emeret Lu*: and were the inspiration for Ricardo's work. The artefacts represented are:

(i)the two masks, *le op*, which evoke death and mourning; (ii) two head-dresses, *daris*, which are symbols of dance; and (iii) three charms called *madub* or *doiom*. One is a tobacco charm which protects tobacco crops and ensures a good harvest; tobacco being an important item used in the maintenance of social relationships. Another is a rain charm, which ensures fine weather for hunting and plentiful garden produce. There is also a turtle charm, which represents the spirit of successful hunting.

Past Times
In former times, everyday life was governed by magic and sorcery. The charms were used to bring good luck, and to grant your desires (such as a successful fishing trip or a plentiful harvest). They were even used to invoke fine weather.

Idagi chose the *le op* masks to signal mourning and death, and the *daris* as symbols of happiness and celebration through dance.

The mask images were used in death ceremonies throughout the Torres Strait. When death occurred, the deceased was disembowelled, embalmed in various oils and laid on a bamboo bench (*takar*). A small fire would be lit to slowly cure the body for mummification. Depending on the status of the deceased, the head would also be embalmed and decorated. This process took months, during which time family members would gather to console each other. Garden produce would be shared and hunting parties would be organised to support the grieving family during the mourning period. Mourning ceremonies were often held at night, when the masks would be worn during ceremonial dances. When mummification was complete, a large celebration consisting of dancing and feasting would take place. On such occasions, the *daris* would be worn. After the celebration, the corpse would be returned and placed in the family house. It was believed that its spirit would live on and protect the family.

Present Times
With the arrival of the London Missionary Society, this practice was banned, and replaced with Christian funerals and church services. Although the people do not produce and worship the charms any more, the concept is still evident in a practice called *ailan kastam*. For example, families still gather together to mourn the deceased, and the mourning period is still lengthy. Families still work to contribute goods and monies to the grieving family during this time. The culmination of the mourning period is now on the day of the tombstone opening, after which a large celebration still takes place. The tombstone is ceremoniously unveiled to signal the deceased is now resting properly in his home.

Reproduced courtesy of Cairns Regional Gallery, Cairns.
Photography: David Campbell

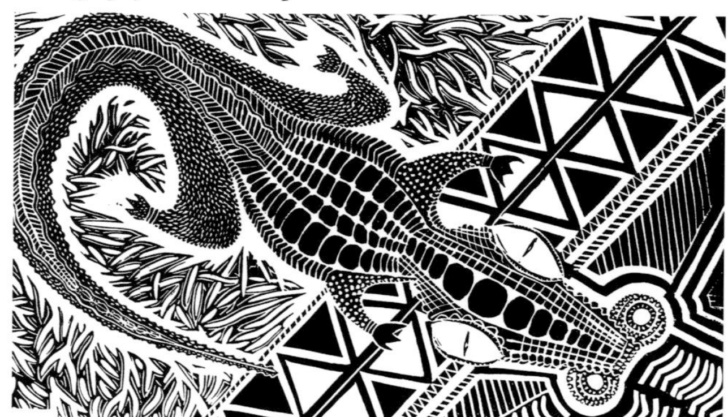

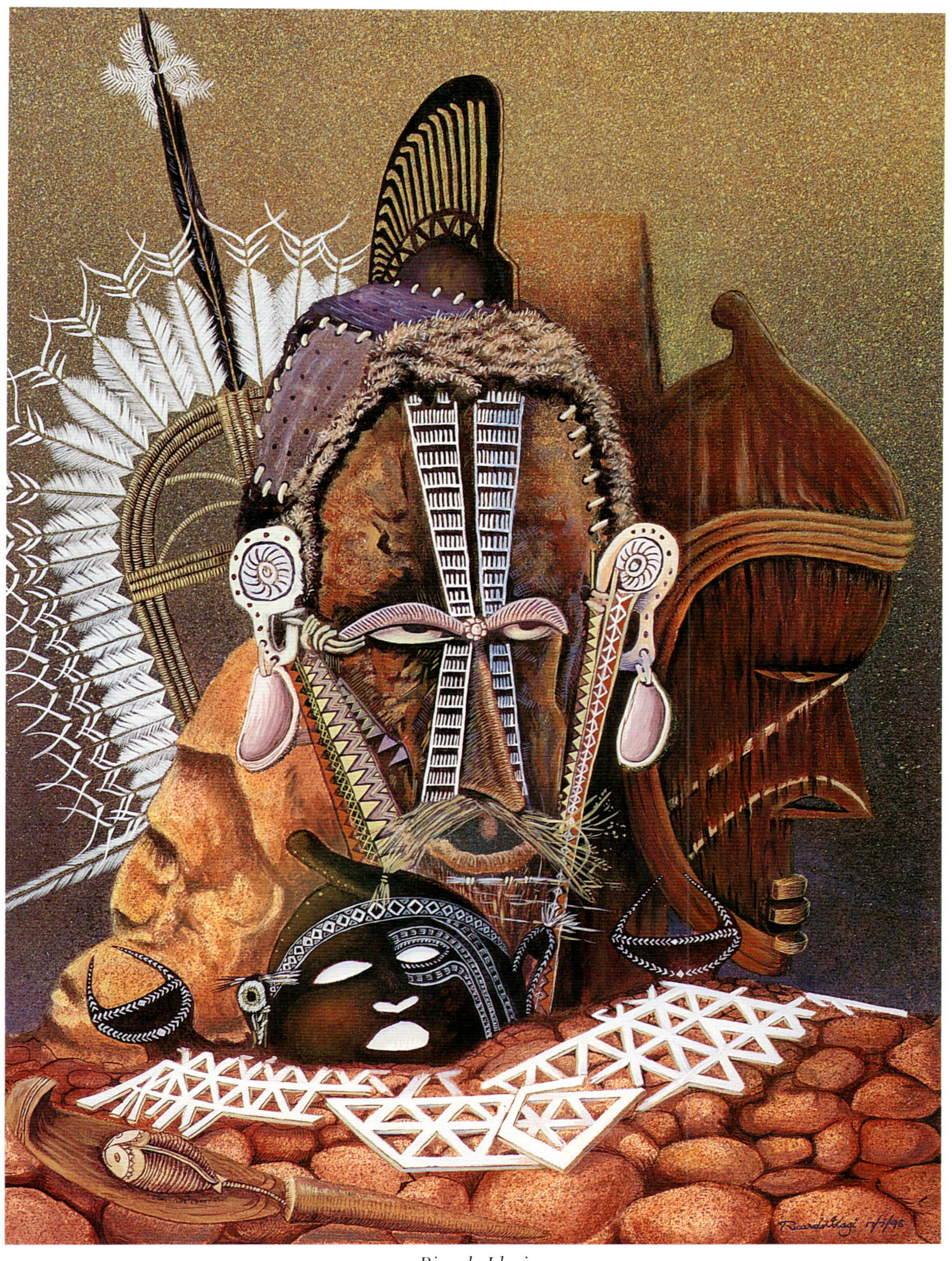

Ricardo Idagi
ARTEFACTS OF THE TORRES STRAIT
BEFORE THE LONDON MISSIONARY SOCIETY'S ARRIVAL

YIRRGANYDJI DREAMING

Patricia Singleton

1998/99
Acrylic on Canvas
133cm x 195cm

This painting relates to the time of creation. The Rainbow Serpent is creating and transforming colour to give to the sea life and the surrounding land.

The barramundi, crab, stingray, turtle, and dugong played an important part in the cultural lifestyle of the Yirrganydji.

Most sea-creatures were a part of the people's diet and remain a food source for Yirrganydji peoples.

The harvest times were connected to different seasons of the year; therefore, with every harvest there was a cycle that prevented the over-fishing of each food source.

Every activity had its own purpose. The oil of the dugong was used for medicinal purposes, and there was the belief that the tears of the dugong brought good luck to the people.

The Yirrganydji Dreaming began in the waters off Double Island near Cairns, North Queensland. The tail of the serpent is today recognised as Scout Island, near Double Island.

Courtesy of the artist.

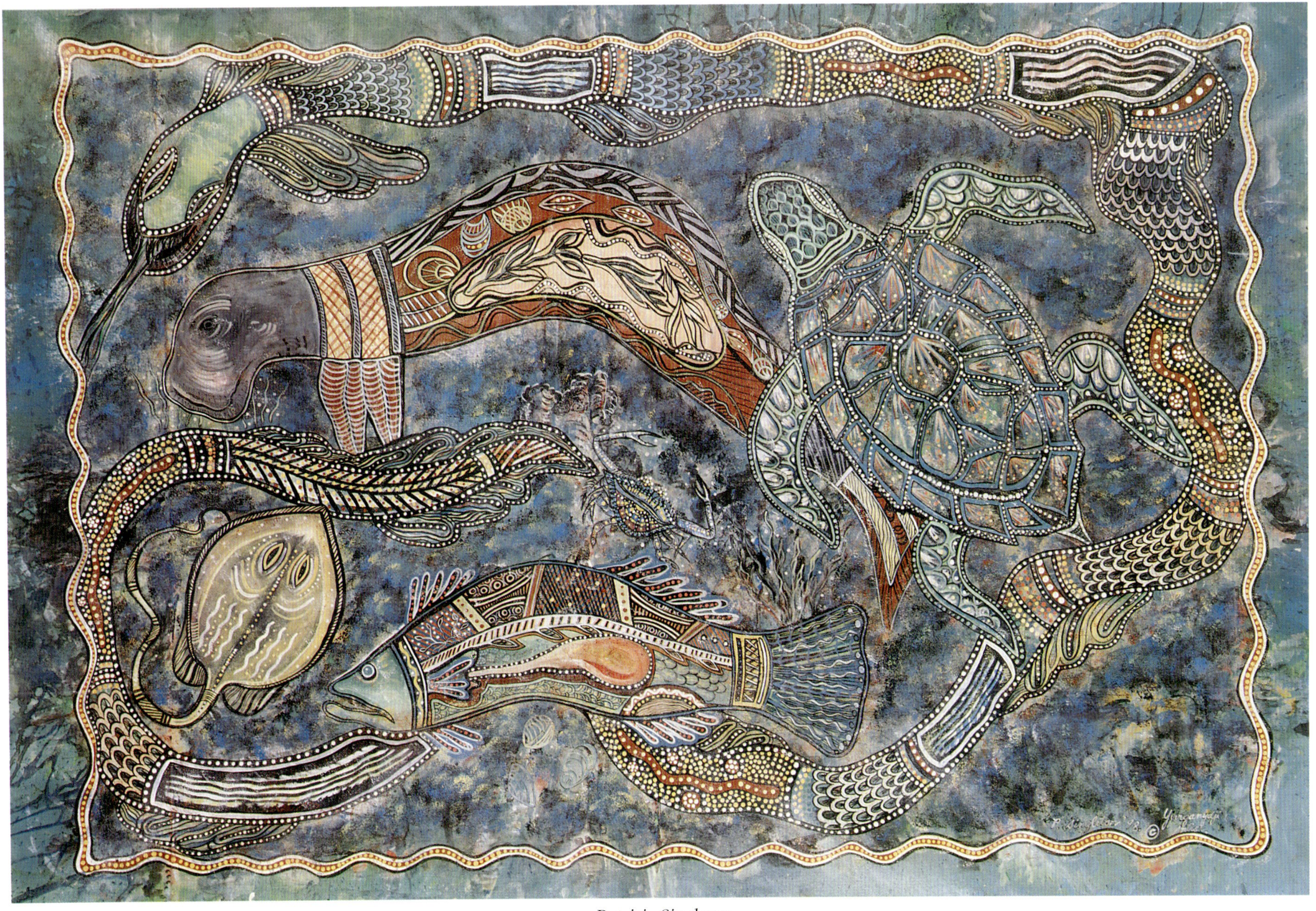

Patricia Singleton
YIRRGANYDJI DREAMING

SHARK DANCER

ANNE ABEDNEGO GELA

1992
Acrylic on Canvas
106cm x 165cm

The long name for this piece is *Shark Dance, Shark Play*. The shark has always belonged to the sea, as do the artist's people. This is the artist's interpretation of Torres Strait Islander traditional dancers preserving culture, and promoting the salt water people.

The sea is the mother of Torres Strait Islander people. She provides the food, and has been part of islander people's way of life since the creation era. The songs and dances about the ocean, and its spiritual and natural forces have also played a major role in islander people's society. It is history being recorded in another way.

Sagul pronounced 'sah' - gool is West Torres Strait meaning *play dance*.

Segur pronounced 'sair' - goor is East Torres Strait meaning *play*.

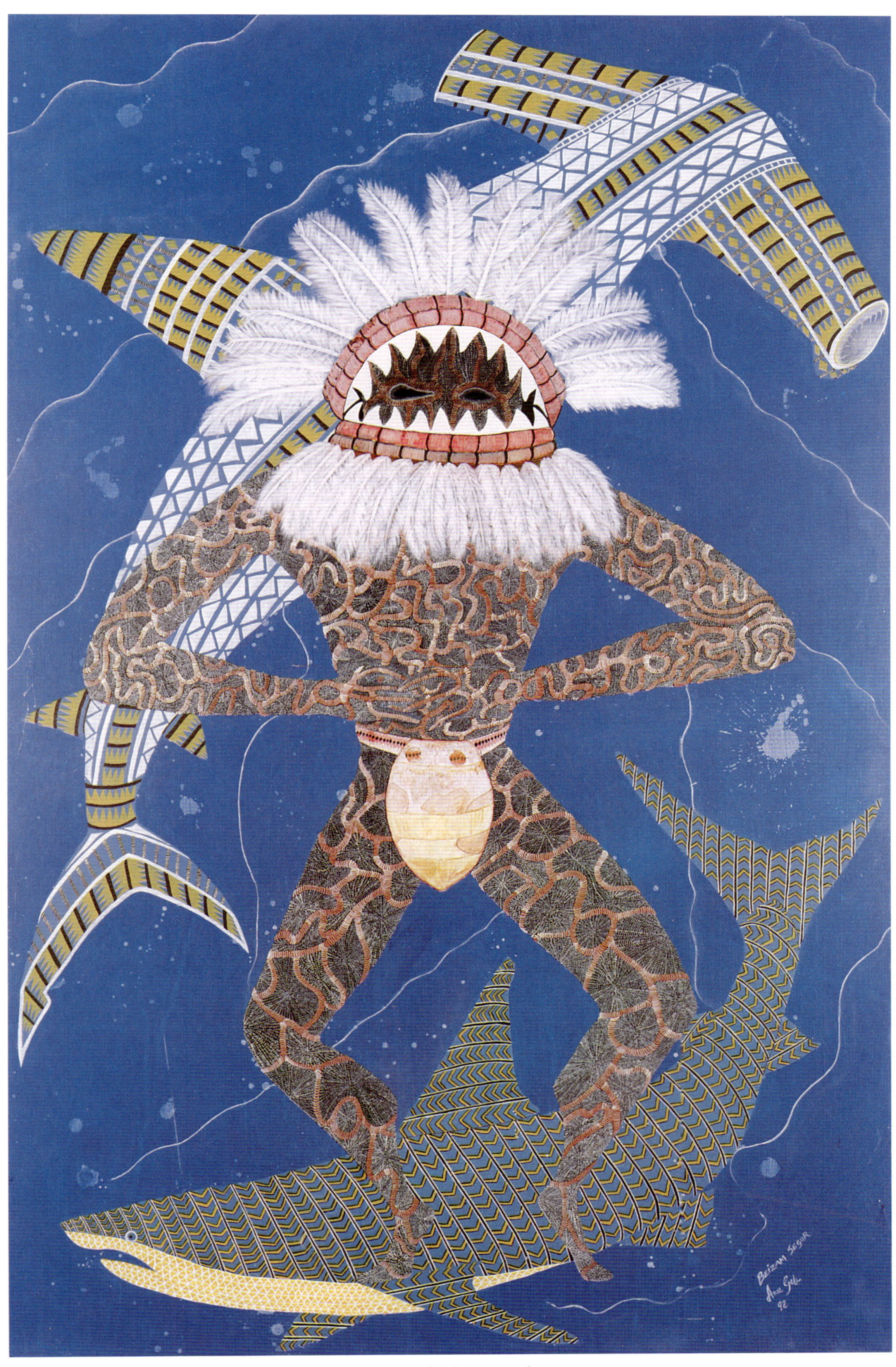

Anne Abednego Gela
SHARK DANCER

IN SEARCH OF...

Zane Saunders

Acrylic on Paper
56cm x 76cm
1999
Private collection

The story of the *Mundagutta*, better known as the Rainbow Serpent, creates a spiritual pathway. A pathway in search of God's chosen people, who are lost, having turned away from the spring of fresh water.

Mundagutta was placed in charge of a selected area of water by the creator spirit. His job was to make sure there was plenty of food to eat and hunt. Young lads out hunting stopped at a familiar waterhole in search of cool water to soothe their thirst. Unaware of the danger they placed themselves and their people in, they threw large rocks into the peaceful waters.

Old Mundagutta arose. Disturbed from his peace, he lifted himself out of the water. Rising high above the trees amongst a thick fog covered by a beautiful rainbow, he made his way along the dry gullies destroying everything in his path. He was searching for calm waters.

Without their source of food and water, many lives could have been lost if it were not for the tribal elders. They spoke in language on behalf of the people, convincing Mundagutta, the Rainbow Serpent, to return to his resting place.

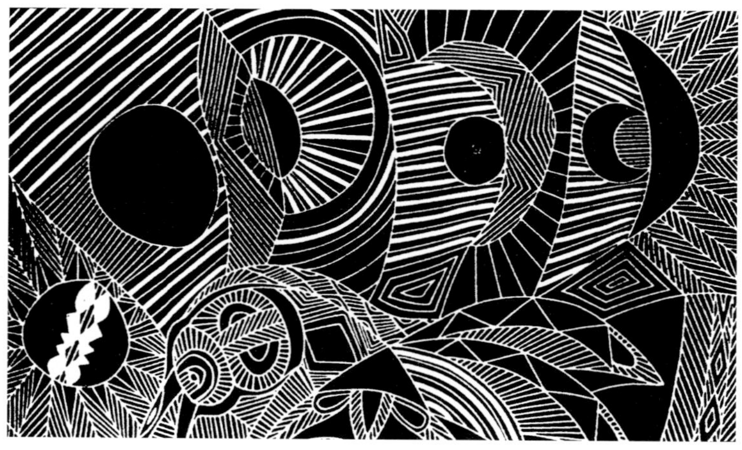

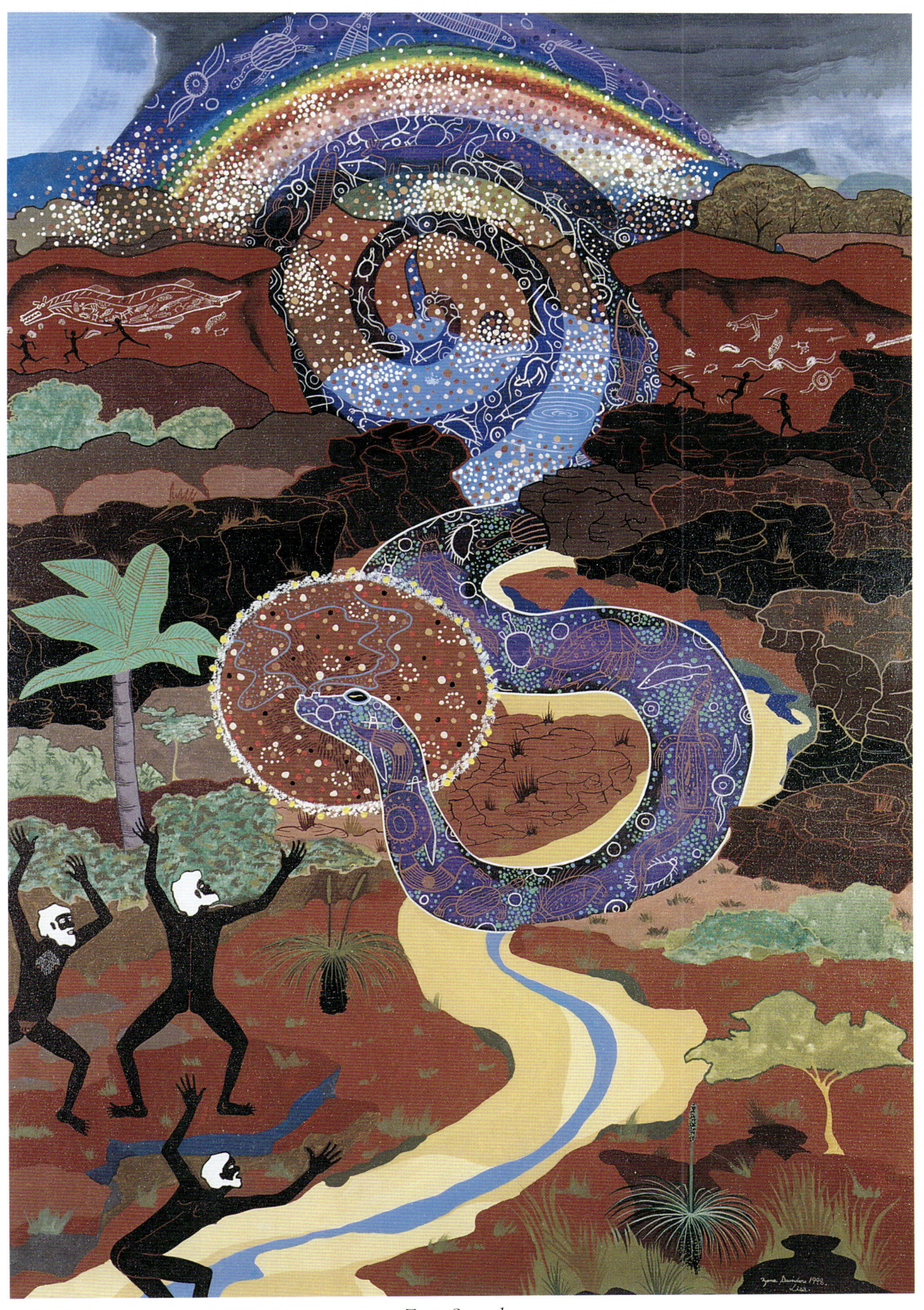

Zane Saunders
In Search of...

HUNTING DUGONG

WANJIDARI (LEANNE REID)

Acrylic on paper
2 pieces: 57cm x 76cm
1996

This painting depicts hunters out on the reef in dinghies spearing dugong, the dugong being a favourite traditional food of the Aboriginal people.

"The sea and coast are extremely important for our people, not only as a source of food, but for our spiritual well-being. Even though we use things like aluminium boats and motors, we have not lost our ties with our country. We care deeply for our country, and everything in it.

We have our own traditional calendar, and other rules, which don't allow hunting, fishing, or gathering at the wrong times, or in the wrong ways. We know the proper seasons to fish, gather and hunt for different foods, so they're protected, and there is always plenty to eat.

Our first concern is to look after our country and resources for our people and our children and grandchildren.

Traditional Aboriginal owners must always have the right to fish, gather and hunt for food for their families and friends, or for traditional or cultural purposes."

(Extract from "Caring for Country, our Coast and Sea: The Lockhart River Community Sea Plan" 1995)
Courtesy of the artist.

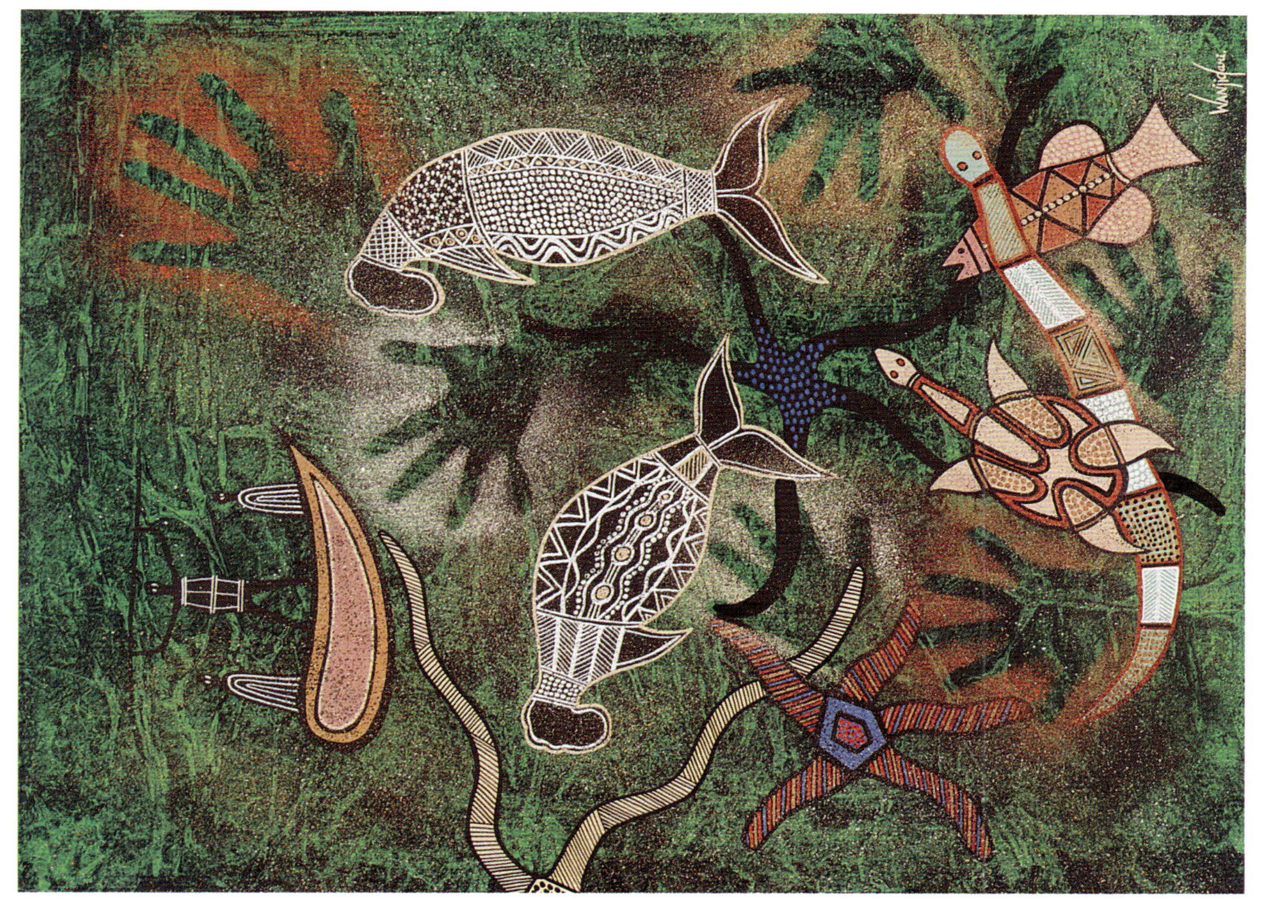

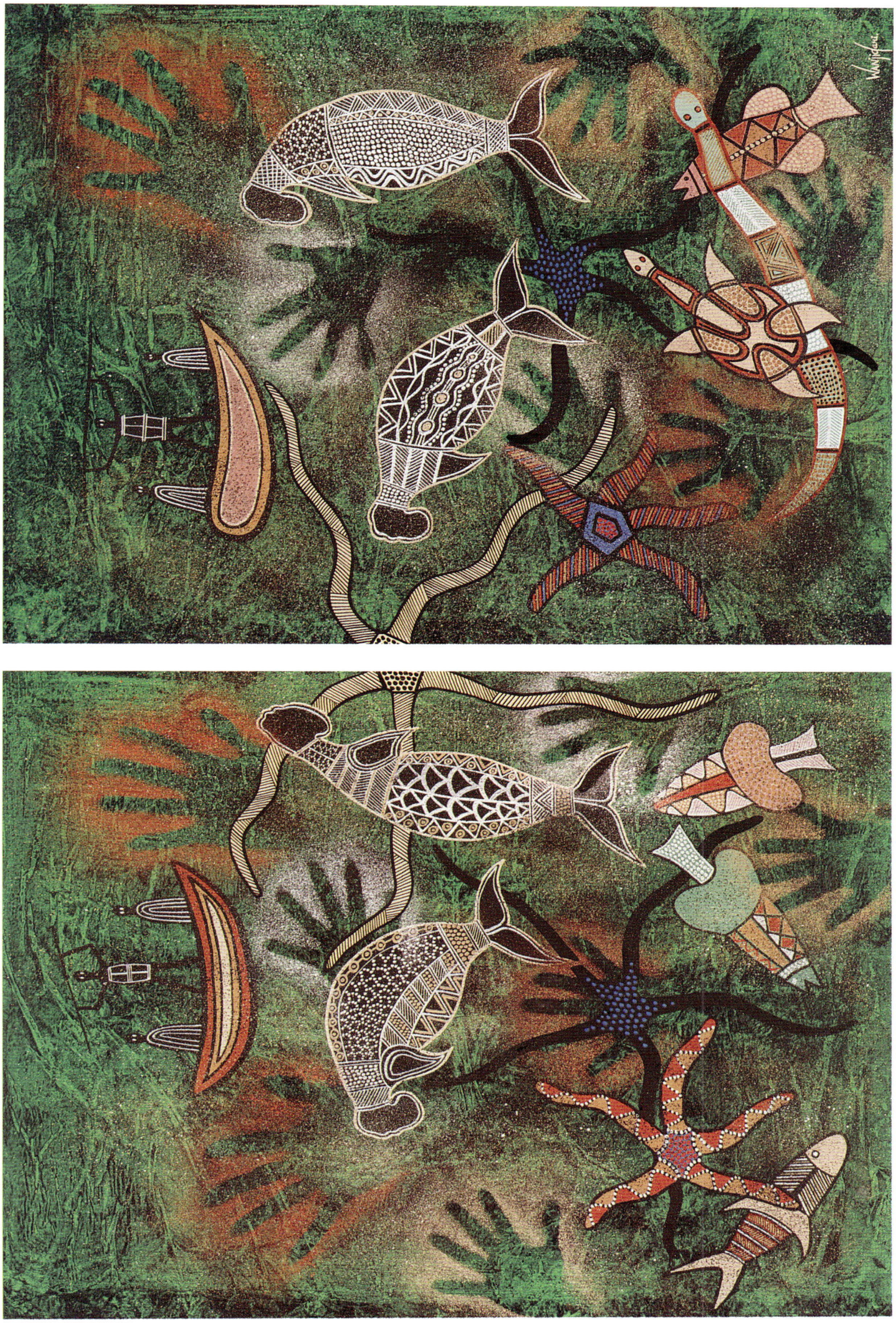

Wanjidari (Leanne Reid)
HUNTING DUGONG

STAGING FLAME

WAYNE KITE

1997
Acrylic and Pastel on Canvas
100cm x 160cm
Private collection

The human *being* is the journey.

The human *experience* is staging within our minds a path that scars the breast of our existence.

The great furnace of dancing energy may burn or warm you. It is not how you make your fire it is how you use it. You are the flame, and through thought energy may burn away the truths of your daily practices. That same thought may also shed the amazing light of understanding from an eagle's point of view, upon you, with compassion.

There is pain before birth. The child is the host and the guest through this process of giving and receiving. Witness the joy in your own journey alike the overwhelming love that a mother has towards the child of her nurturing. For every day is a birthday, we return from the spirit world of dreams to be born again in our human bodies.

Sleep is only for those who close their eyes towards the truth of reality; reality is forever opening our eyes towards greater truths. When we see, we want to see more and in doing so we grant ourselves the wings of wisdom.

Fly with me and share your light. Shine when you speak, for the serpent is awaiting to drown you with all his love. You are the reflection in his eye.

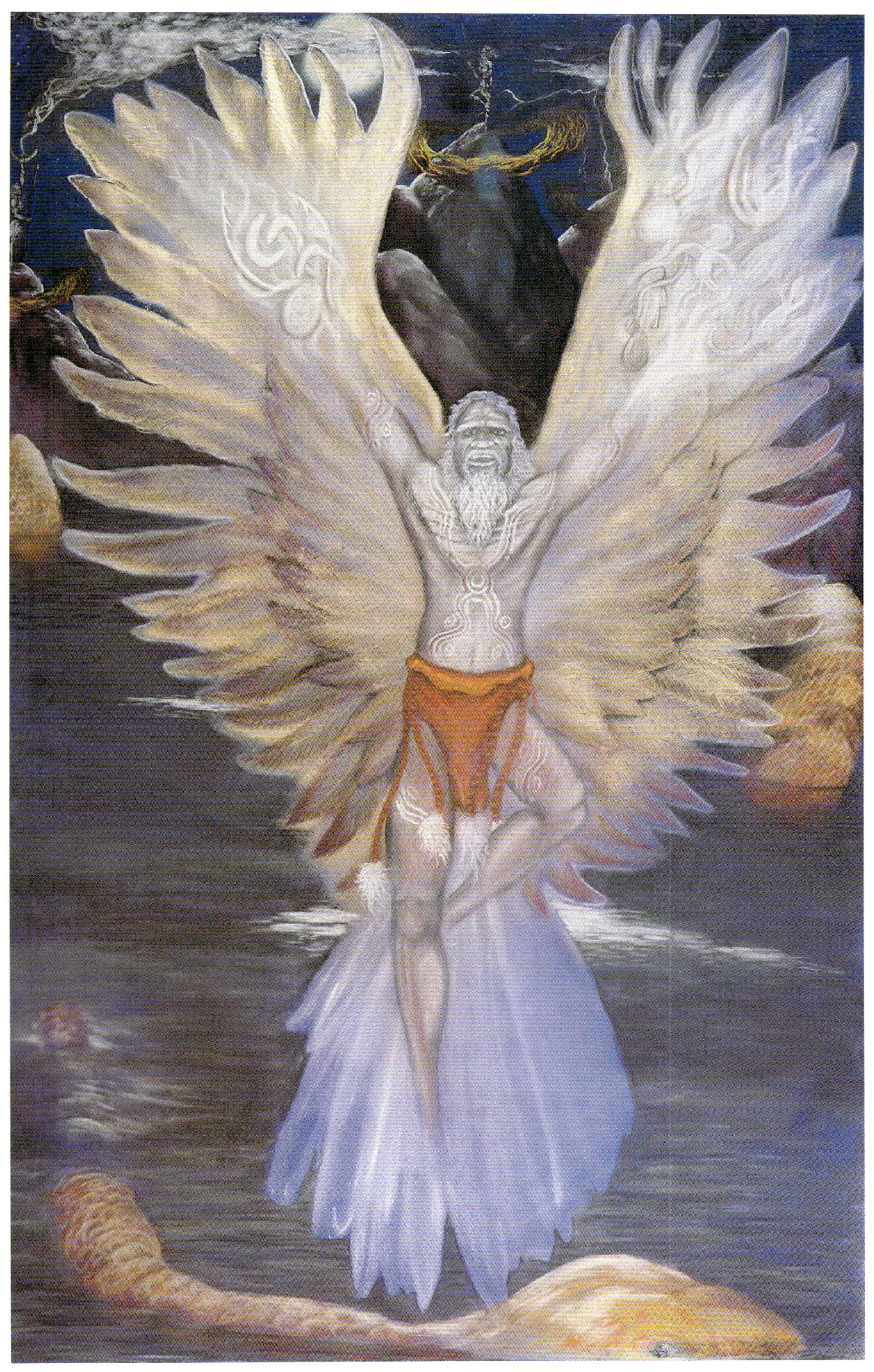

Wayne Kite
STAGING FLAME

SERPENT CREATION

Mary Cummins

Batik on Cotton
1997

The batik symbolically recreates the totem of the artist's Grandfather.

The infinity depicts the stars, reflecting the eternal question: "Where do I come from ?"

The dots in circular motion represent the cycle of life-death-rebirth.

The artist's greatly respected Grandfather, Sid Serico, was known for his strength and wisdom. The depiction of the Grandfather's totem, *Munda*, in an intertwining manner is the artist's way of respecting his great strength and cultural integrity.

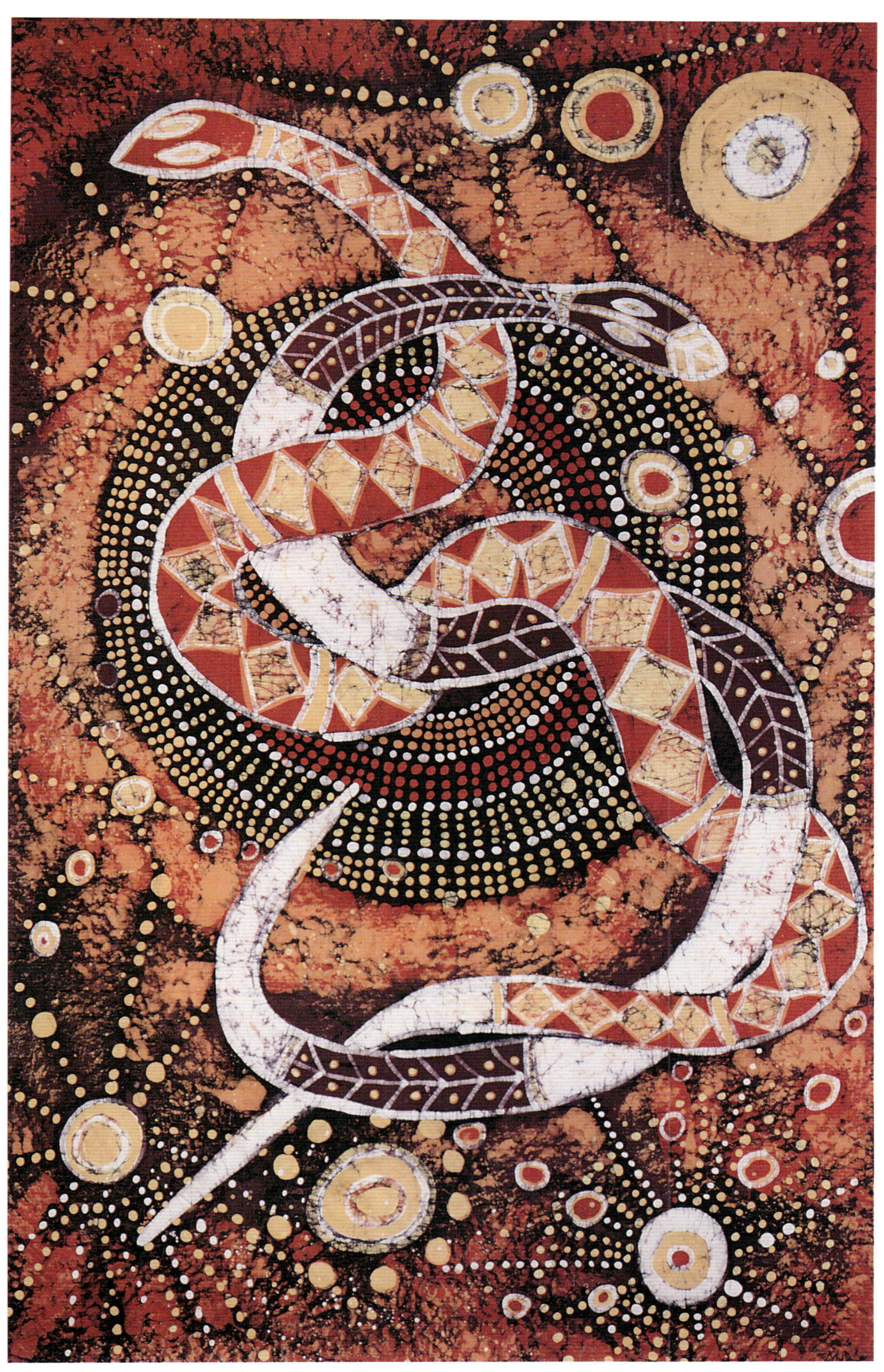

Mary Cummins
Serpent Creation

CREATION PAINTING

DANIEL GEIA & COLIN WIGHTMAN

1992
Acrylic on Canvas
196cm x 214cm
Faculty of Aboriginal and Torres Strait Islander Studies - Tropical North Queensland Institute of TAFE Collection.

This large canvas is about the creation of the planet, and the land animals and sea creatures that live upon it. In 1992, when this work was painted, Daniel Geia and Colin Wightman were close friends and fellow students at TAFE. They decided to work together to tell the creation story.

Daniel, who is from Palm Island in Queensland, chose to portray the creation of the seas in his part of the design on the bottom half of the canvas using images of dugong, manta ray, stingray, squid and the saltwater turtle.

Colin, who is from Toomelah in New South Wales, painted the land creatures depicted in the top half of the canvas. The kangaroo, emu, and the long necked freshwater turtle are his.

Both artists worked on the central symbol - the serpent of creation.

Courtesy of the artists.

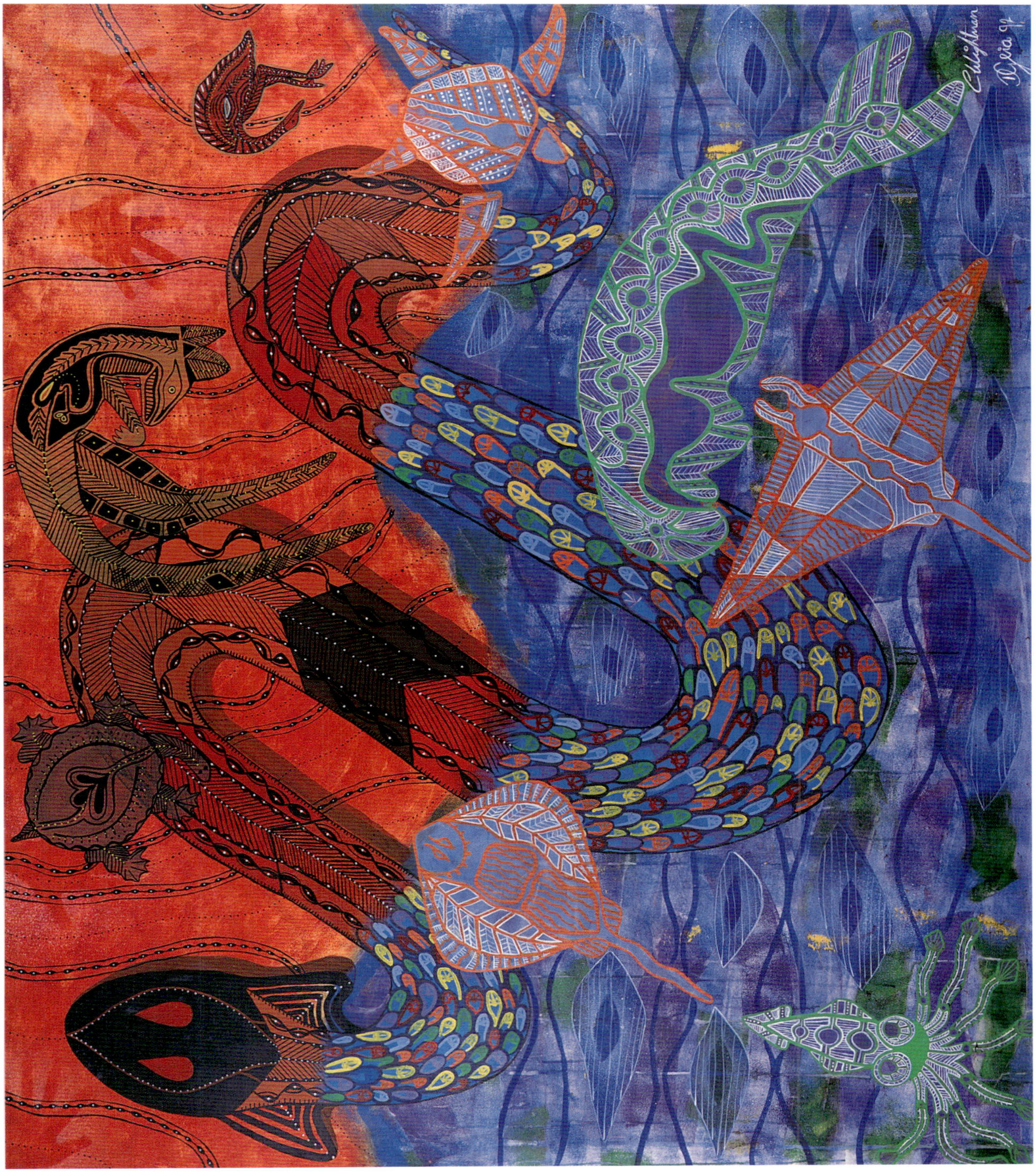

Daniel Geia & Colin Wightman
Creation Painting

EELS

Lisa Michl

Acrylic on paper
56cm x 76cm

This painting is one of a recent series, inspired by the creatures of the artist's homeland.

The white dots on the eels represent how they move in the water. The red ochre, yellow ochre, and black, represent the many different creeks they have to swim through during their lifetime. From youth, they travel up from the sea into the creeks and water ways where they spend much of their lives . When it is time to mate, they return to the sea where their young are born, and the cycle begins again.

Courtesy of the artist.

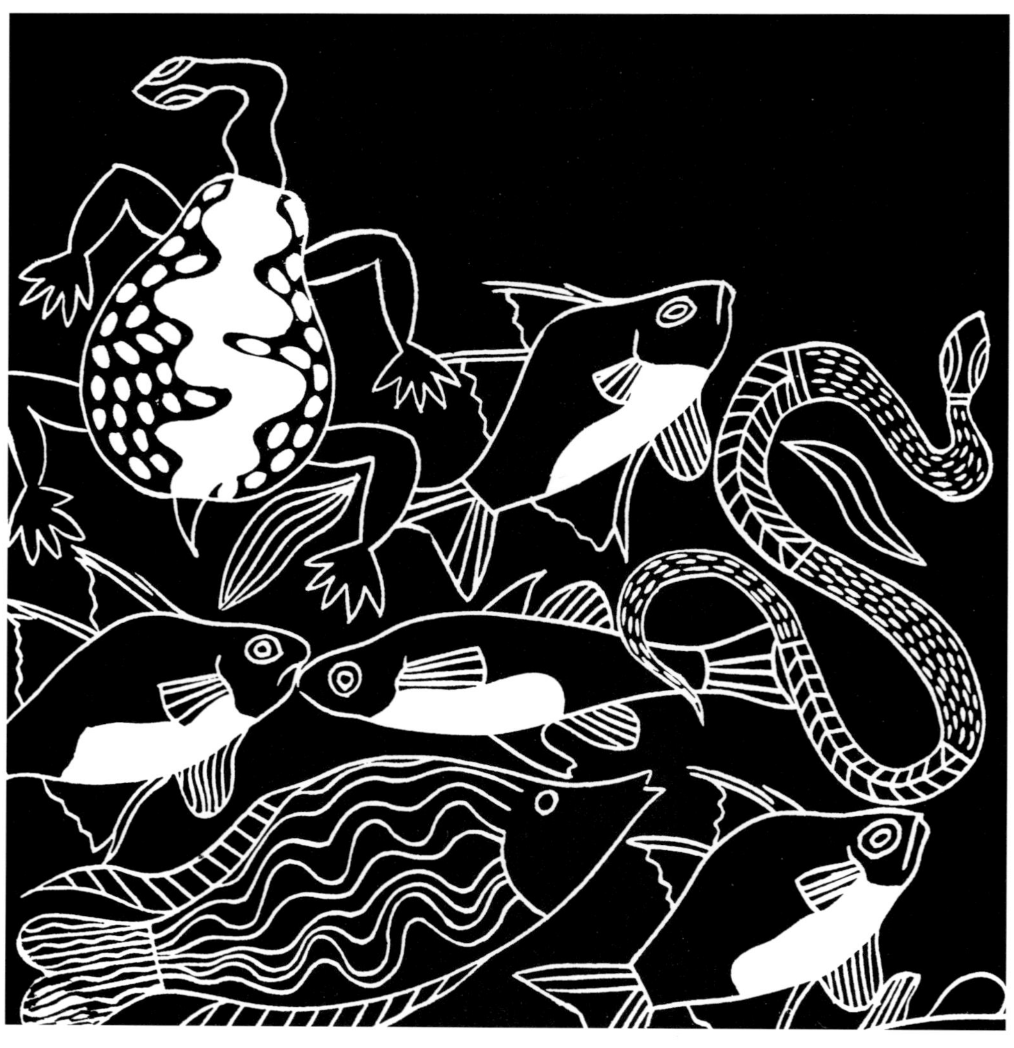

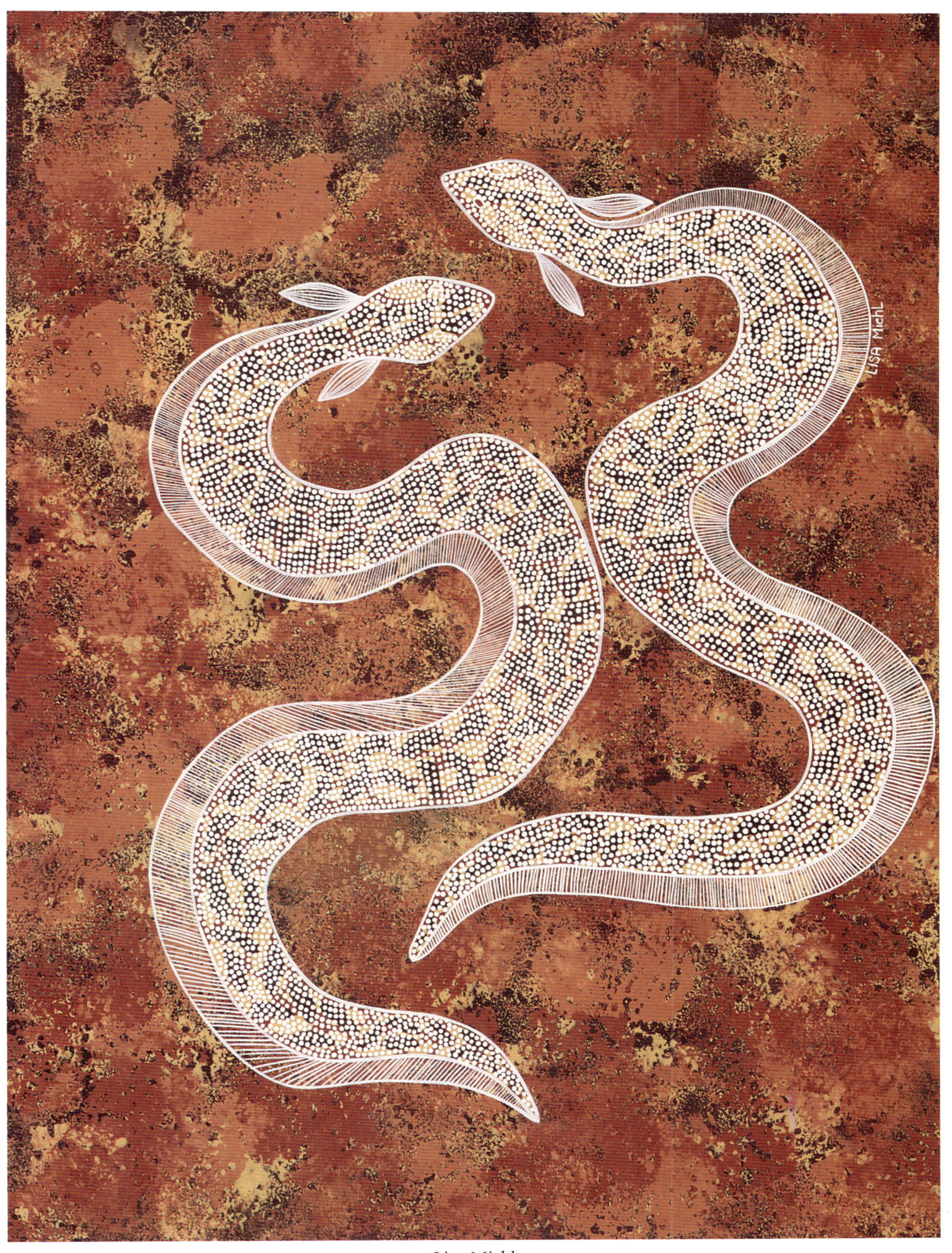

Lisa Michl
Eels

BLUE SHARK

PRISCILLA SEDEN

Acrylic on paper
56cm x 75cm
1994

This vibrant painting was used for a poster produced by VETEC Department of Employment, Vocational Education and Industrial Relations, an initiative of the Division of Employment and Training.

Blue Shark is typical of Priscilla's use of sea images in her work, combining strong, decorative design and bright colour. Priscilla screenprinted many beautiful lengths of fabric, and t-shirts while a student at Cairns TAFE. These designs were much admired when shown in various fashion parades in both Cairns and Brisbane.

The inspiration for Priscilla's shark painting is from an early memory she recalls from a time when she lived on Thursday Island. Priscilla writes:

"When I was about twelve years old, my family took me fishing in our small boat. The day was lovely, the sky beautiful, and in the ocean I saw lots of yellow coral with waves moving all around them. On the other side of the island, near Sadiar Beach, we stopped the boat and started fishing.

After a while I saw the sky change from light to dark, and could hear a storm not far off. My skin felt cold, and it started spitting with rain. The boat began to rock as the waves built up around us.

Just then I hooked what I thought was a small fish, then suddenly the line became very hard to pull in. I was struggling with the line, and it started to cut my hands. My hands were bleeding, but my family encouraged me to keep pulling. To our surprise we saw that I had caught a big shark.

I cut the line and let it go. I still remember, with wonder, being such a little girl catching such a big shark."

Courtesy of the artist

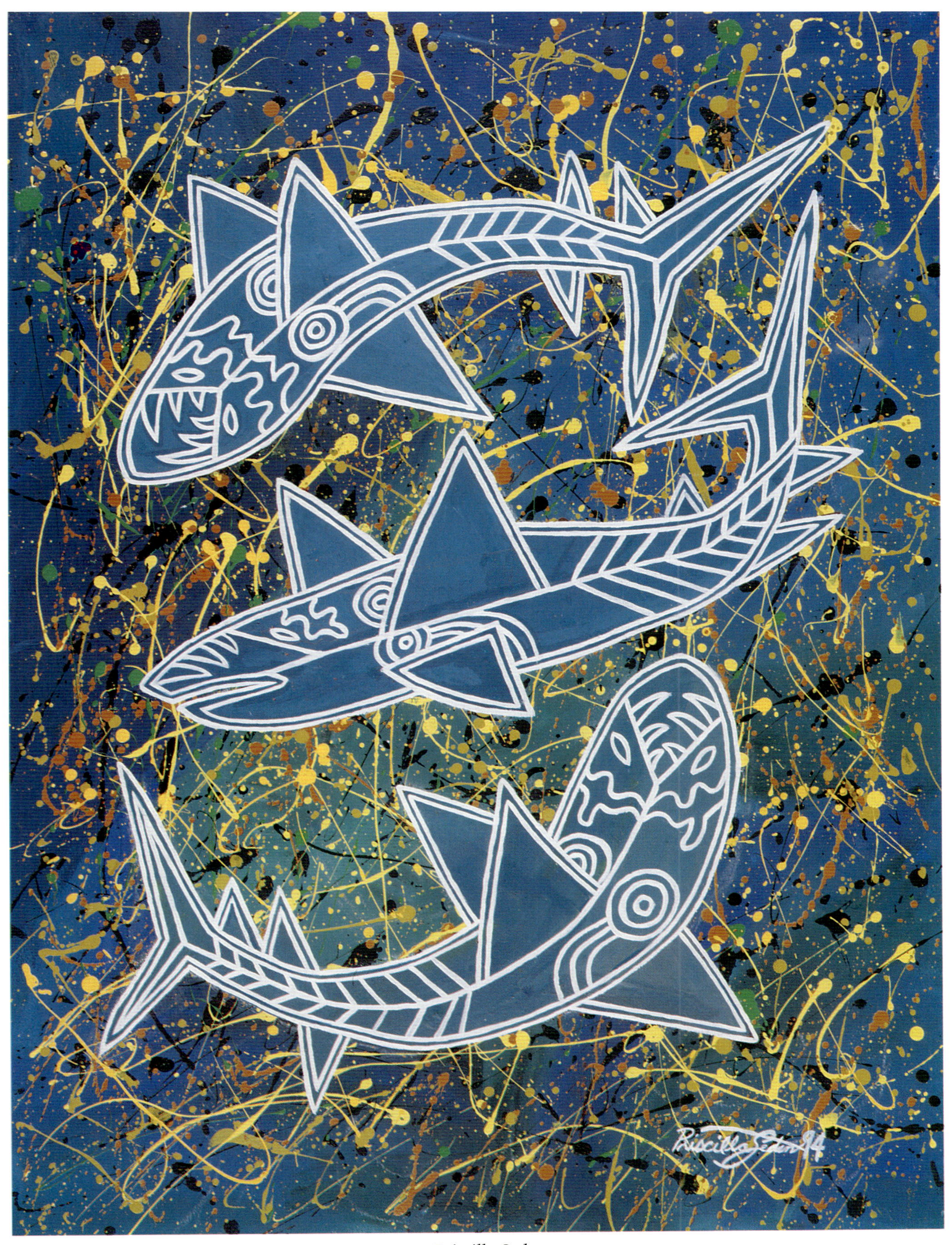

Priscilla Seden
BLUE SHARK

FOUR BROTHERS

Glen Mackie

Acrylic on Paper
38 x 76cm
1999

The four brothers came in their canoes from a place along the coast of Papua New Guinea.

The names of the four brothers were Malu, Sigai, Kulka and Saeu.

Malu went to Murray Island, Kulka went to Aurid, Saeu went to Yorke Island and Sigai went to Yam Island.

Sigai took on the form of *Kurrs* (hammer head shark) and became the object of hero worship from the people.

After the warrior head-hunters had fought a war, the severed heads belonged to Sigai, the hammerhead shark, and to Maiau, the crocodile.

But always, the greater number of heads were claimed by Sigai.

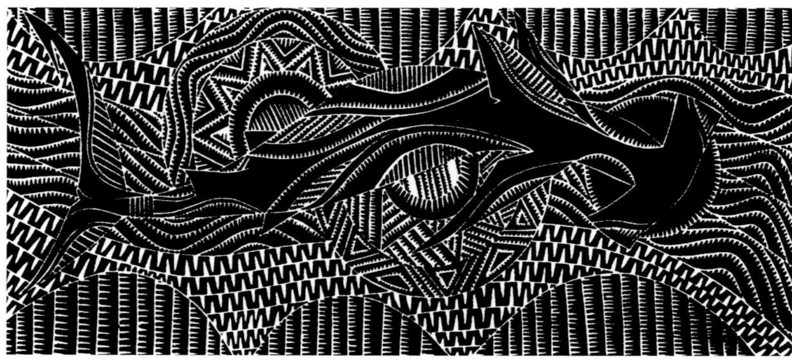

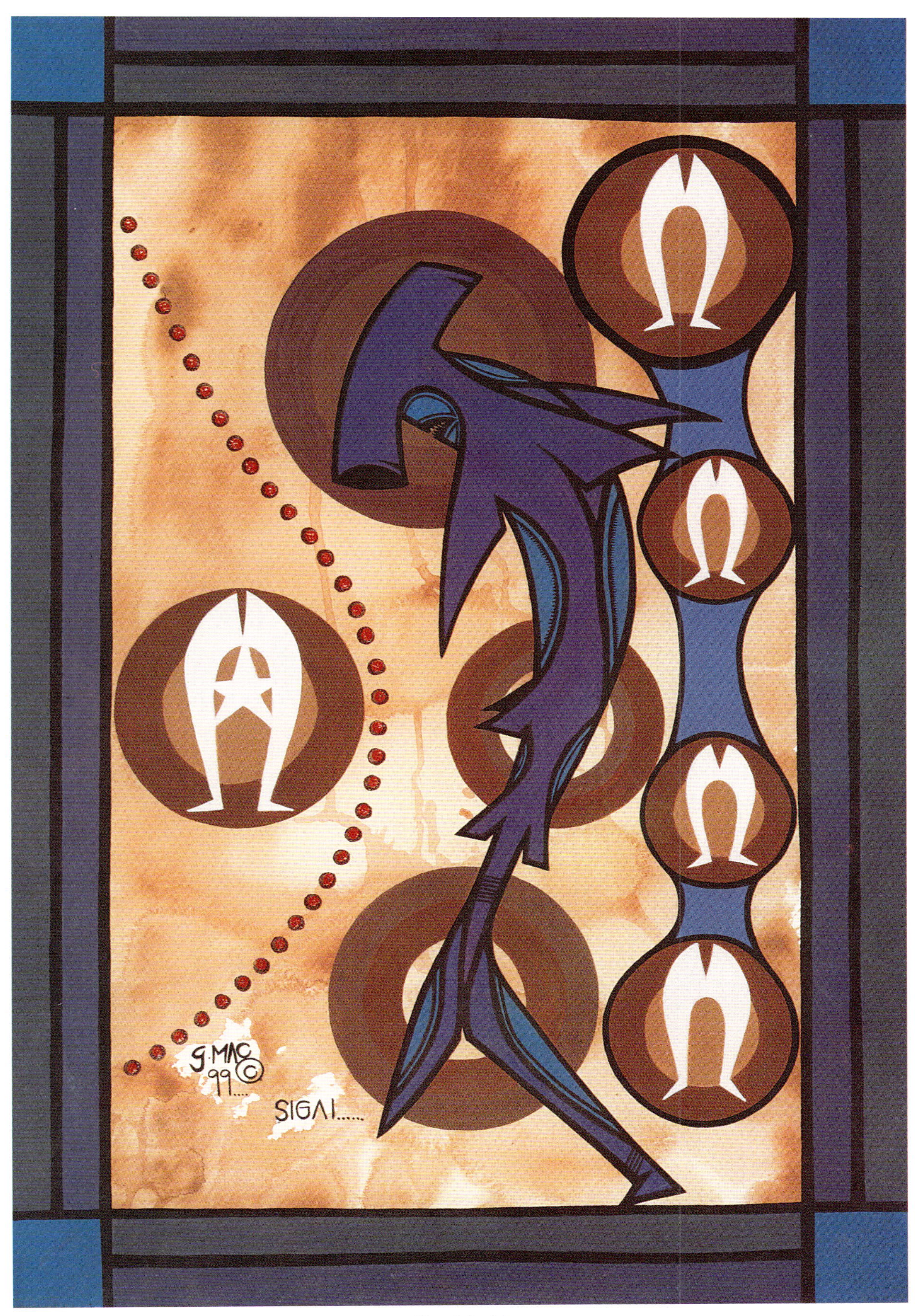

Glen Mackie
Four Brothers

THE LEGEND OF THE BOULDERS

Bindur Bullin (Paul Bong)

Acrylic on Paper
56 x 76cm

In the tribe was a very beautiful young woman, Oolana. The tribal elders were proud of Oolana, because of her absolute beauty. Also in the tribe was Waroonoo, a very old, very wise and respected elder. The chief was most pleased with both of them: Oolana because of her unusual beauty, and Waroonoo because of his wisdom and great tribal knowledge. It was decided that these two should be given in marriage to each other, and so it was done. The tribe was well satisfied and the couple seemed quite happy.

Later, during that time, a wandering tribe came through the valley, and as was the friendly custom of the Yidinjis, they made the strangers welcome and invited them to stay. In the visiting tribe was Dyga, a very handsome young man. All eyes were upon him for his grace and beauty. At first sight Dyga and Oolana fell in love. So great was their attraction for each other they arranged to meet secretly. Knowing full well that their desire for each other would never be permitted, they ran away. Oolana knew she could now never return as she was rightfully married to Waroonoo. She and Dyga journeyed well up to the valley, spending wonderfully happy days together as they camped under Churichilam, near the water's edge.

The two tribes had been searching for them, and it was at this spot that they came upon the two lovers. The wandering tribesmen seized Dyga, forcing him away calling how they been shamed, and how they would travel far away, and never return. The Yidinjis had taken hold of Oolana and were dragging her back, forcing her to return with them to the rest of the tribe. Suddenly she broke away and violently flung herself forward into the gentle waters of the creek. She called and cried for Dyga to return to her here, but the wandering tribe had gone and with them her handsome lover.

"Would he ever return?" she thought to herself, and at that very instant she struck the water. A tremendous upheaval occurred. The land shook with terror and sorrow, as Oolana cried for her lost lover to come to her. Cast up to the surface, she gradually merged with the stones and the water. Oolana seemed to become a part of the stones as if to guard the very spot where it all happened.

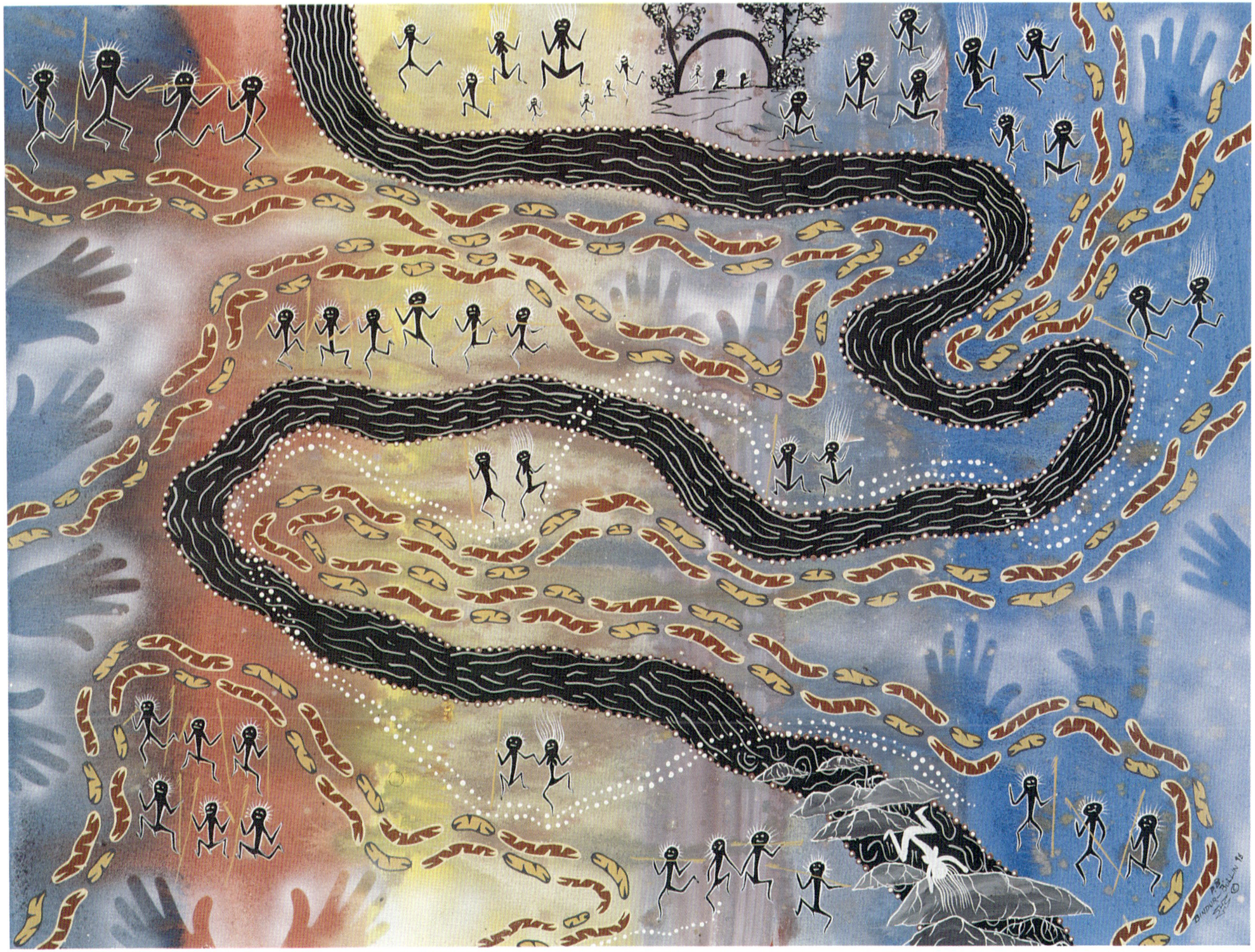

Bindur Bullin

The Legend of the Boulders

BADULGAU DTHOERI

ROBERT MAST

Gouache on Paper
38 x 76cm
1999

"This painting shows the traditional Badu Island headdress of the Torres Strait featured in the centre. The other artefacts featured were all used in warfare, such as the shell which was used like a horn to alert the people of danger, and the drum (warup) used to accompany war dances. The club (gabagab) and the bows and arrows (gaigai and thaiyak) were used on the battle grounds.

Today these artefacts are only used in dancing, for special ceremonies such as the 'Coming of the Light' (the arrival of the missionaries), tombstone openings, and weddings.

The design in the background, going across the painting, shows that the culture will never die for generations to come."

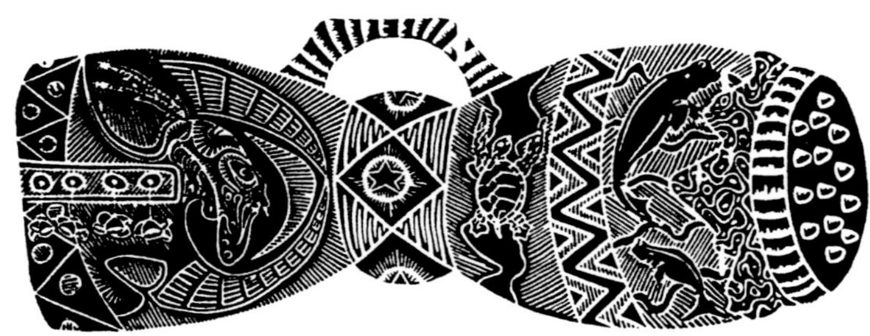

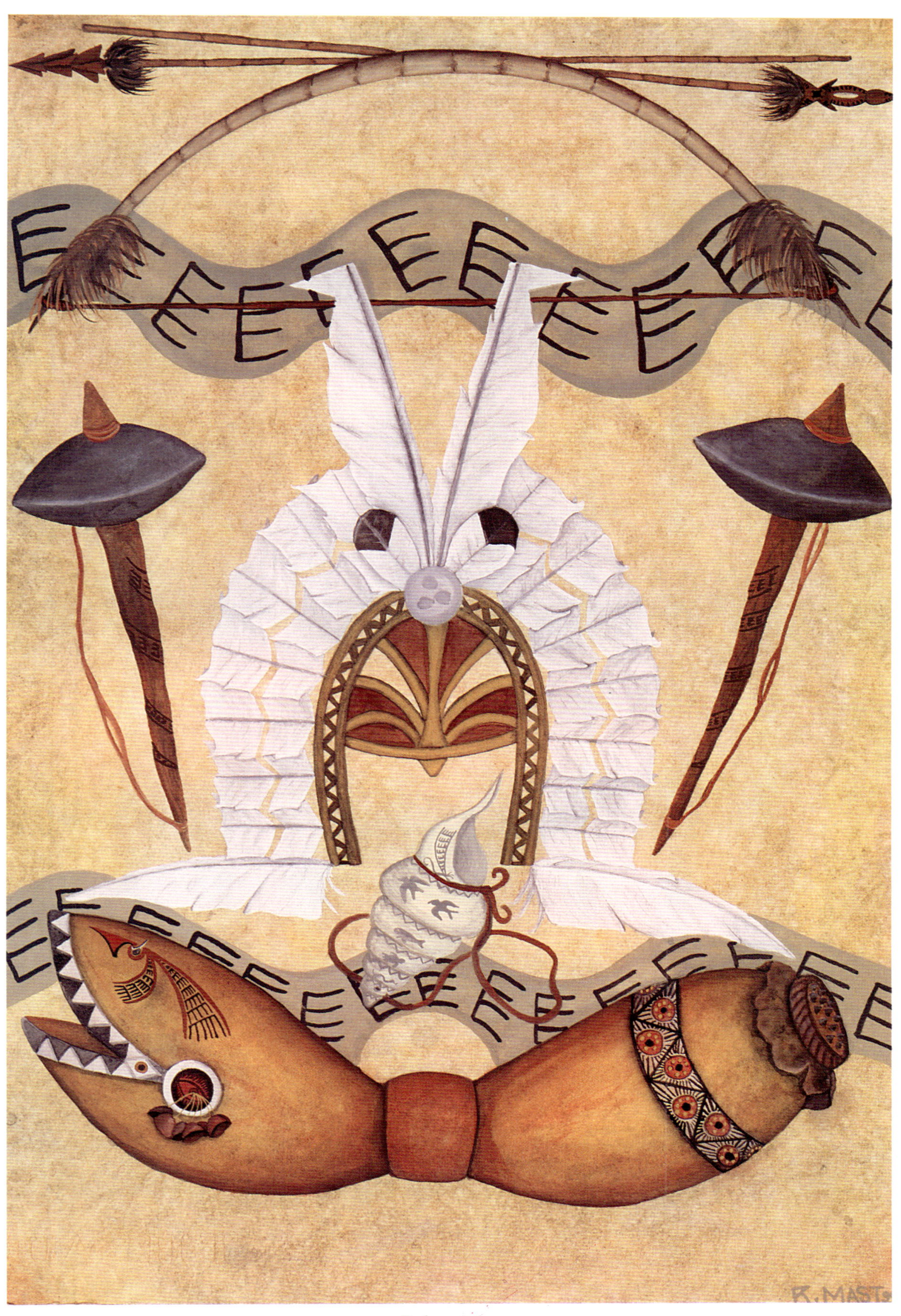

Robert Mast
BADULGAU DTHOERI

BUUTMAROO

Mabel Edmund

Acrylic on Paper
56 x 76cm
In the collection of the Gladstone City Council

This painting depicts childhood memories of the artist, Mabel Edmund. She says:

"As a young girl, I grew up on the banks of the Fitzroy River. I can recall the family going fishing and catching plenty of eel, barramundi, catfish and crabs. There was always a good supply to be caught and cooked. As we had no electricity where we lived sixty years ago, we used to salt or smoke the fish that were left over.

On Pink Lily Lagoon, the bright pink lilies would grow as big as dinner plates. When they had finished flowering, my two brothers Johnny and Cecil, and my cousin Walter used to go in a boat to gather the pods which were full of nuts. They would put them in a bag and bring them home to eat. We would also go catching porcupines high up in the mountain

There was always an abundance of food at our home."

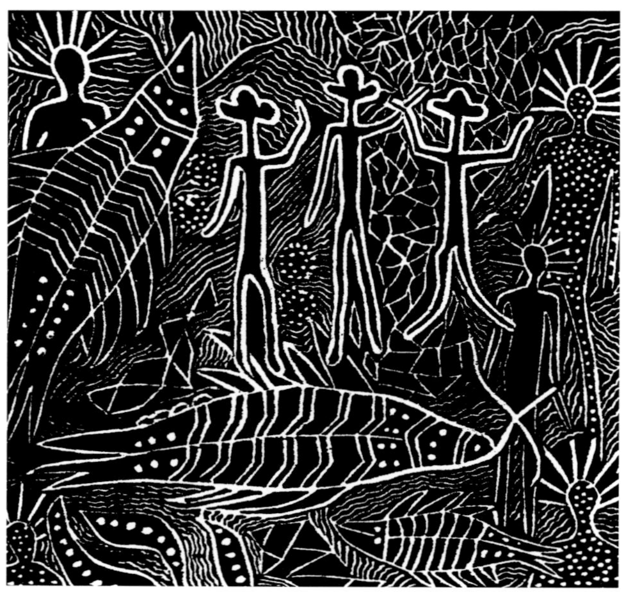

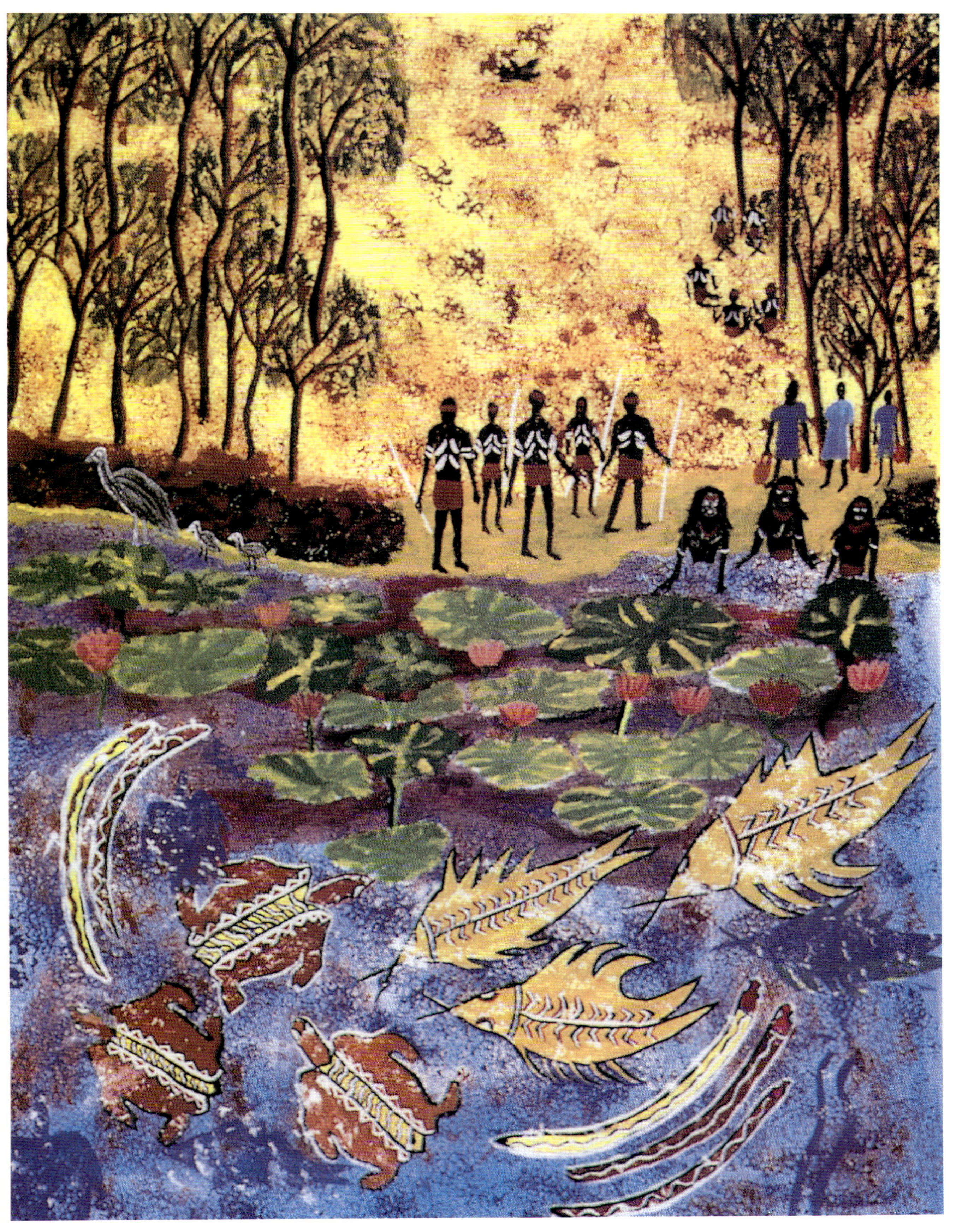

Mabel Edmund
Buutmaroo

GOODI
(THE ANCIENT BARRAMUNDI)

Leon Burchill

Acrylic on Paper
56 x 76cm

The artist's mother comes from the *Kuku Yalanji* people in Far North Queensland. This painting tells a story that originates from her clan.

Goodi lived in the sacred rivers of the Daintree where he would feed constantly. He controlled the different tide levels, as depicted in the painting by the colour change in the dots. He did this to keep *Bilgamore* the Ancient Crocodile away from him.

In those days, *Goodi* could walk on land with his fins to search for food on the river banks. His body was transparent, in order to camouflage and protect him from predators.

The *Kuku Yalanji* people ingeniously used green ants as a method for catching the barramundi for food. The green ants, which contained acid in their bodies, would stun the fish when digested, making them easier to catch.

Goodi's role is one of great importance to the survival of the *Kuku Yalanji*, because of its ability to control the food chain in the rivers by regulating tide levels. When the tide becomes low, it is safer to hunt.

The barramundi is also an important totem, a sacred symbol of guidance.

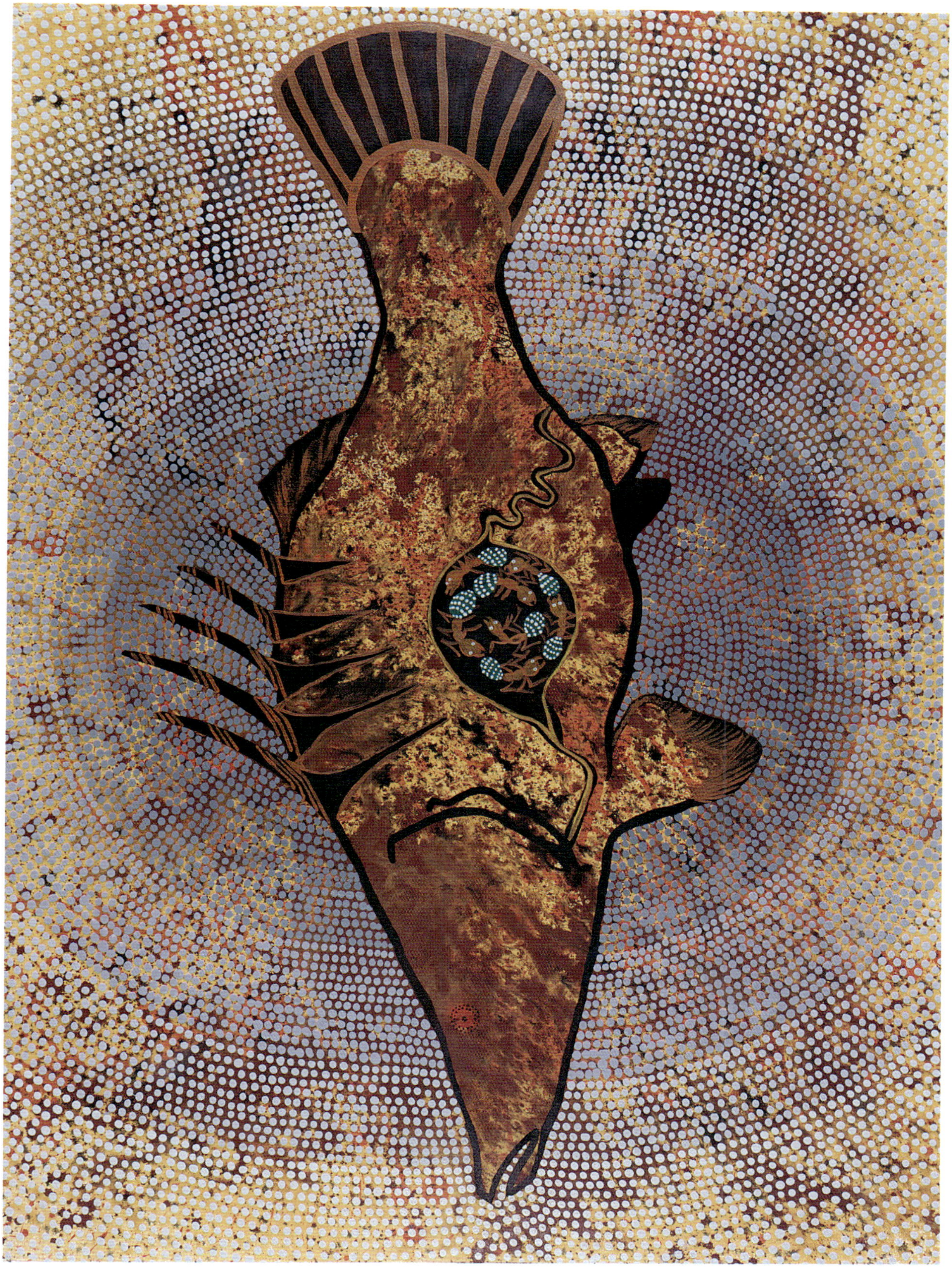

Leon Burchill
GOODI (THE ANCIENT BARRAMUNDI)

SHARK HEAD

GLEN SHEPPARD

Acrylic on canvas
75.5 x 99.5cm
1996
Private Collection

Modern art, materials and techniques inspire this artist as much as life in the nearby rainforests of the Cairns region. He chooses and arranges colours, shapes and lines on canvas or paper, in order to illustrate his joy and appreciation of all things living.

His admiration of land and sea animals because of their long history on the earth is clear. Although these things are still a part of the artist's modern lifestyle, he enjoys painting them because it connects him with Dreamtime spirituality.

About his painting *Shark Head*, Glen writes:

"I started this picture after seeing a story on the television news the night before. The story featured tiger sharks. The colour on the canvas is strong and bright, to catch the eye, so that you may know that the sharks are out there in the sea.

The tiger shark is a mankiller, and is found throughout all of Australia's warm waters, from northern New South Wales, along the coast of Queensland, into the Gulf of Carpentaria, the Northern Territory, and into the tropical waters of Western Australia.

The small tiger sharks at the top and bottom of the painting are done in black and white, like I mostly do my main subjects. They are then surrounded by colour to make them stand out. The human figures are brown and limp and in pieces, to represent what is left after the shark has gone. The big white teeth have some spots on them, like the way some food stays on after a meal.

The eyes stare straight ahead to see what is coming close to its mouth, which is open ready to attack.

The news story was still in my mind when I painted the lines in the background. They are the life lines of the tiger sharks in different parts of the seas."

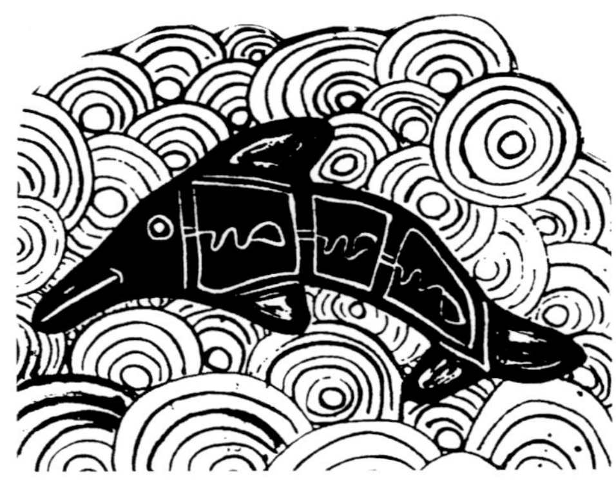

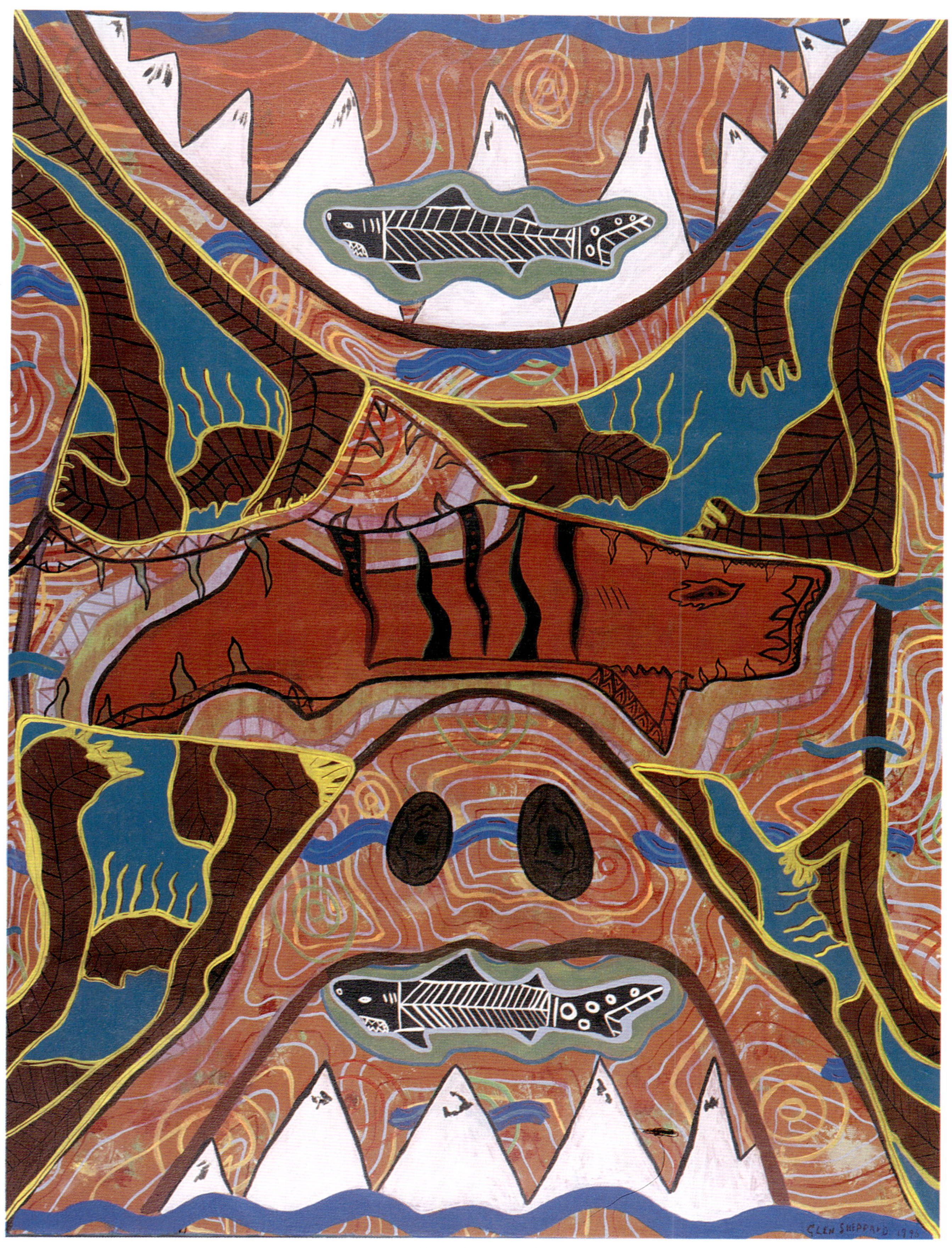

Glenn Sheppard
SHARK HEAD

DANCING BROLGA

Patty Morris

1996
Acrylic on Canvas
200 x 250cm

In the Dreamtime, the Anta Moola sisters left human baby spirits in the lagoons on Cape York, where they were looked after by old women, the *Kweelucs*, so they couldn't wander off and get lost.

When the Anta Moola sisters, whose names were Marbee and Nardoo, had finished with the baby spirit business, they travelled east towards the coast, towards the island where their future husbands, the Lizard brothers lived.

Soon they found they were being followed by that greedy man *Gidja* the Moon, who wanted the Anta Moola sisters for his wives. *Gidja* followed Marbee and Nardoo until, finally, he caught up with them.

The Anta Moola sisters didn't like *Gidja*, so they decided to trick him and escape. To do this Marbee told *Gidja* that she and Nardoo would dance for him. As they danced, the magic sisters were surrounded by campfire smoke as they changed into dancing brolgas, and flew away up into the sky.

During their long journey to the coast, Marbee and Nardoo created many places. Finally, they reached the coast and sat down on a mountain to wait for the Lizard brothers to come for them. They waited so long, sitting up among the clouds on top of the mountain, that they turned into stone, where they still wait today for their future husbands to find them.

Patti recalls a time in 1988, when she was with her foster parents travelling in the Northern Territory, when they took an early morning river trip in the Kakadu National Park, leaving just before dawn. Patti writes:

As I sat in the boat on this beautiful dark river I saw the sun rising and the morning sky turning pink and blue. It was so quiet, and then, on the riverbank, I saw and fell in love with this wonderful bird, dancing with its long legs outstretched in the early morning light.

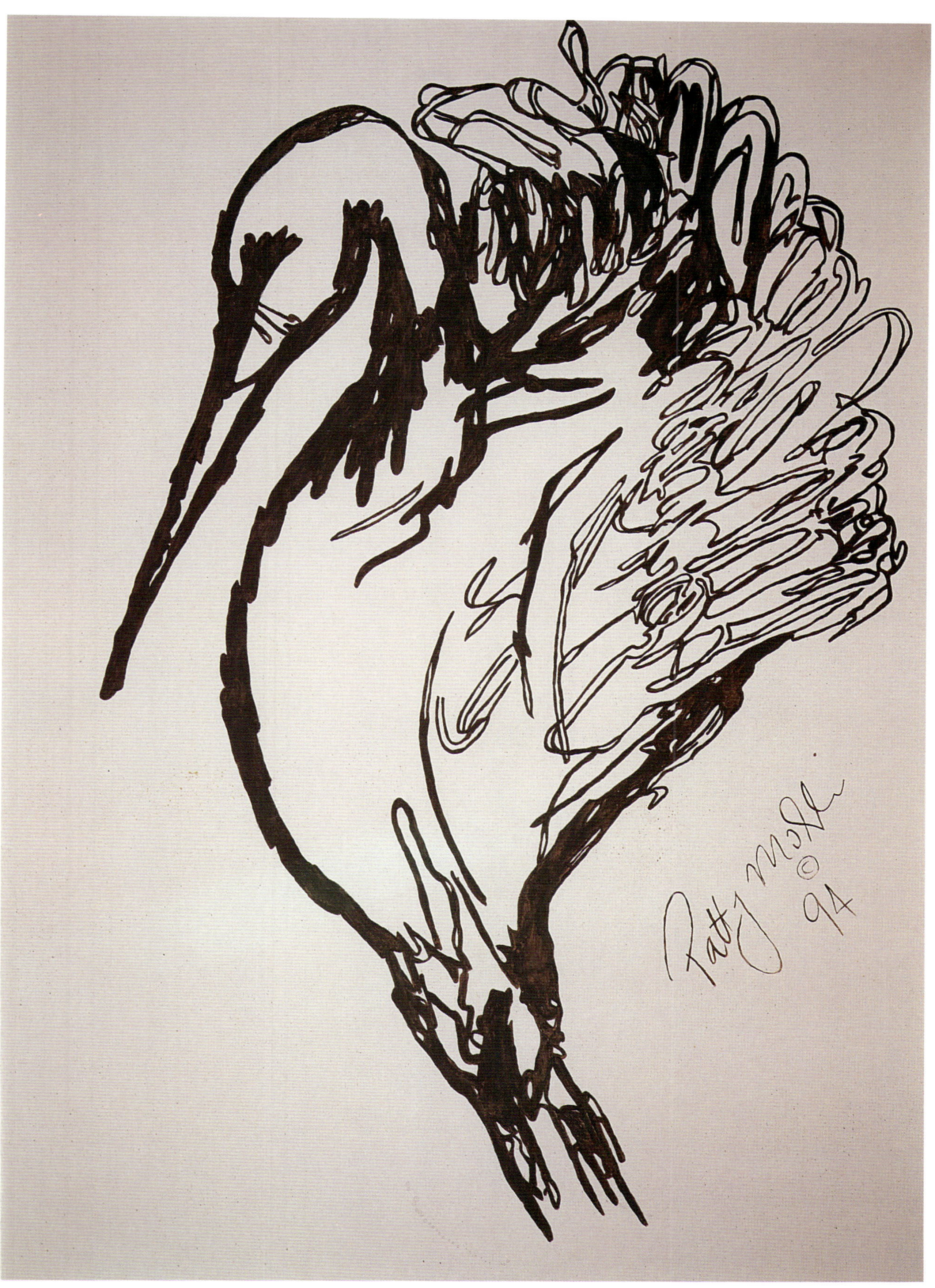

Patty Morris
DANCING BROLGA

OUR MU-YI BUB

Blair Malthouse

1999
Linocut Print
56cm x 76cm

This picture is of a mother dugong showing her calf how to find seagrass to eat.

The title *Our Mu-yi Bub* is the mother using the regional dialect word for food *Mu-yi* (Mah-yee) and telling the baby that this is the food he will eat when he is weaned off her milk.

Seagrass crops are being destroyed by commercial fishing fleets, primary industry run-off, private commercial ventures, and coastal tourism expansion. If this degeneration of seagrass continues, the only way that future generations will be able to relate to dugongs, and their American cousins, the manatee, is through film, video and depictions such as mine.

Photo courtesy of the artist.

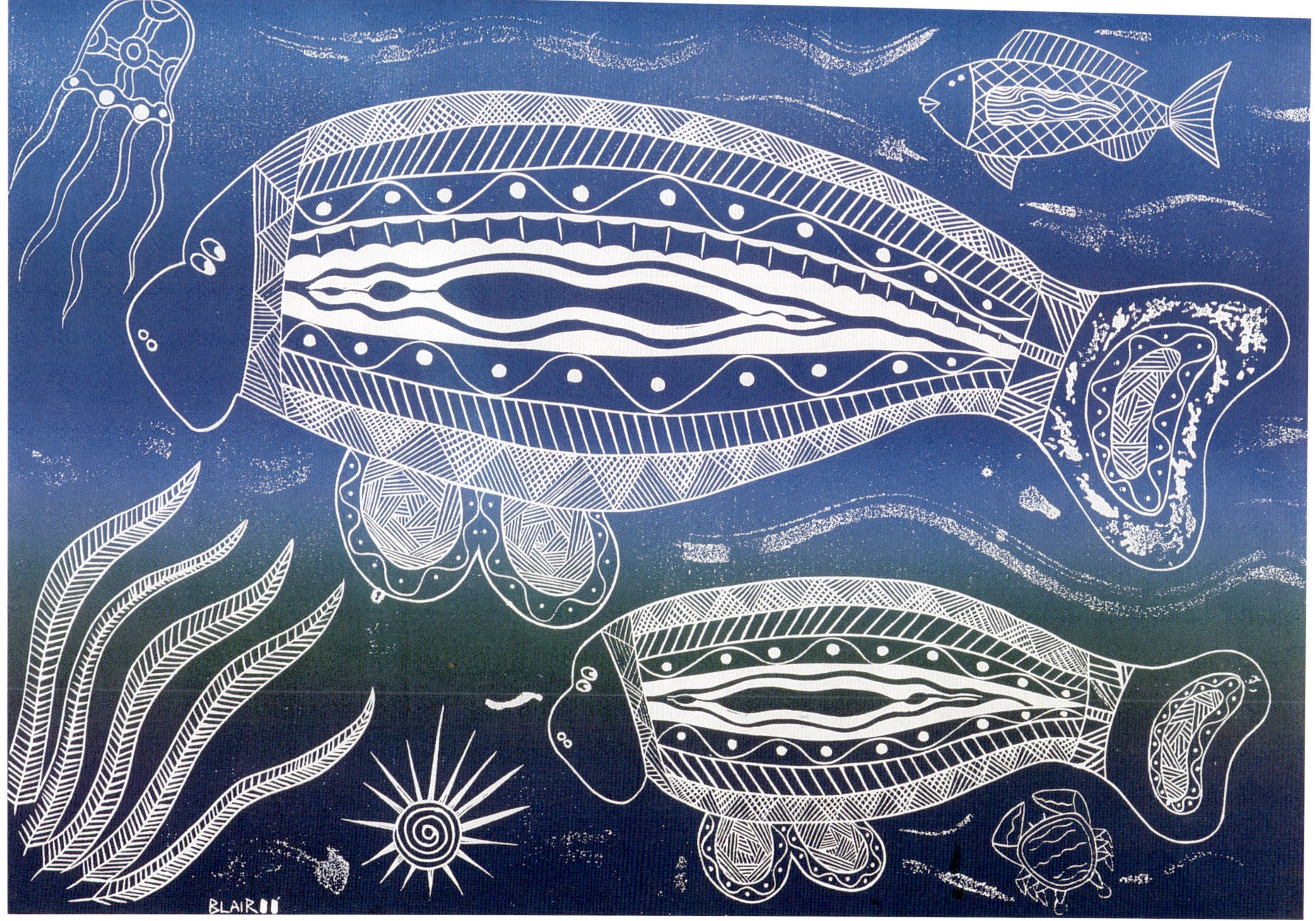

Blair Malthouse
OUR MU-YI BUB

LAGAU DUNALAIG
(ISLAND LIFESTYLE)

LAURIE NONA

Linocut Print
56 x 76cm
1998
National Gallery of Australia Print Collection

This intricate design is best described in sections:

The Flared Tail of the Crayfish
The design and pattern represents the two sea currents in the Torres Strait that determine the times at which the people of the Torres Strait can hunt and gather crayfish, dugong, turtle, fish and shells. On either side are two shovel-nose sharks which symbolise these currents. In the artist's language these currents are called *Guthath* and *Kulice.*

The Body of the Tail
The six sections symbolise the six dialects of the Straits. The designs in these sections represent the human tongue.

The Last Section between the Tail and the Head
The tight spiral represents the old culture of our people which is emotionally centred within every person in the Straits- a strength of culture.

Mid-Section of the Head with the Warrior Image
This area represents the tensions of living in mainstream society, the obstacles we have to learn in order to survive. It is the stress that drives our young people to crime, particularly those who live away from their islands - live on the mainland. Without their culture they turn to crime. The young warrior represents the young people on the mainland who grow up without their culture. The young warrior in my print is waking up to realise that he must re-find his culture symbolised in the designs all around him.

The Dari (Headdress)
The solid white area is the shape of the Torres Strait Island Head Dress worn by the cultural dancers nowadays, and worn by warriors in the old days.

The Legs of the Crayfish
The patterns in the part of the legs closest to the body represent the pearl shell. The pattern on the bottom section before the feet depicts the trochus shell.

The Eyes of the Crayfish
The eyes are also the eyes of the Torres Strait Island pigeon, which is symbolised in the patterns that flow up the first section of the crayfish's feelers until meeting a coconut leaf design, a small section representing a mud crab and another coconut leaf.

The Pattern on the Antenna
These represent the flow of the Coral Sea and sea cucumbers. Other patterns within this print are two squid holding turtle eggs at the top of the crayfish. On their bodies are patterns representing turtle tracks, and the two feelers at the mouth of the crayfish represent the shark.

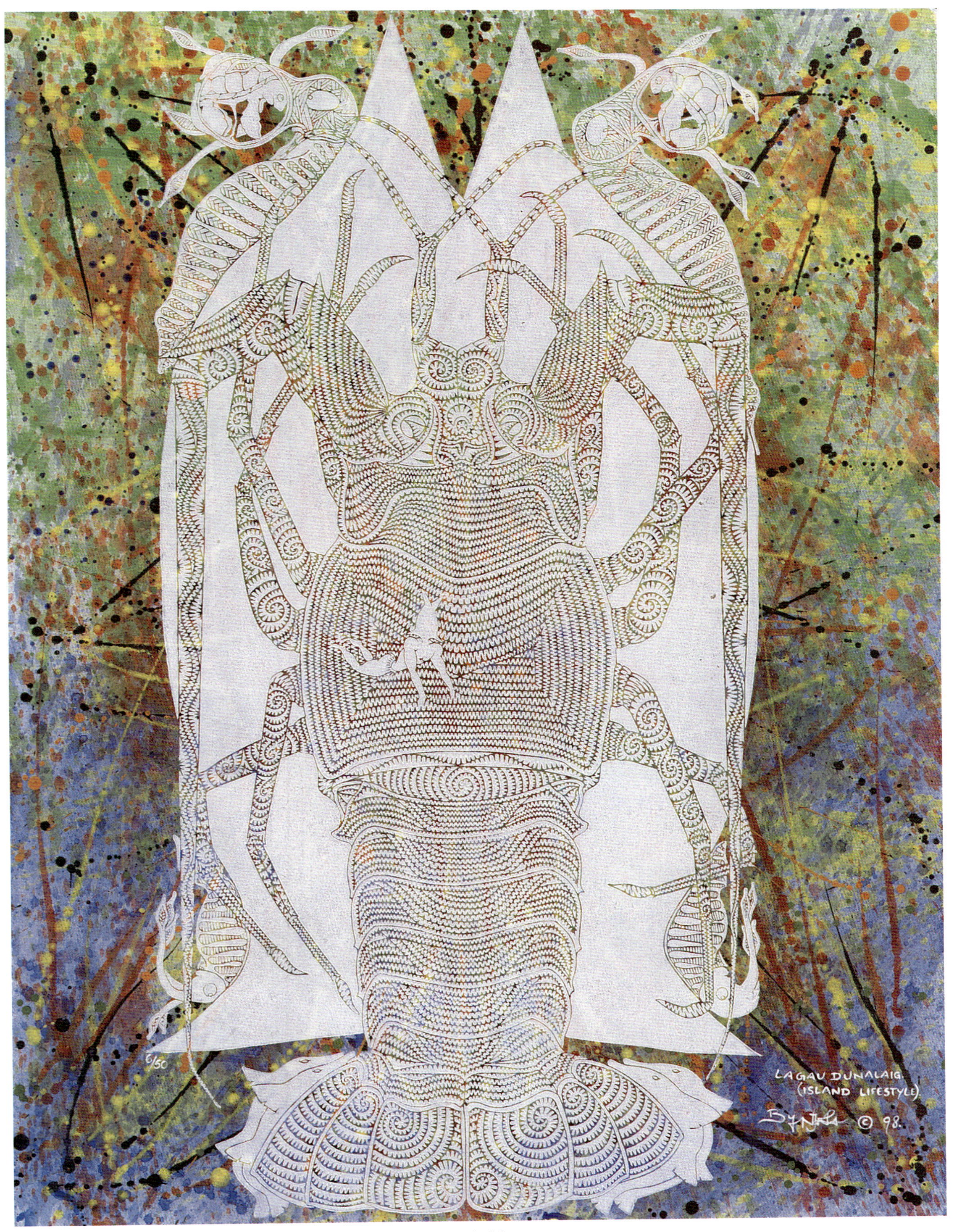

Laurie Nona
Lagau Dunalaig (Island Lifestyle)

PLATYPUS

SAM WASON

Woodblock Print
21cm x 29.5cm
1998
Private collection

The story of the platypus is set in the places where he hunts for food, particularly in fresh water outlets and rivers.

The platypus has come out of his riverbank burrow, and starts stretching out lazily, getting warm from the sun in preparation for hunting. He carefully looks for any signs of danger before slowly floating to the surface of the water. From this position he can look below for any movement on the river bed. He can see the small freshwater crayfish, small fishes and other favourite foods.

When he sees any movement, he dives quickly, skimming along the bottom turning over leaves, small rocks and pieces of wood.

The hunt begins.

The platypus is covered in waterproof fur all over his body except for the feet and bill. The bill looks a bit like a duck's bill and is soft and rubbery.

The platypus is found in most Eastern Australian streams and rivers from Cooktown in the North to Tasmania in the south.

Courtesy of the artist.

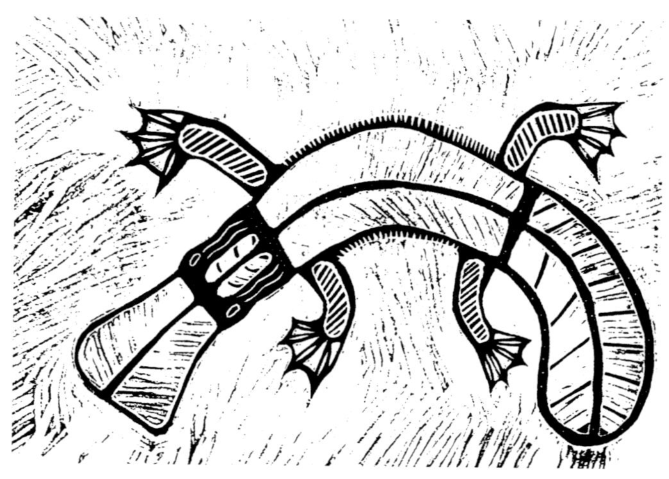

Sam Wason
Platypus

SELF PORTRAIT

VERNON AH KEE

1993
Pastel on black paper
51cm x 63cm

This self-portrait is about identity. The artist recognises that for many Black people whose families have a history of dispersal and displacement, Aboriginal identity is often all that remains.

Vernon Ah Kee describes the artwork in a personal context: "The image in *Self Portrait* of myself against an ochred background reflects my thinking and feelings for Black peoples' right to cultural expression as opposed to White peoples' tendency for cultural suppression."

"Essential to the effectiveness of *Self Portrait* is a sense of directness and sureness. It reveals aspects of me. Aspects of intensity, fight, struggle and anger. While these traits do not shape me absolutely, they do to a large degree exist as significant attributes of my identity."

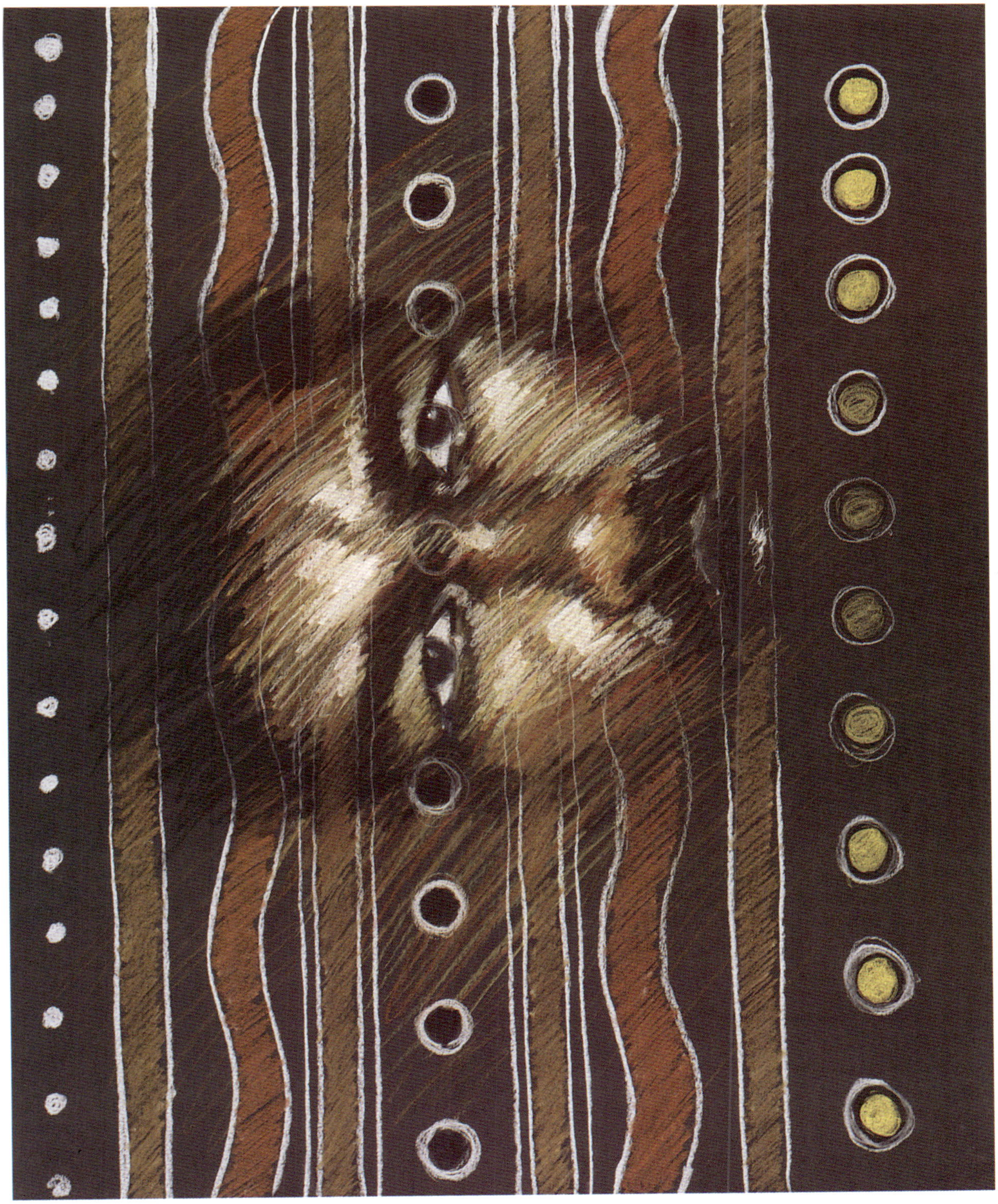

Vernon Ah Kee
SELF-PORTRAIT

PORTRAIT OF MY GREAT-GREAT-GRANDFATHER

Walter Raymond Lui

1999
Watercolour pencil drawing

Walter writes:

"The drawing I have submitted was produced using watercolour pencils. The man in the drawing is from Darnley Island in the Torres Strait (North East Australia). This man is one of my ancestors, my Great-Great-Grandfather. He originally came from the island of Lifou in the Loyalty Isles, married and settled in the Torres Strait. He was known by his family name as Lui Gope, but his countrymen addressed him as Gope-Tanu. Tanu being the village in Lifou where he came from. This name was eventually changed in the Torres Strait to Getano which is carried on within the Lui clans.

He is the father of Joseph (Yosepa) Lui (my Great-Grandfather) who was one of the first islanders to be ordained to the Deaconate together with Poey Passi in 1921. Later in 1924, two more islanders Sela Gaby and Captain Oth were also ordained.

The series of bands and patterns which run across the background, are selectively put into place in order to give some feeling of his essence as a man and of his culture. Some of the bands are not traditional. They are my own patterns designed to express both traditional and contemporary art.

The seagull featured in the composition is my family's totem."

Photo courtesy of the artist.

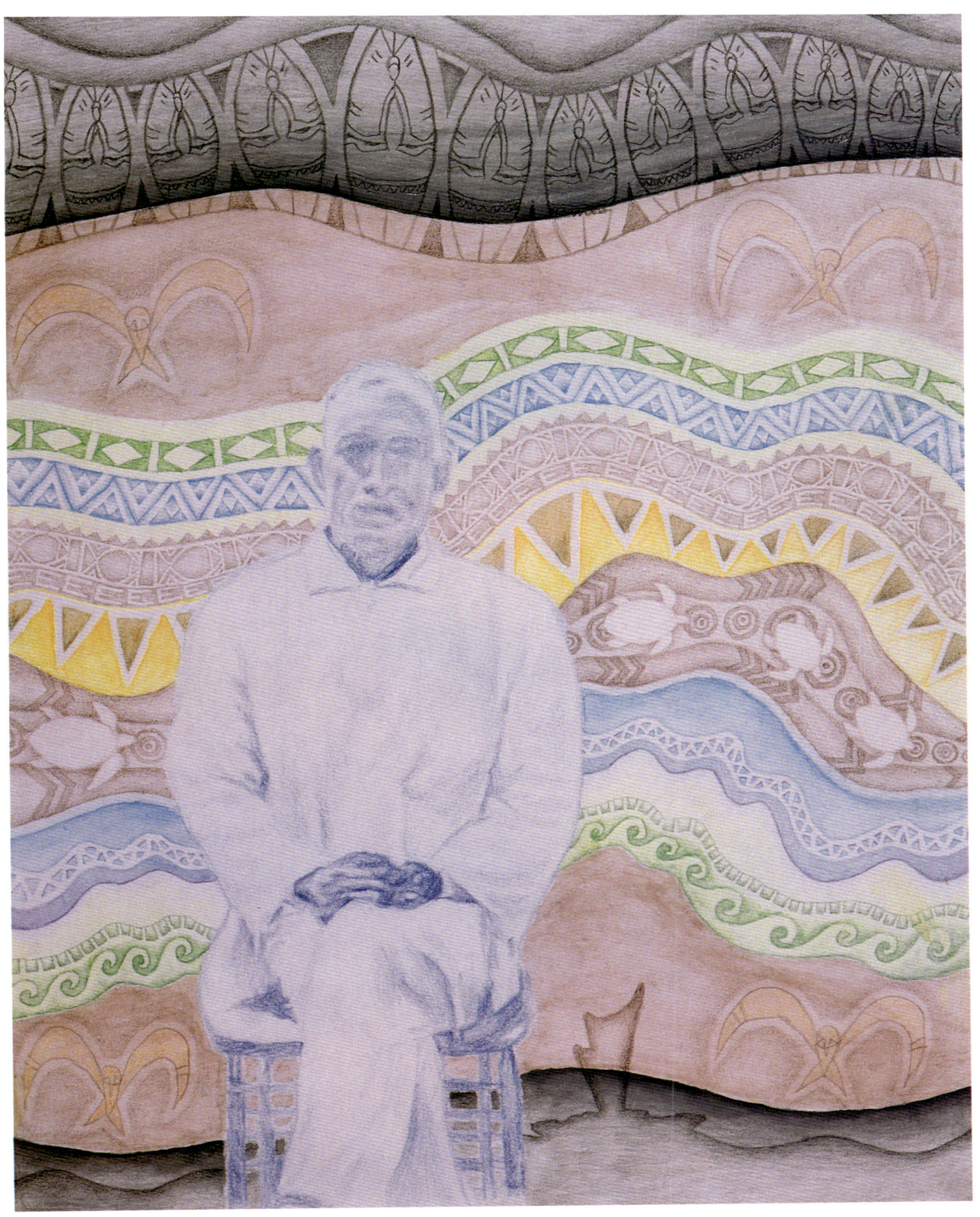

Walter Raymond Lui
PORTRAIT OF MY GREAT-GREAT-GRANDFATHER

Pink and Purple Waterlily Dreaming

Ethel Sambo

1998
Acrylic on Paper
38cm x 76cm

The pink water lily in the painting is the artist's dreaming, and the purple bud of the water lily is her aunty Maureen's dreaming. According to Aboriginal myths and legends, the spirit of every Aboriginal child is found in certain objects, such as the water lily, trees, plants, animals, rocks and sea creatures. According to the artist's grand-mother, water lilies are where her family's spirits were found.

Most water lilies are found in fresh water ways and billabongs, so during the artist's formative years, considerable time was spent camped around the billabongs, hunting for traditional foods like the magpie goose and the long-necked turtle, and fishing for barramundi. Other edible food was collected, including the water lily. They collected the stems, which taste like celery when eaten, as well as the flowers. The males of the clan would throw boomerangs into the billabong and accidentally they often got tangled with the vines and weeds of the waterlily, never to be found again.

The patterns on the stem of the waterlily represent the movement in the water, and the pattern on the boomerang is the mangrove worm. The mangrove worm is the totem of the artist's clan (the *Mari-amor*) who originate from the Daly River area in the Northern Territory.

The brown border around the painting represents the edge of the billabong.

Courtesy of the artist.

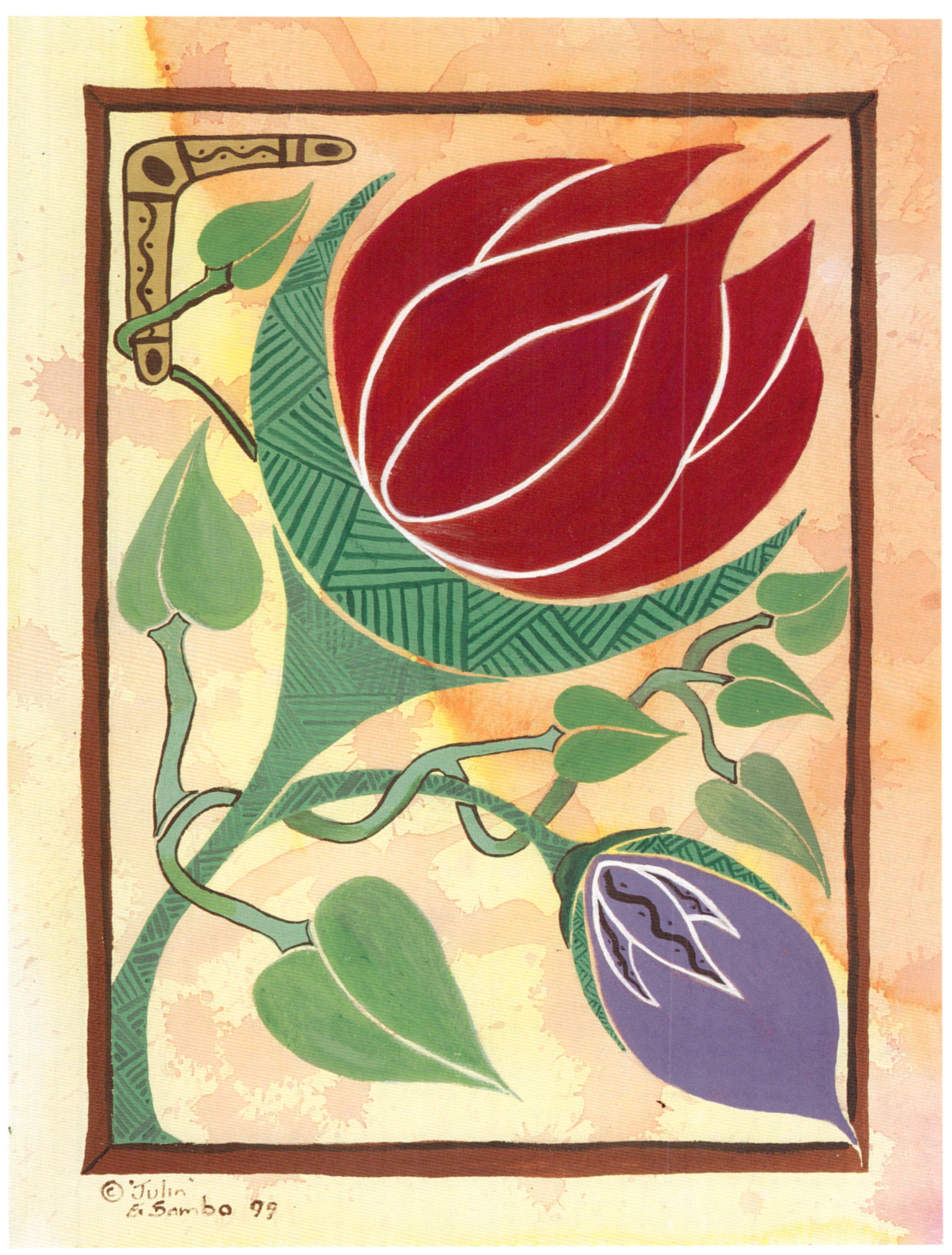

Ethel Sambo
Pink and Purple Waterlily Dreaming

MANGROVE MUDFLATS

MUNGANBANA (NORMAN MILLER)

1998
Linocut Print
40 x 54cm

The mangrove mudflats along the Cairns Esplanade were the inspiration for this artwork. During morning and evening walks, the artist would see and hear not only human movement, but the elements and animal life: the ocean, wind, waves, birds, fish and crabs. The egrets wading around in the mangrove mudflats pictured on the left and right of the painting are decorated with traditional Aboriginal designs. The crab in the centre is framed by two fishes, one above, one below.

This is a limited edition lino print.
Courtesy of the artist.

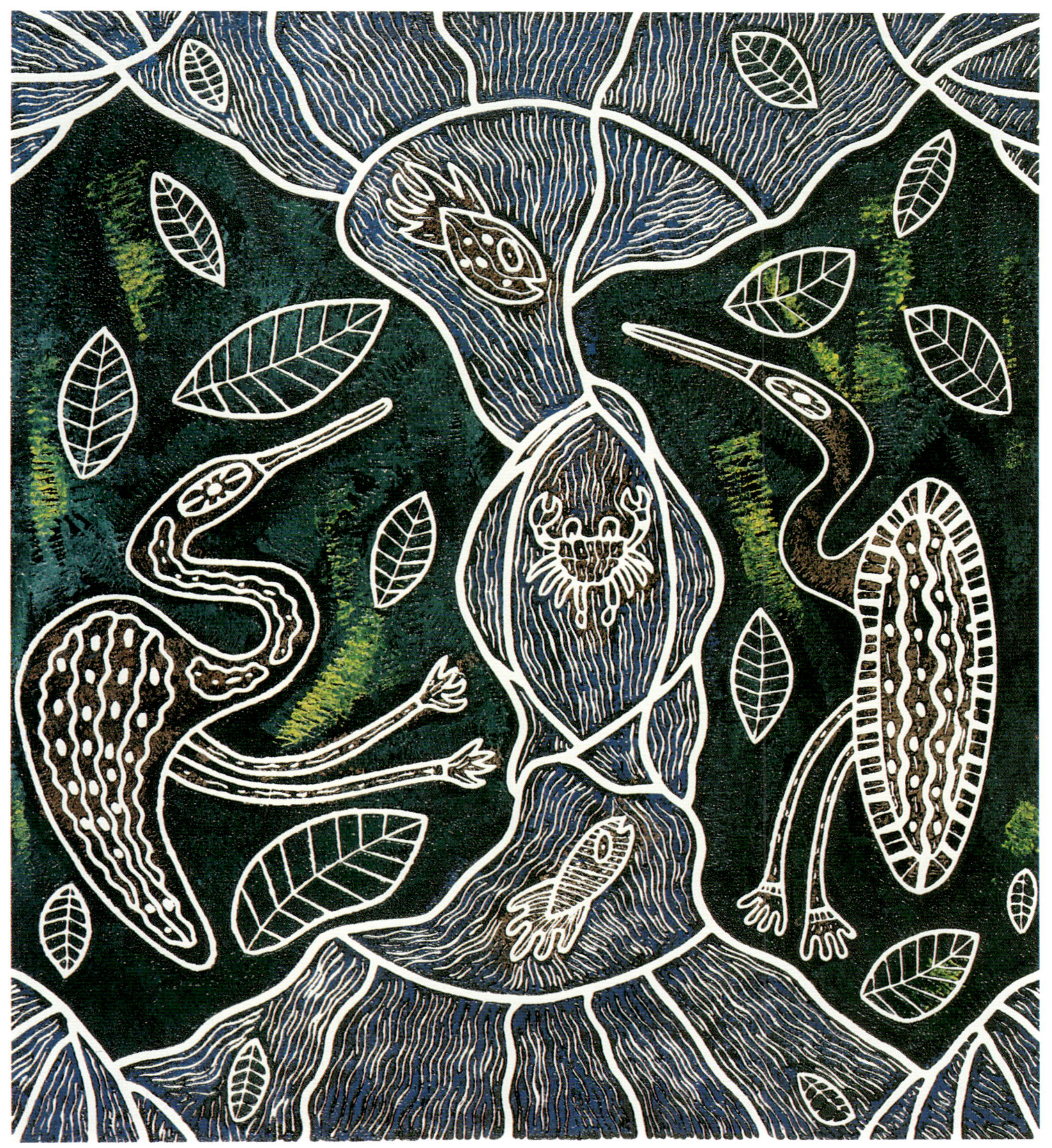

Munganbana (Norman Miller)
MANGROVE MUDFLATS

DJUBBA (TREE GOANNA)

MATU (BRIAN O'BEIRNS)

Red cedar carving
1999

Matu chooses his timber carefully. He may walk many days before finding the piece that will suit his idea for a carving. The main timbers Matu uses are red cedar, black bean, black palm, Huon pine, rosewood and others. These woods are mostly scrub woods, but Matu also collects from the rocky mountains, desert areas and swamps which are also sources for suitable timbers and roots. Matu appreciates the texture and grain of roots that have grown between rocks. The pressure that the rocks provide leaves the roots with a compact, tight grain different from all other wood types.

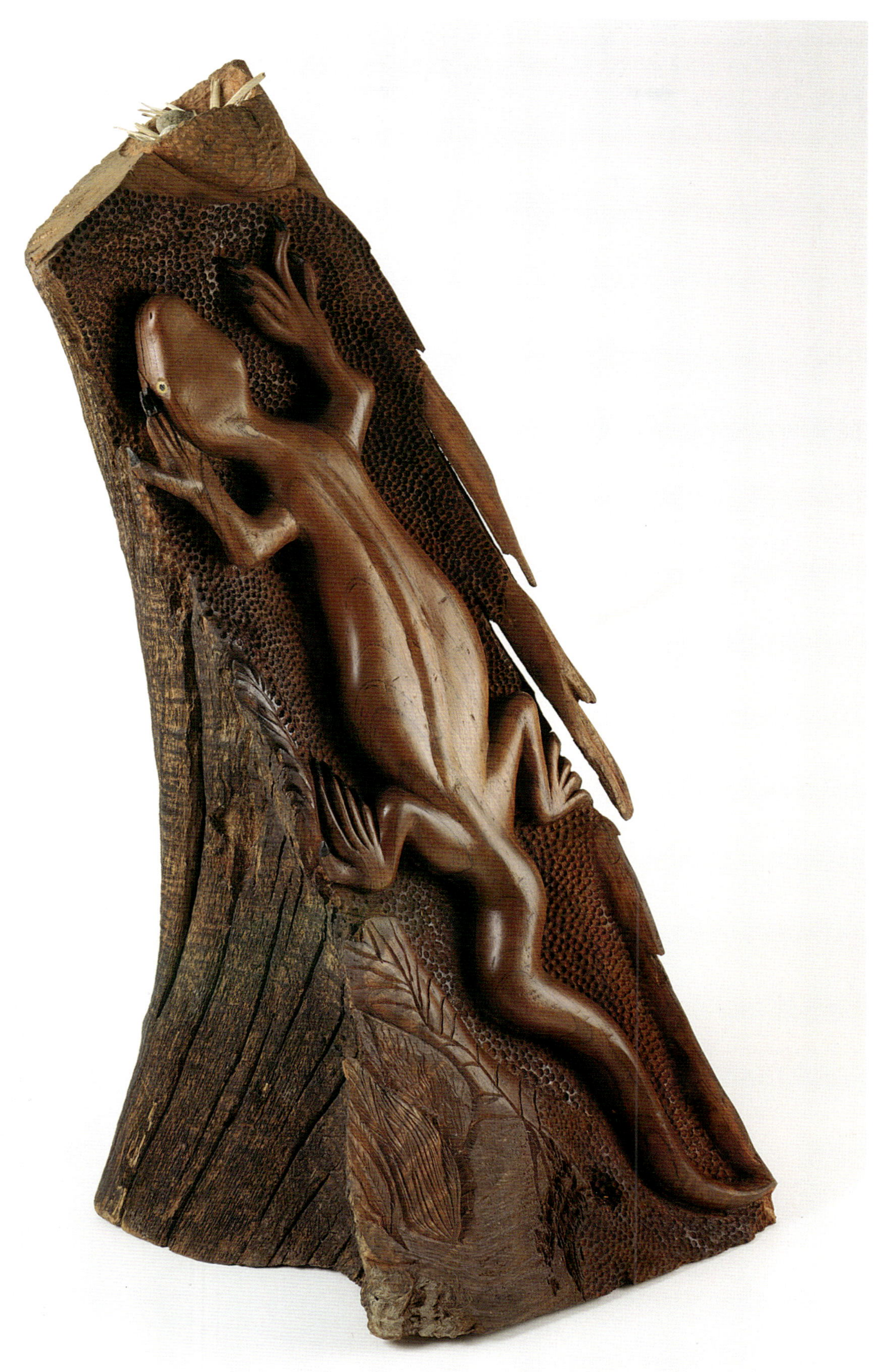

Matu (Brian O'Beirns)
Djubba (Tree Goanna)

THE BLACK HOLE IN THE SKY

Shirley Christian

Batik on Silk
1985
Private Collection

In 1999 Shirley wrote:

"The image I have used on my batik depicts an Aboriginal legend about death. It is believed that after death our people go through the black hole situated in the Milky Way.

I saw this phenomenon when I was on Mornington Island, just before the start of the initiation ceremony I was attending to see my eldest son Stephen initiated into tribal ways.

I was asked by my Tribal son and Stephen to go with them, look up into the night sky and tell them what I saw. First I saw clouds shaped like arrows pointing Eastwards. I was asked to look again. This time, for the first time in my life, I saw the legendary 'Black Hole', right in the middle of the Milky Way.

Word got to the elders and the next night when the initiation ceremony began I was part of the ceremony from beginning to end as my son was initiated into the tribe.

The Mornington Island people (Lardil) adopted my family into their tribe. My eldest son was given the name Warrigal (Dingo). I was given the tribal name of Waal (Morning Glory). This name refers to the small woolly clouds that can stretch across the sky for miles around Mornington Island. I was told that these clouds are in the Dreamtime, and that the only other place you can see such clouds is in Mexico.

White people who have near-death experiences have told of travelling through a dark tunnel at the end of which is a bright white light. When Aboriginal people go through the black hole in the sky, they have the same experience and enter the Spirit World."

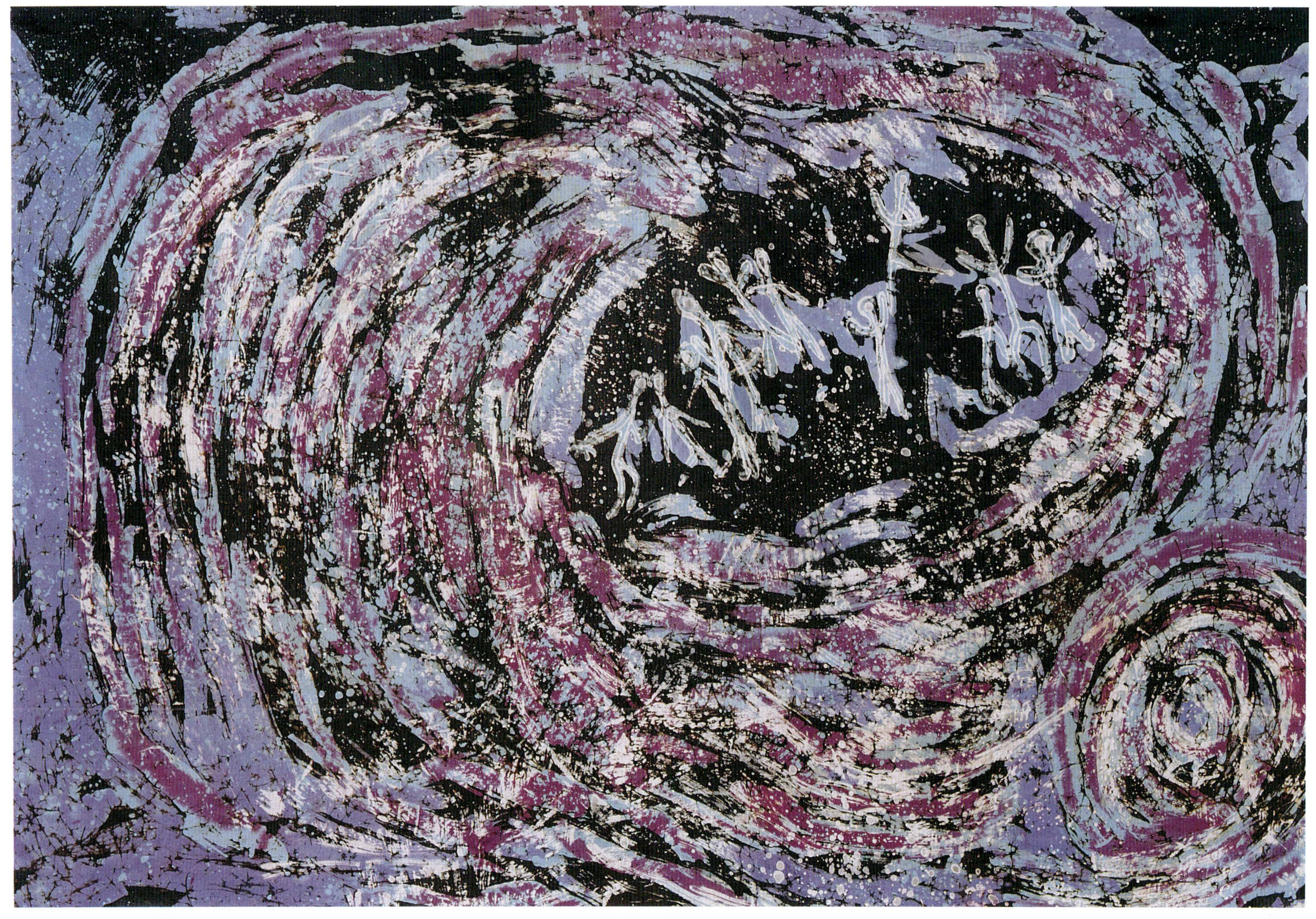

Shirley Christian
THE BLACK HOLE IN THE SKY

KAH
(ECHIDNA MAN)

Gordon Landers

1994
Acrylic on Paper
56 x 76cm

A long time ago back in Aboriginal mythological time, there was a man who belonged to a clan whose people thought he was a good person, but in fact he was a good-for-nothing person. He would steal other people's belongings and their women. The elders knew he was a thief, so they chased after him and were tracking him for days and nights before finally finding him. The no-good-person grabbed one of the women by the hand and ran away with her.

The elders pursued both of them throwing spears to stop them. Every one of the spears stayed quivering in their backs, and both were also speared through their noses. The no-good-person could not run any further, and the elders were gaining on him. He quickly decided to hide in an ant hill and covered up any tracks he and the woman had made. When the elders came to the ant hill where they were hiding, they could not find the runaways so they went back home.

In the ant hill, the man and woman began to change into *Kah* the echidna. The yellow soil fell on them and the spears turned into quills. Their finger-nails turned into claws, hair became fur and they lived on white-ants and honey-ants.

The honey ants are considered *Nun-na* (food) for Aborigines. That is why the echidna (*Kah*), which symbolises all no-good-persons, their women and their babies, is hunted today.

Courtesy of the Artist

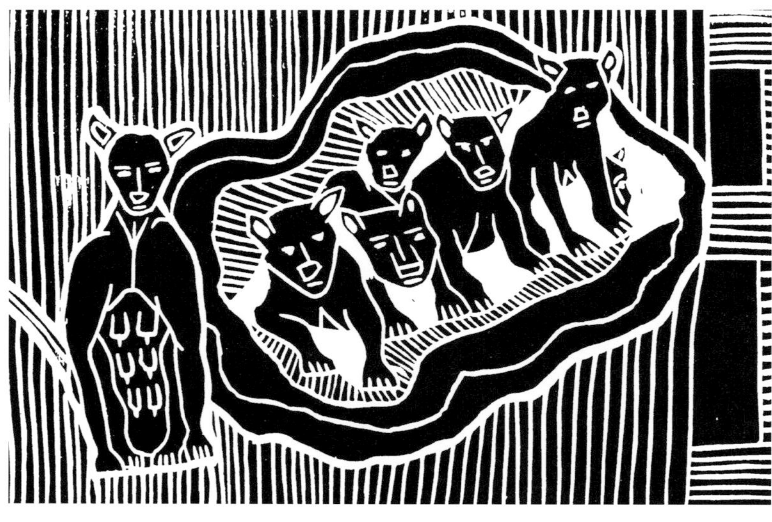

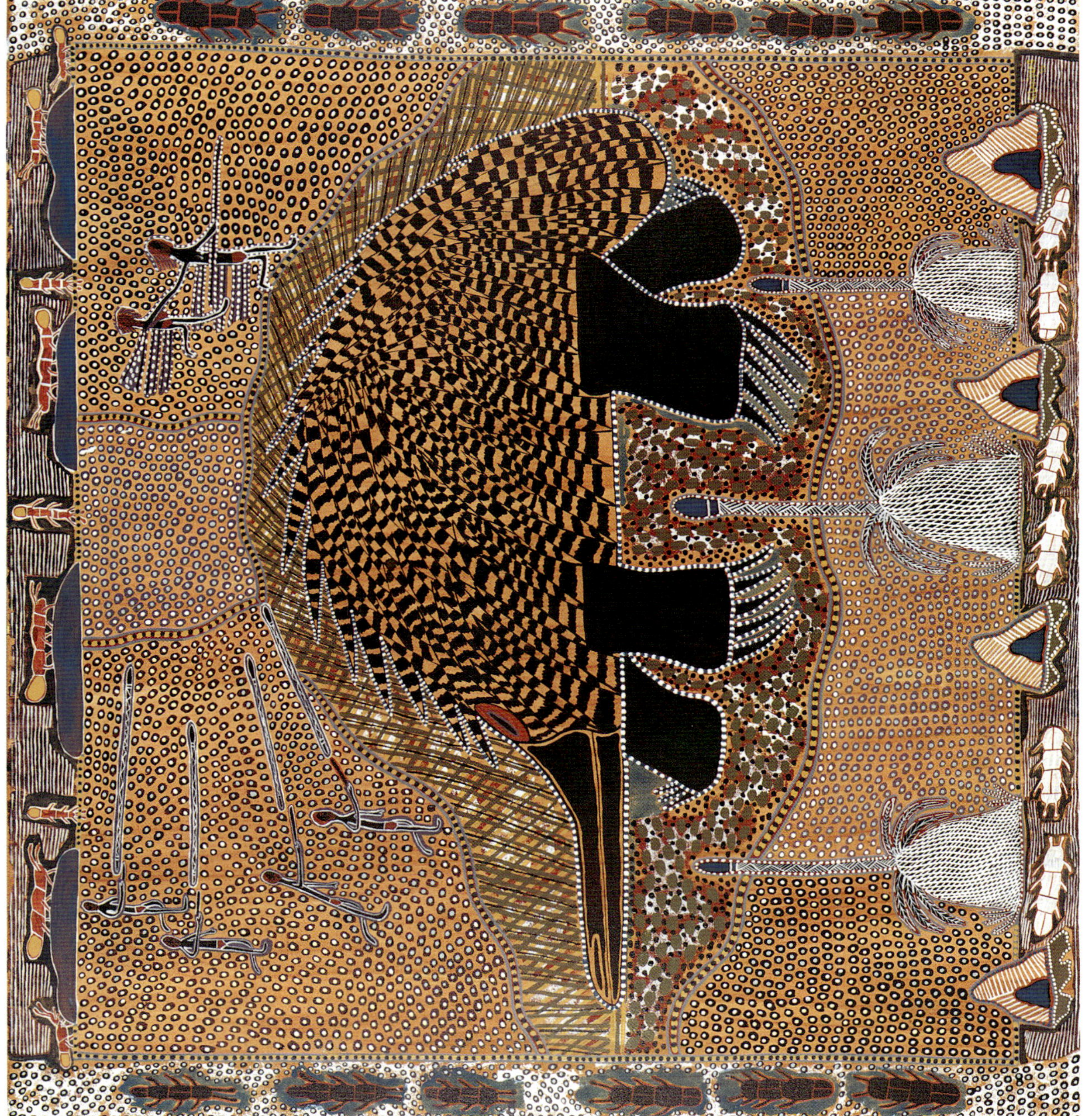

Gordon Landers
KAH (ECHIDNA MAN)

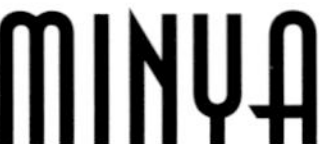

Marilyn Kepple

4 Images - Acrylic on Paper
34.5cm x 27cm each
Cape York Land Council Collection

The connections between Marilyn Kepple's images and her identity are not just coincidental. The paintings reflect her care for her country and her strong sense of tradition. These images are reflective of the spiritual and natural world.

Within each image is contained the rhythm of the water/ sea and the coursing of the landscape. As most of Marilyn's paintings depict the bush and sea creatures, they also represent important traditional foods and locations of her people.

Using textures and layering of design behind the kangaroo, goanna, turtle and barramundi, each of the four pieces creates a unique story of place and tradition.

Text: Courtesy of Arone Meeks

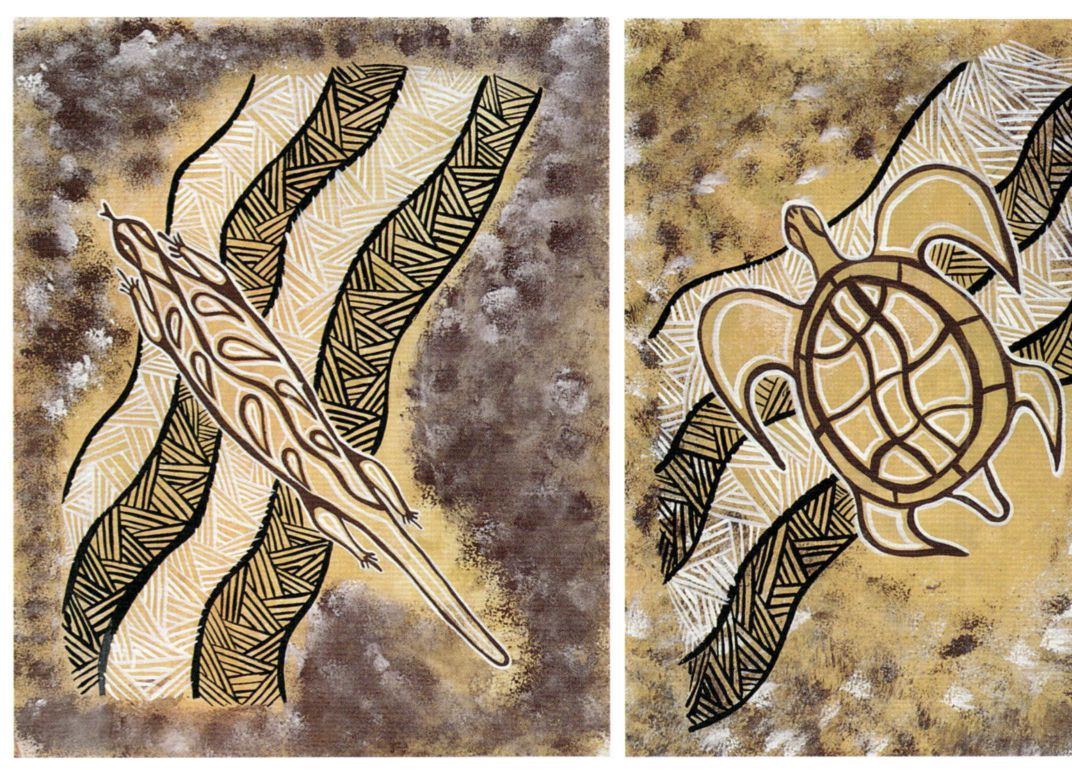

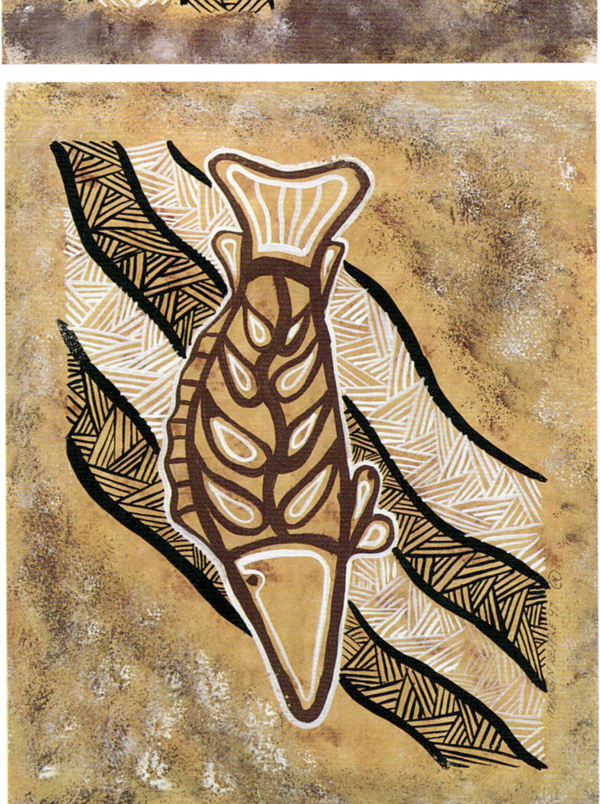

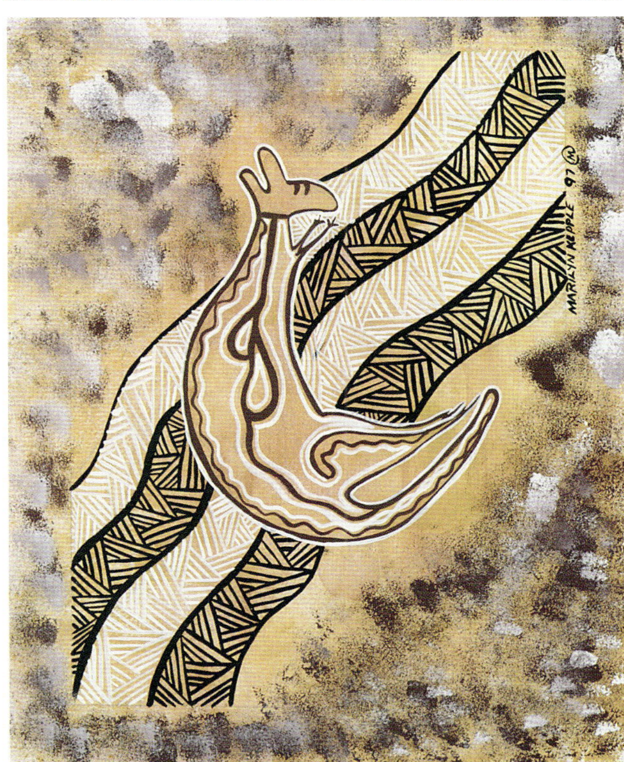

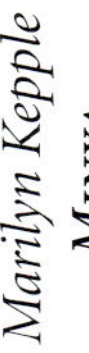

Marilyn Kepple
MINYA

WOMEN'S DREAMING PLACE

Linda Kamara Myers

1994
Lithograph
33 x 48cm
National Gallery of Australia, A.C.T. Collection

This lithograph is based on a true story.

The image shows a dreaming place only for women on the Todd River. One of the sacred objects in the dreaming place was destroyed by bulldozers when the Northern Territory government was attempting to build a recreational dam.

Work on this dam was stopped when there was a protest rally by the local Aboriginal people and the custodian from Alice Springs.

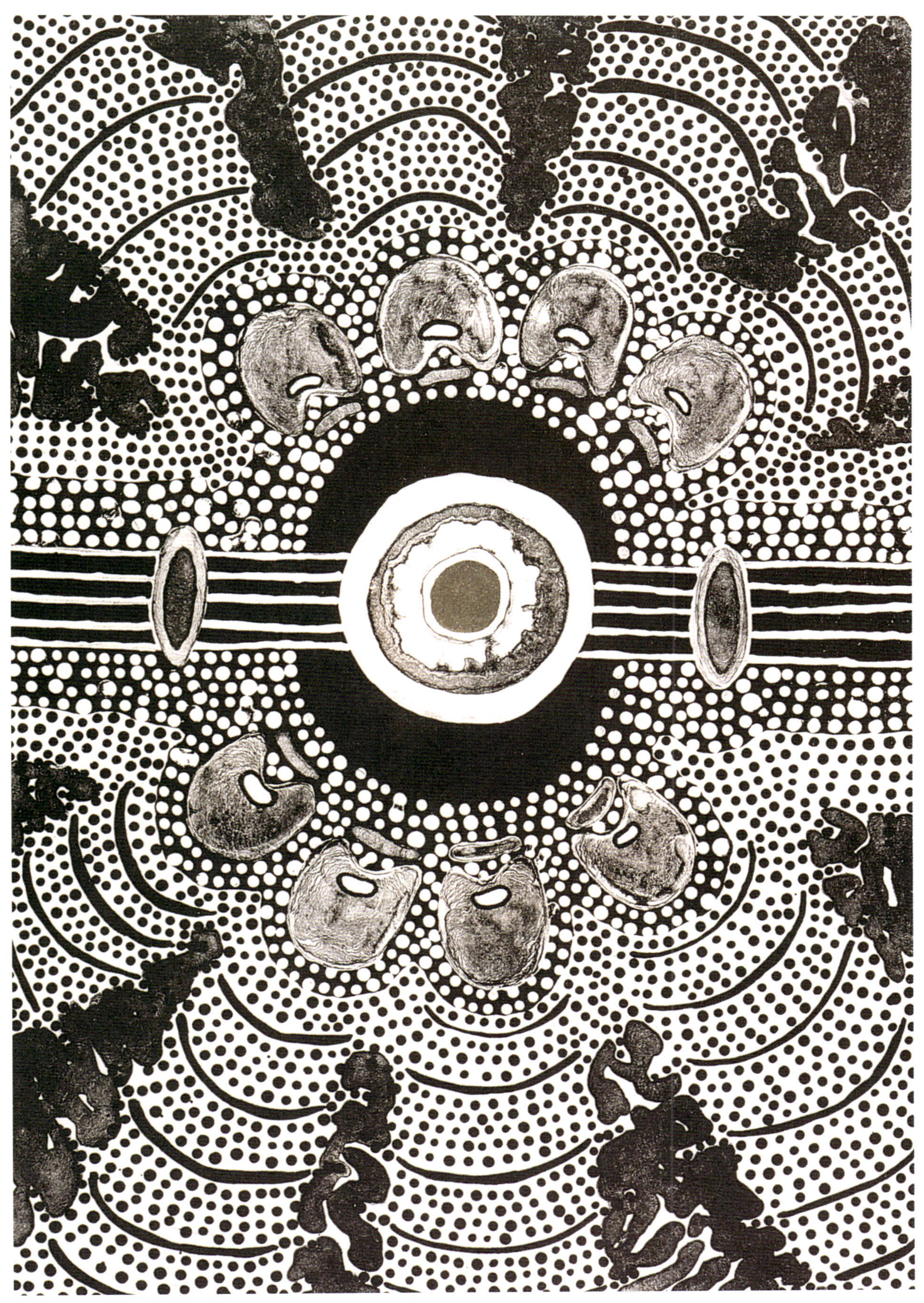

Linda Kamara Myers
WOMEN'S DREAMING PLACE

SEVEN SISTERS

Shelley Monkland (*Djarainj*)

1997
Linocut Print
40 x 52cm
Private Collection

The *Seven Sisters* is based upon two ideas. Firstly, there are various Aboriginal Dreamtime stories about the Seven Sisters, and secondly there is a more personal meaning in that my Mother had six sisters. All of these seven sisters have been very important in my life.

I originally produced only a small edition of seven of these prints to give to my Mother, and her sisters, my Aunties, as gifts.

The backgrounds are coloured from rainbow to ochre colours.

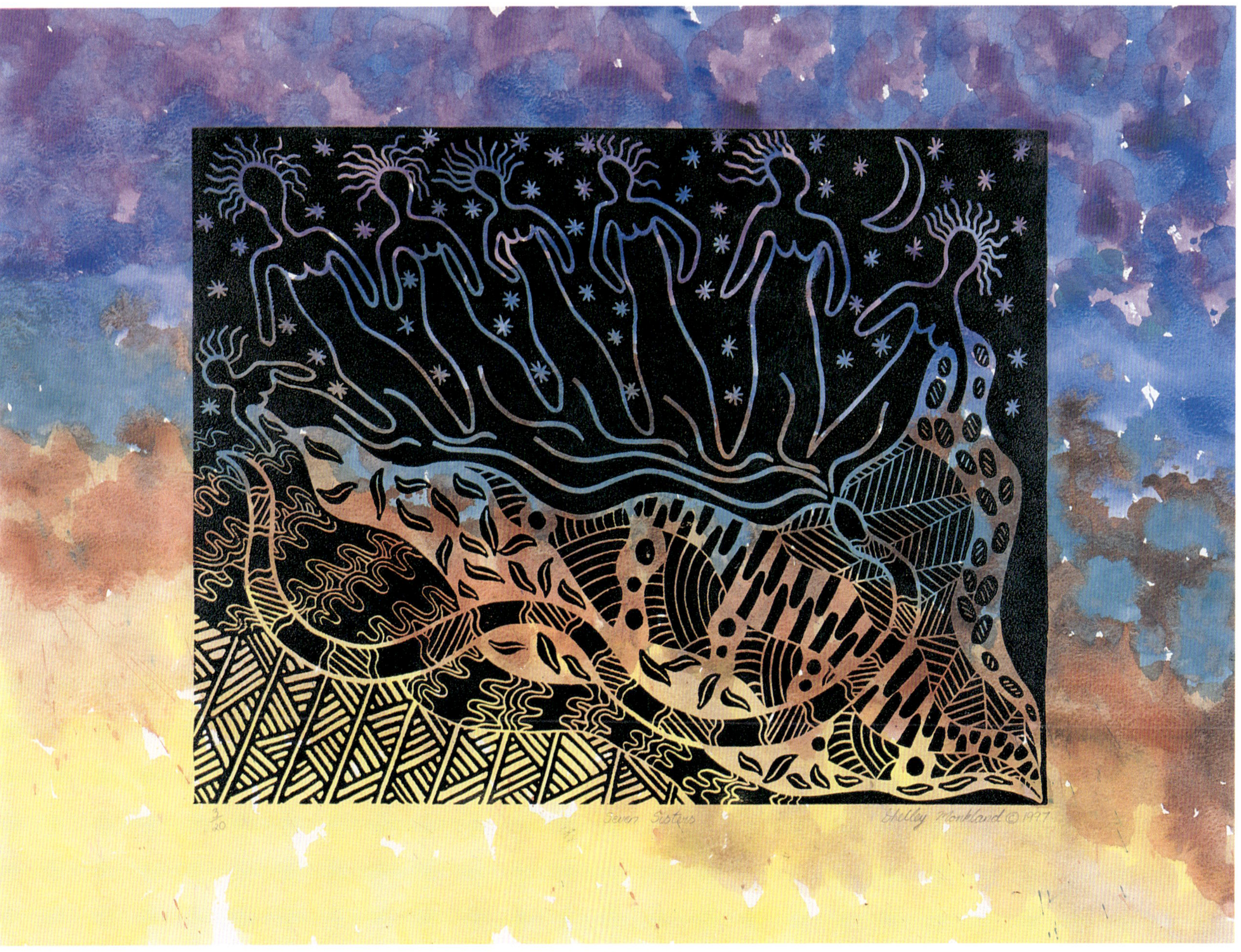

Shelley Monkland (Djarainj)
Seven Sisters

MA REMBELING - LONG NOSE SUGARBAG
(WILD HONEY BEE)

SHAUN KALK EDWARDS

Acrylic on Paper
56 x 76cm
1997

Kokoberrin Language:
Warrekeng nganduw, Parth la wedarr Kokoberra, Pa wanggenang ngantuw ngalaw kulaaw.

Shaun writes:

"During a Ranger training course held in our country (Kokoberra Parth la wedaar) in 1996, the old men (Pa wanggenang) showed the rangers how to make fire sticks (ngantuw ngalaw kulaaw) and where to find sugarbag.

I painted *Ma Rembeling* in 1997. It is an image I saw on my way to collect sugarbag (wild honey bee). We passed a clump of Ma Peal (cabbage tree palms) and in them was a mob of crimson-winged parrots. Until then, I hadn't had the chance to see so many of these parrots at one time so close up.

The colours of these parrots inspired me to paint this picture using bright colours, something I have been introducing into my work in recent years. I used to only work in traditional earth colours."

Note: The parrots described by Shaun are the Red-winged parrots Aprosmictus Eryythropterus, also called the Red-winged Lory, and Crimson-winged parrots.

Source: Cayley, N. W. What Bird is That.

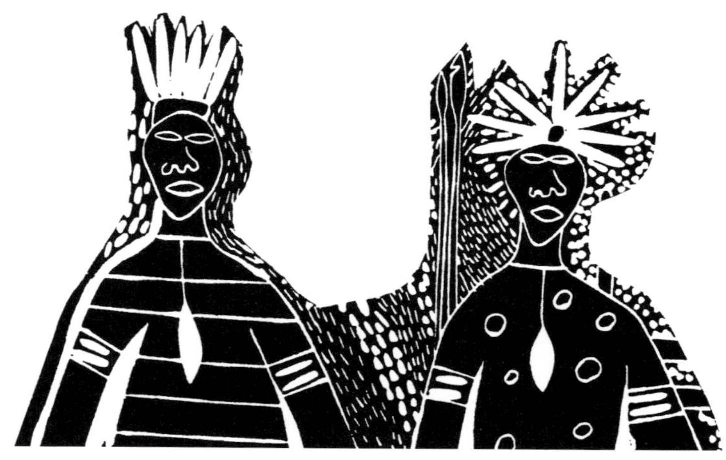

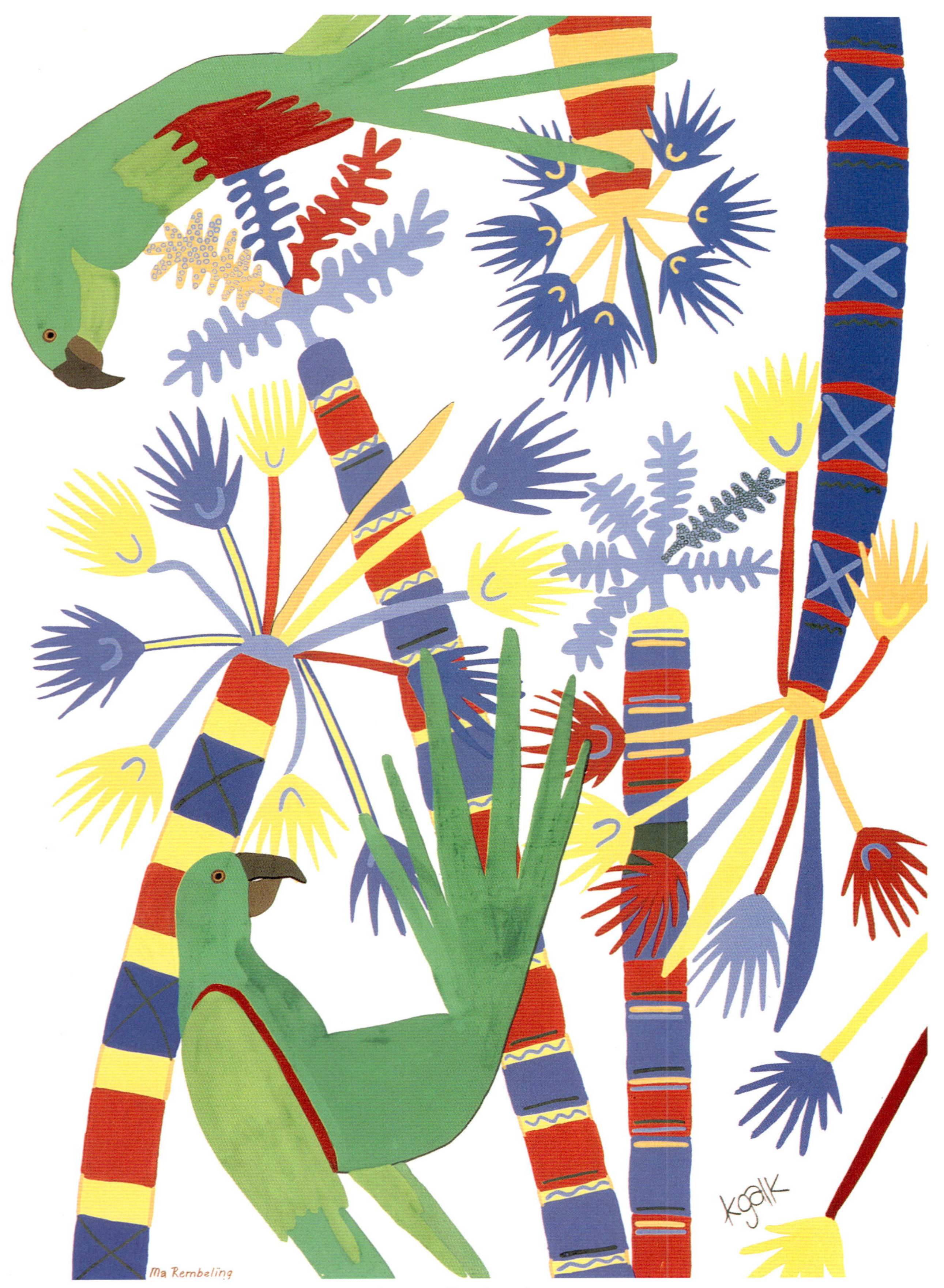

Shaun Kalk Edwards

Ma Rembeling - Long Nose Sugarbag (Wild Honey Bee)

MUM & DAD'S PILLOW TALK

JANET FIELDHOUSE

Ceramic sculpture
17 x 30cm
1999

The theme for this sculpture is the intimacy between two people contemplating life from youth to old age.

The male and female figures resting on the pillow represent the close relationship between two people who have been married for many years, sharing a long life of hardship, love and the bringing up of their children. The figures are not touching and are facing away from each other on the pillow. This is to symbolise the closeness of their relationship and marriage, where the difficulties they have faced together make the need to consolidate their love no longer apparent. They know each other so well, and their love for each other is understood even though it is unspoken.

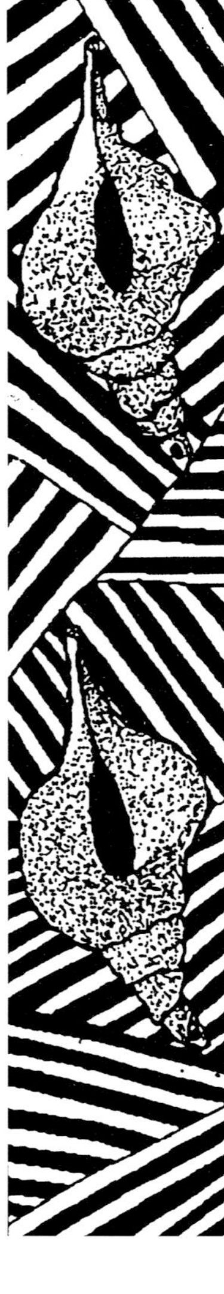

The piece is made from Feeneys Raku clay. The base is formed from coils and the figures are solid sculptures. The sculpture was biscuit fired first to 1000 degrees centigrade for strength, and then sawdust fired. This process involves sitting the piece in a container of sawdust, in this case a metal garbage bin. The sawdust is set alight, the lid placed on the container, and the sculpture is then left to slowly smoulder for 24 hours.

The porous clay is stained with the carbon produced by the smouldering sawdust, giving a variety of smoked brown to black colours.

This technique of firing requires only a comparatively low temperature and glazes are not utilised.

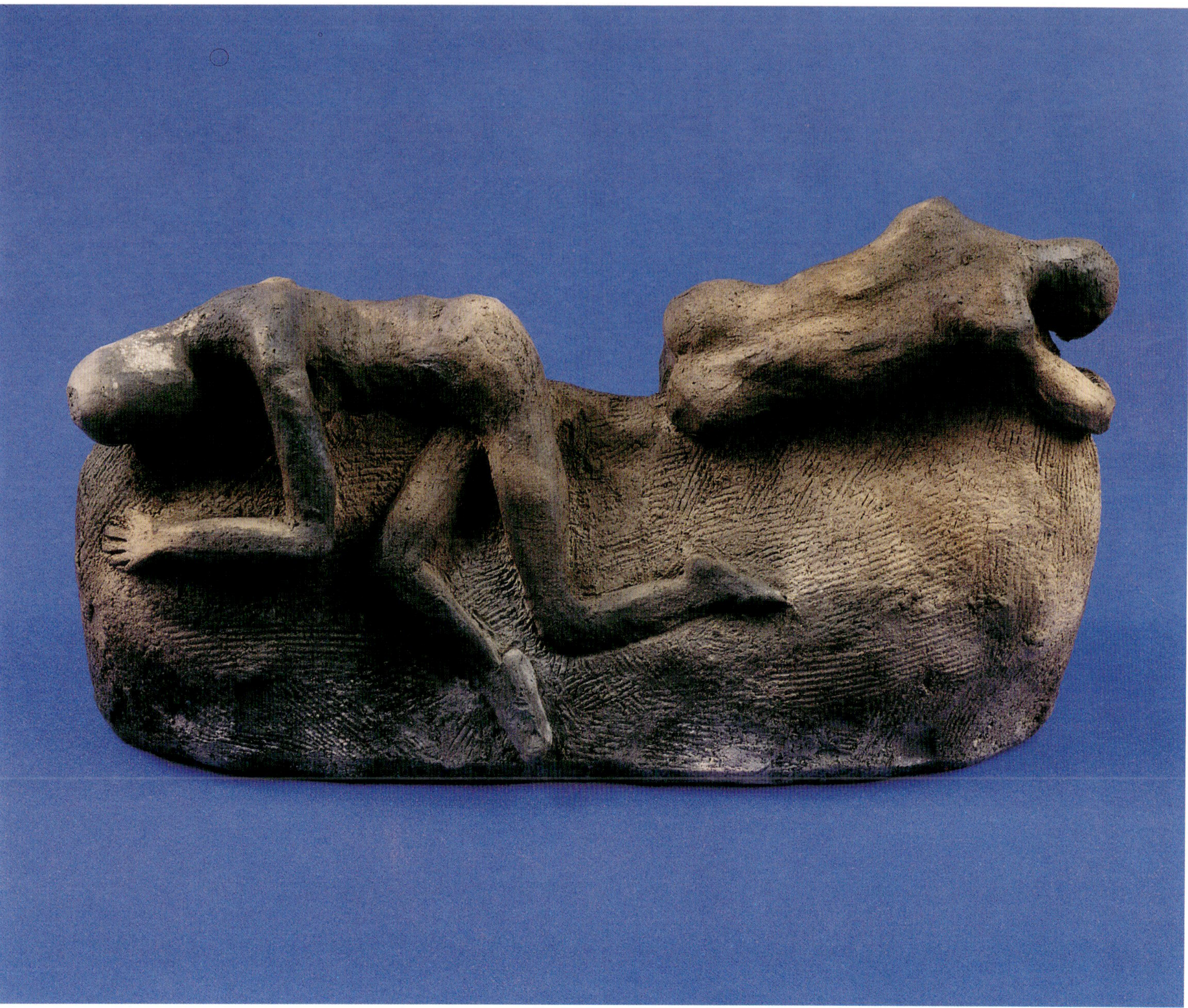

Janet Fieldhouse
Mum and Dad's Pillow Talk

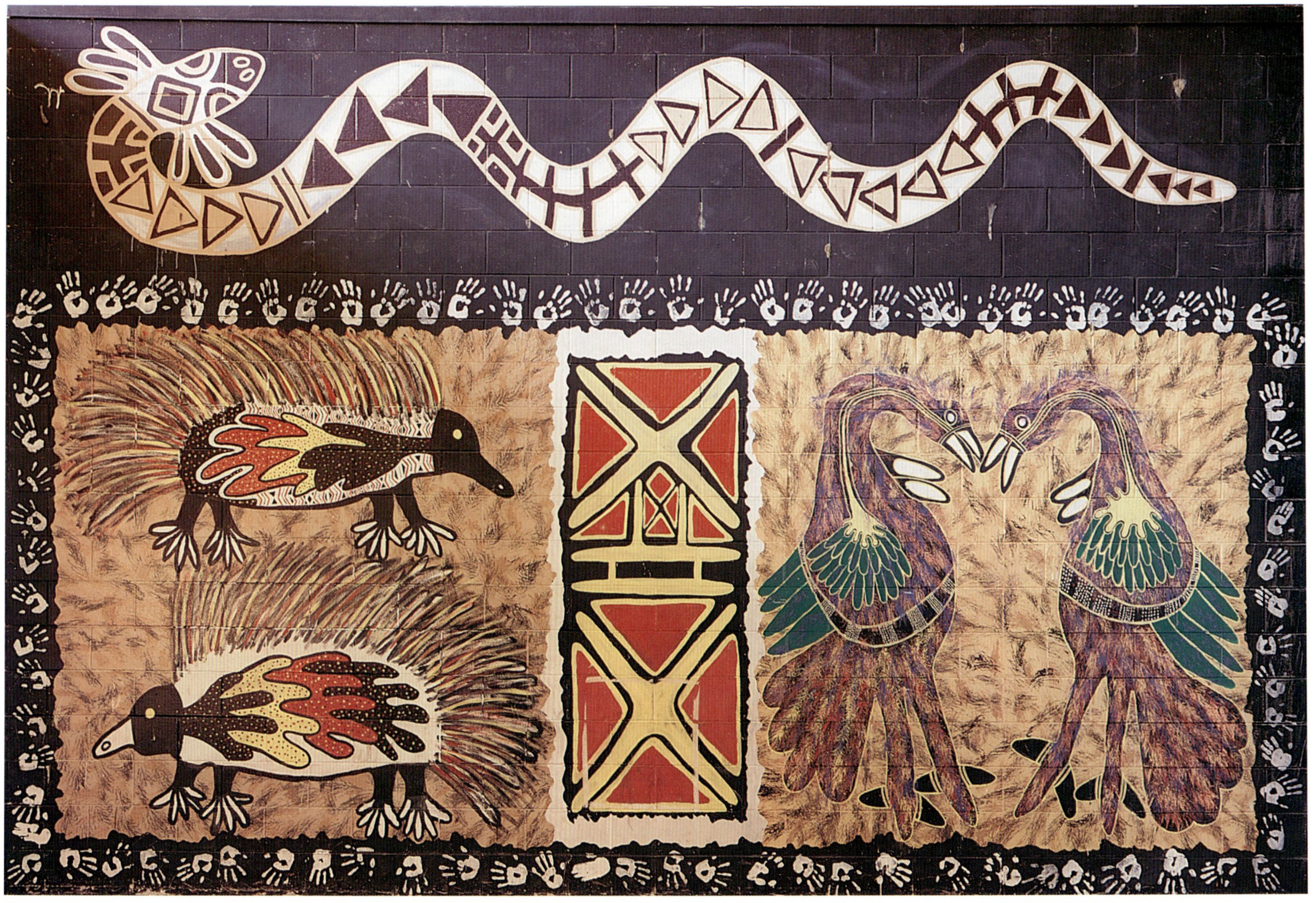

Zane Saunders
SMITHFIELD STATE HIGH SCHOOL MURAL

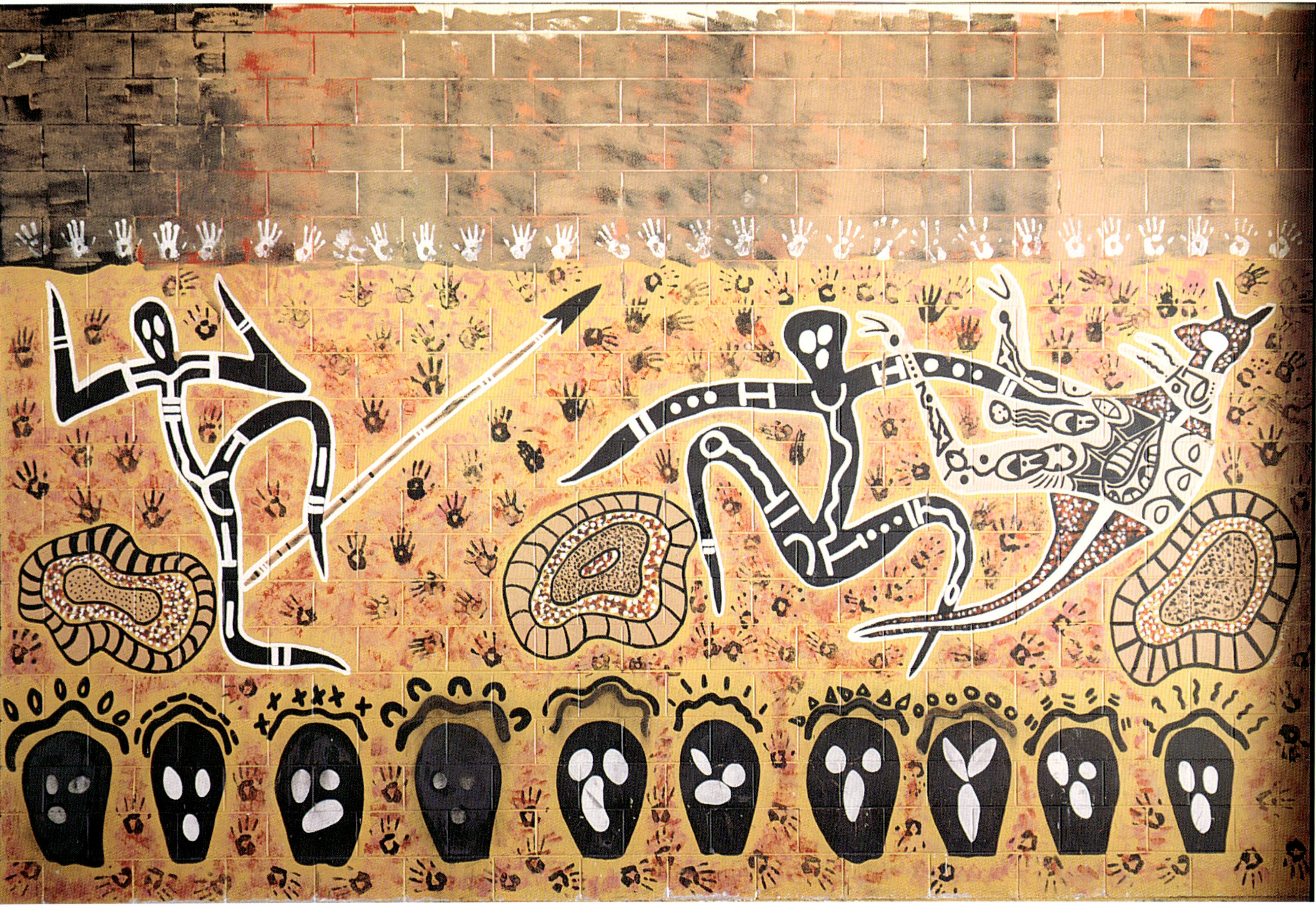

Frank McLeod
SMITHFIELD STATE HIGH SCHOOL MURAL

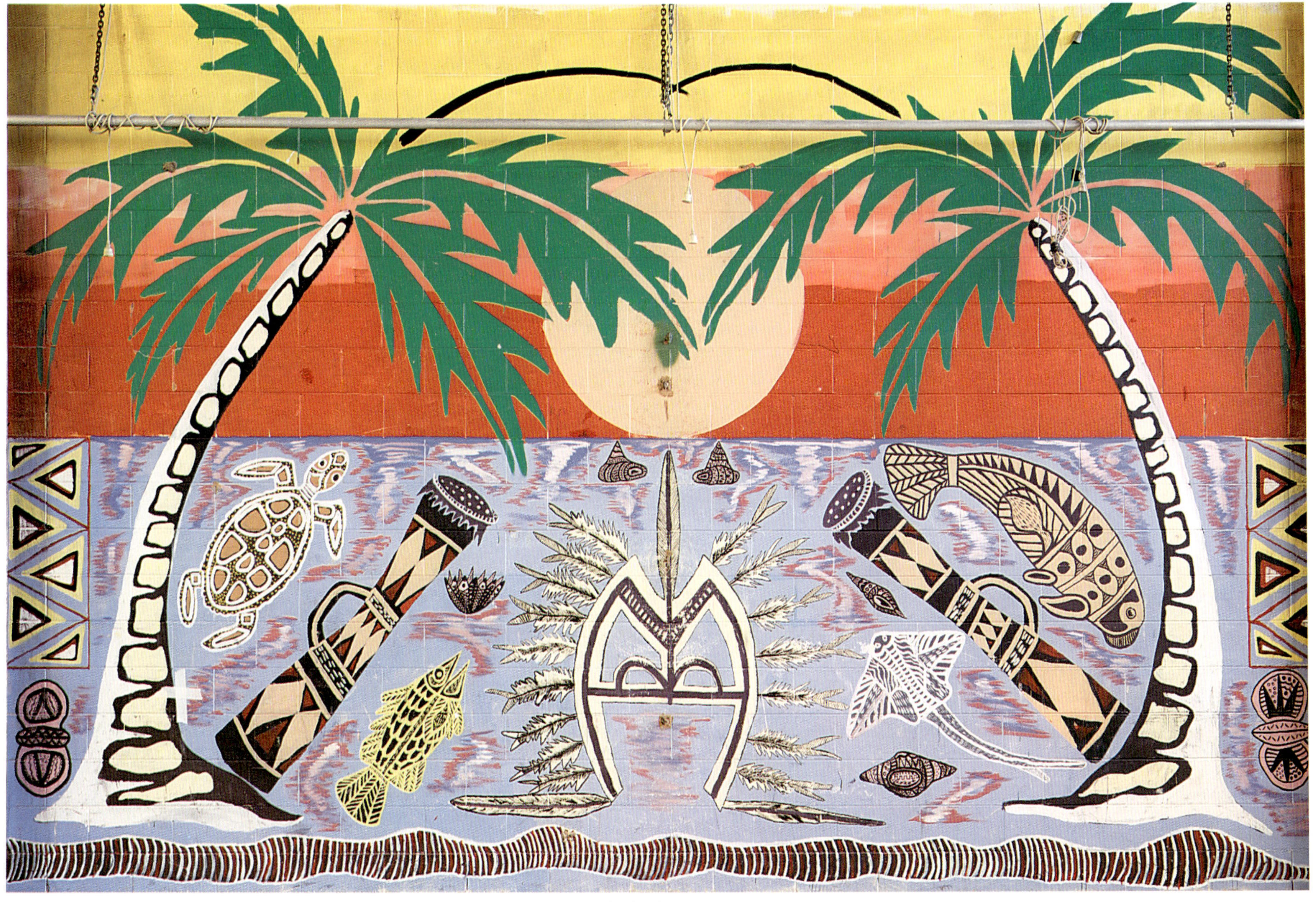

Tatipai Barsa
SMITHFIELD STATE SCHOOL MURAL

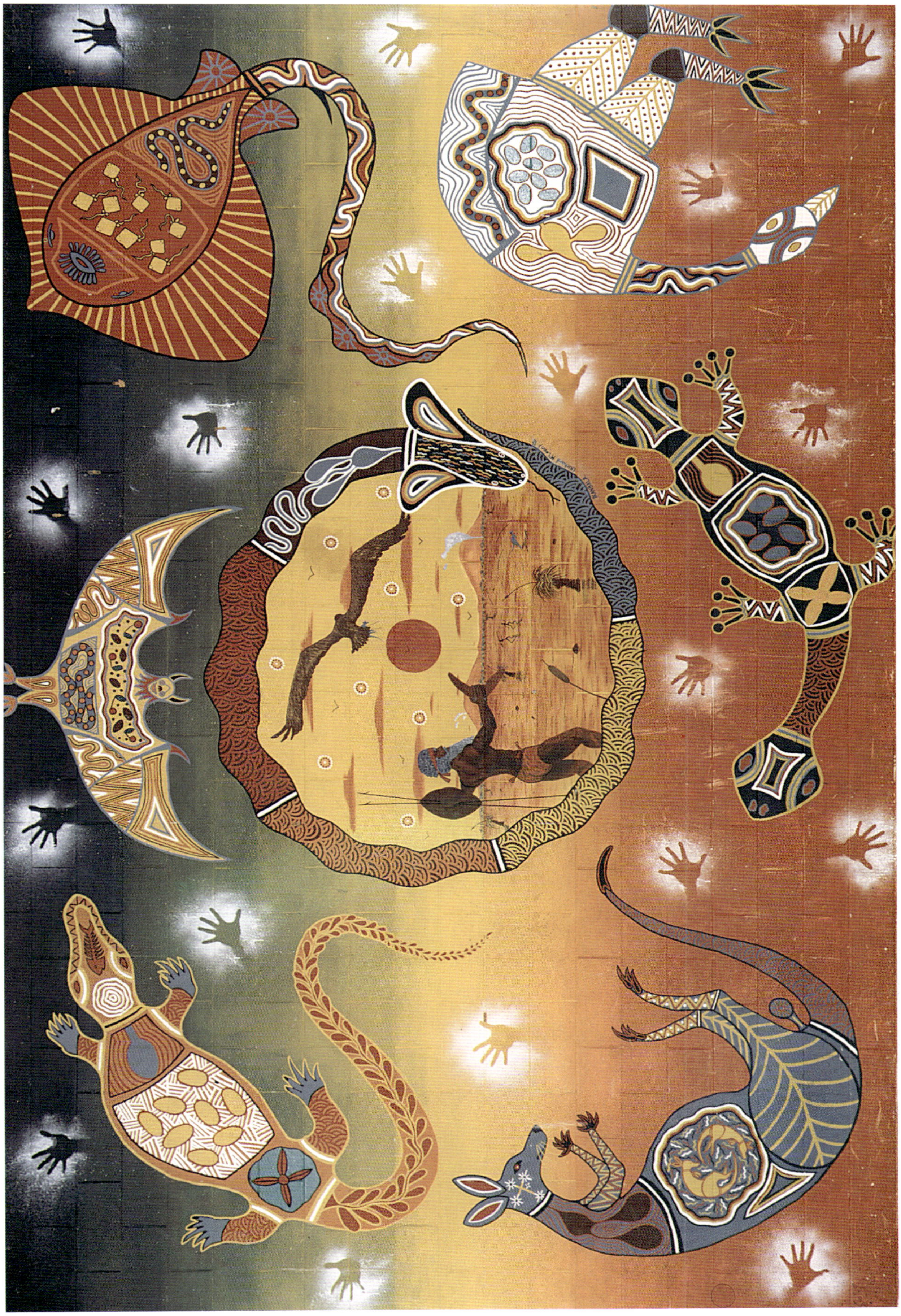

Ikanbala - Richard McLean

Woree State High School Mural

Elder Enoch Tranby was commissioned to paint this mural at Woree State High School in 1995. Located in the school's Multi-purpose Shelter, the mural depicts in the background the landscape as seen from the doorway of the building, looking across to Red Hill. Behind the Red Hill is the Southern Cairns suburb of Whiterock. The next year, students Richard and Robert painted the murals shown on pages 71 & 73 along the same wall.

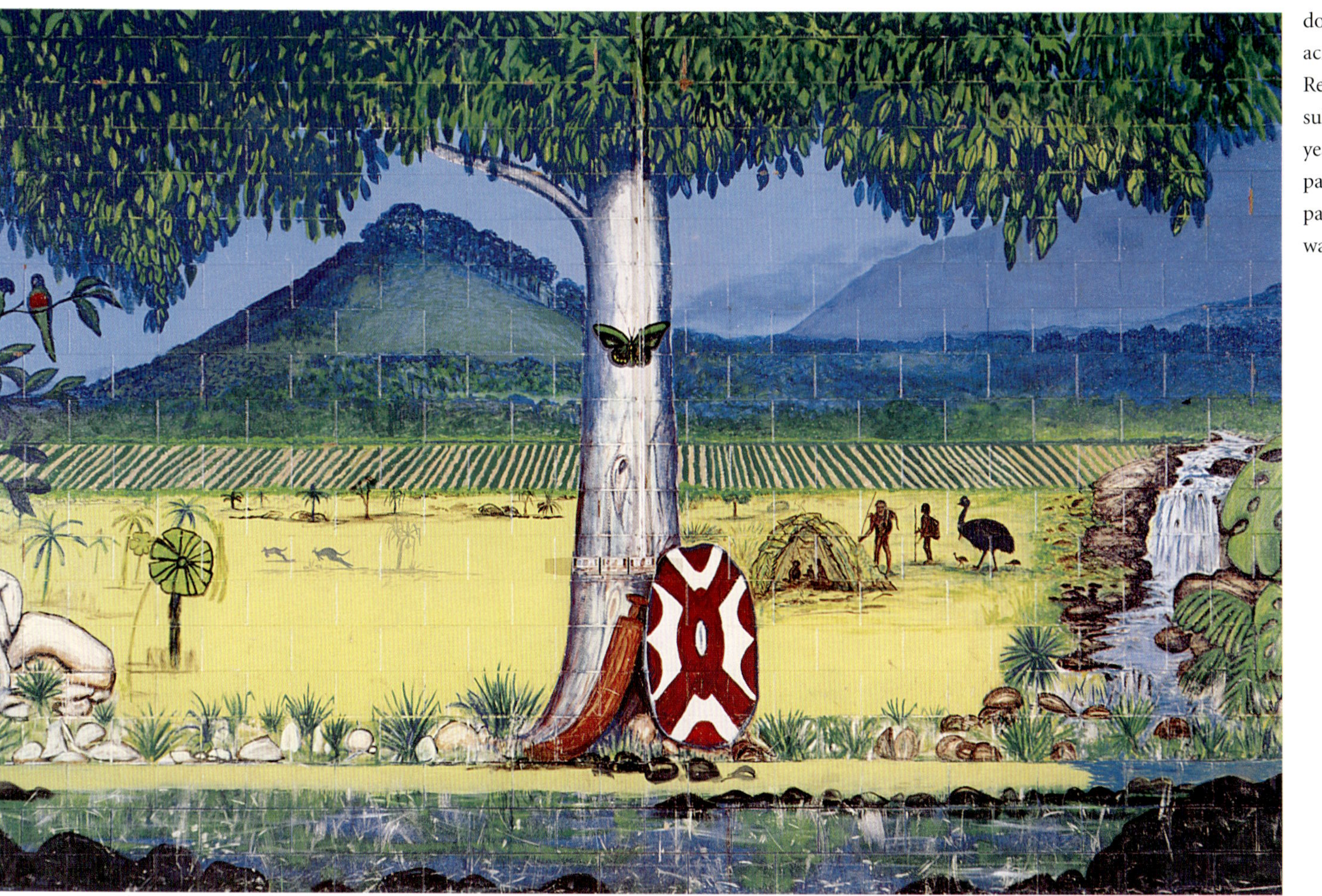

Enoch Tranby
WOREE STATE HIGH SCHOOL MURAL

Robert Mast

Woree State High School Mural

CAIRNS NORTH STATE PRIMARY SCHOOL MURAL

Colin Higgins, James Meeks, Dennis Nona, Brian Robinson

Acrylic on board.
130 x 260cm
1992

The art of Australia's two Indigenous peoples - Aborigines and Torres Strait Islanders - represents one of the longest continuing traditions of art known.

Indigenous art appears in a wide range of forms and media: from ancient rock paintings and engravings, to temporary body decoration, ground paintings and sand paintings, bark paintings to sculpture in wood and woven fibres. In recent years, introduced media such as linocuts and other printing techniques, synthetic paints and canvas, and computer technology have given Aboriginal and Torres Strait Islander artists other avenues for their creative expression.

The work of contemporary Indigenous artists is clearly recognisable. Many have left aside the traditional ochre colours of their ancestors and opted for a more vibrant colour palette. Even though the colour spectrum may have been altered, many Indigenous artists and artworks still retain various facets of tradition: images, motifs, strengths and themes.

This painting depicts the various iconic images which portray both Indigenous cultures of Australia. It focuses on the traditions of hunting, food gathering, and activities associated with these aspects of the cultures.

Representing Aboriginal Australia are the stylised images of certain fauna, such as the lizard or goanna, the snake and the fresh water barramundi. Depicting the Torres Strait Island people are images of sea-faring creatures such as the dugong and the octopus. Note the various markings inscribed onto and around each animal. These markings have been stylised from the traditional etchings of both cultures. Surrounding the central images are depictions of two throwing boomerangs, a spear and a harpoon, which were traditionally utilised for hunting these and other animals.

The drum represents the festivities taking place after a successful hunting trip. Dances would have been performed using this and other instruments to portray the hunt. The collection of this food would ensure the survival of each Clan group.

Text by Brian Robinson

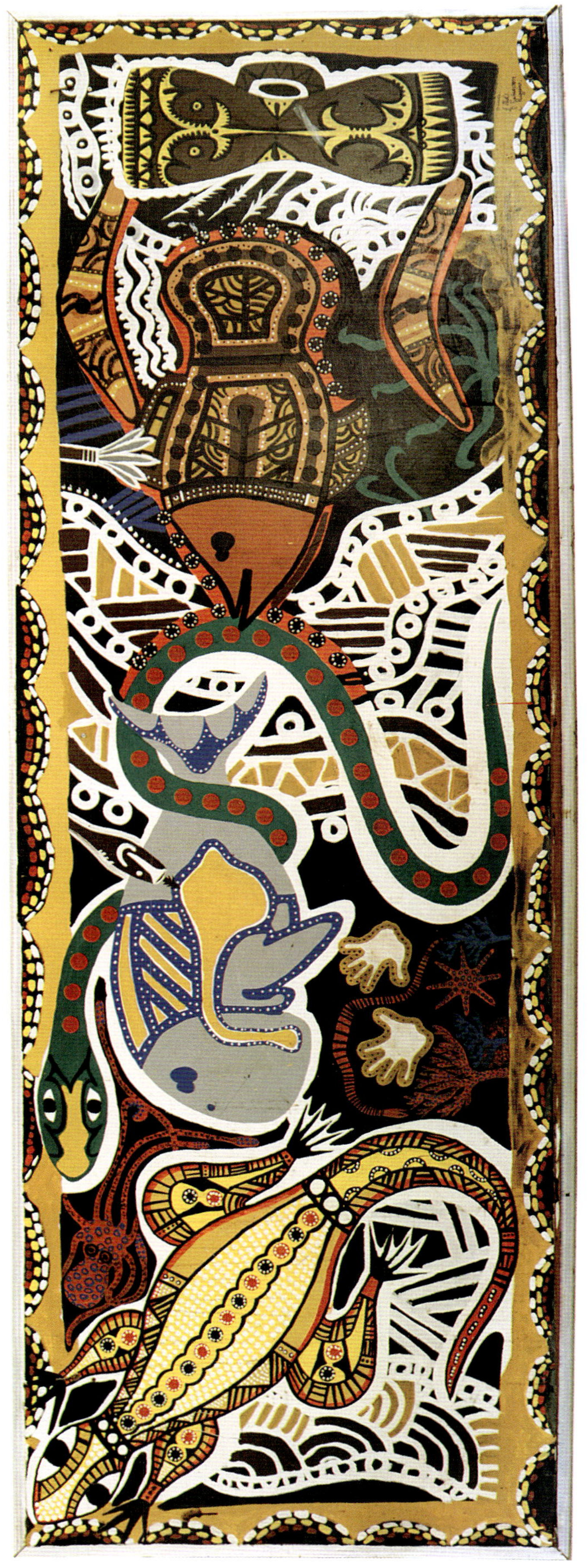

Colin Higgins, James Meeks, Dennis Nona, Brian Robinson
Cairns North State Primary School Mural

Caravonica State Primary School Mural
Cairns

Lynette Snider, John Gee, Shane Gorry, Nicholas

1995

This wall mural in the grounds of the school was painted in 1995 and is a fine example of the many murals painted in the local schools during the National Aboriginal and Islander Day Observance Committee Week, known as NAIDOC Week. These murals were painted in a spirit of reconciliation - no money was involved - and the young primary students (both black and white) participated in the painting of this mural, even if just to leave a handprint on the wall.

Today the school staff is very proud of this mural which can be seen as people motor up Kamerunga Road, a busy tourist road that leads to the Tjapukai Aboriginal Cultural Park and the Skyrail Rainforest Cableway.

Both the Aboriginal and Torres Strait Islander cultures are portrayed in this mural, with the two flags painted in the top corners - the Aboriginal flag in the photo is half hidden behind a tree branch. No one would have been happy for the photographer to cut the branch down and that includes the photographer himself, but the Torres Strait Islander flag can be clearly seen in the top right hand corner of the mural.

The whole wall is vibrant with images of cultural artefacts, land animals and flora, sea creatures such as dugongs and starfish, and just under the branch the Torres Strait Island pigeon can be seen, identified easily by its white feathers and black tipped wings and tail.

While photographing the mural, many of the older primary students came up to point out their work, to fit their hands in the prints made four years ago to show how much bigger their hands are today and to say how exciting it was to work on this mural.

Note: This mural was a collaborative venture undertaken by the ASSPA (Aboriginal Student Support and Parental Awareness Program Committee) and the School.

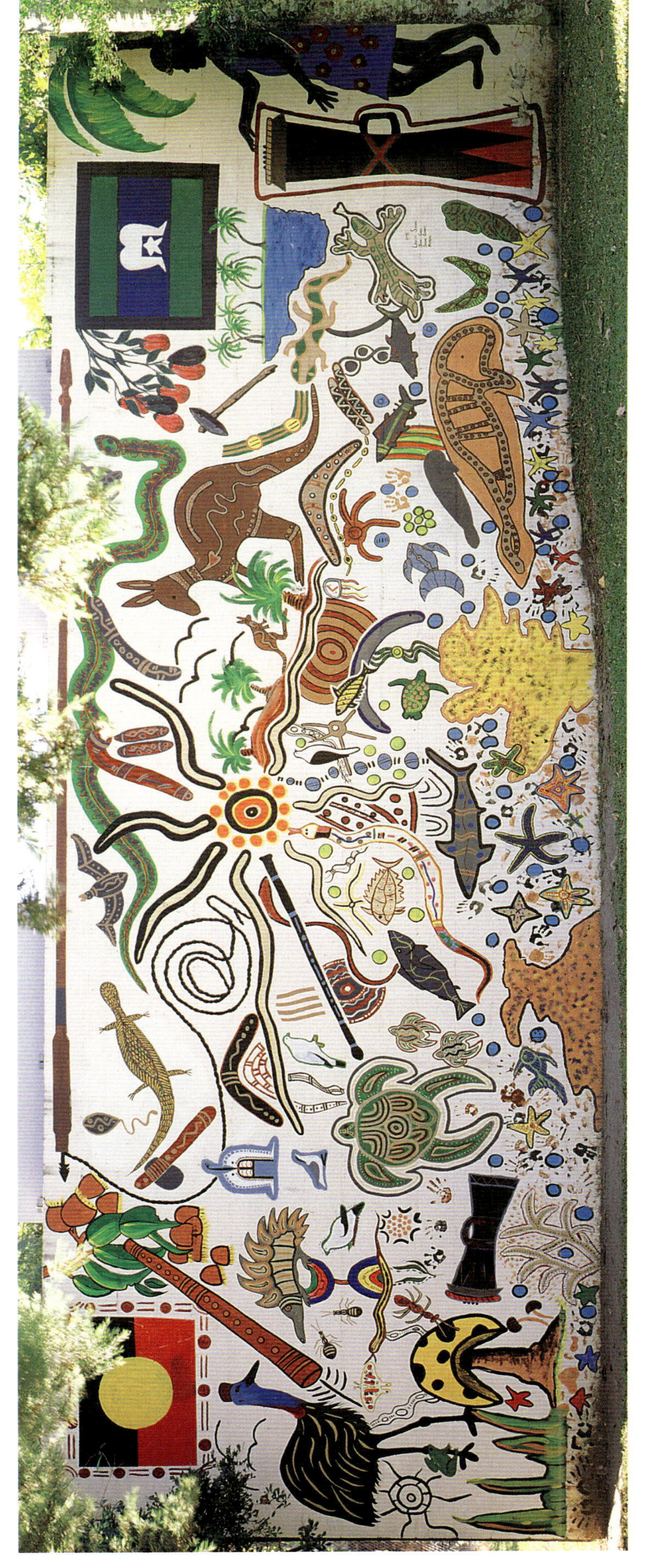

Lynette Snider, John Gee, Shane Gorry, Nicholas
CARAVONICA STATE PRIMARY SCHOOL MURAL
CAIRNS

GURRURU
(BROLGA DANCE)

DEBORAH COTTER

Acrylic on Canvas
1997

When Gurruru Brolga danced, this signified to all creatures that the rains would soon arrive. This in turn, saw the regeneration of the land and water supplies. Animals would soon be plentiful. This meant that there would be food and water for all living creatures.

The dance of the brolga is stately and graceful. Sometimes the birds soar to a great height during the dance. These elaborate displays, consisting of a variety of elegant dancing movements, may also be associated with courtship.

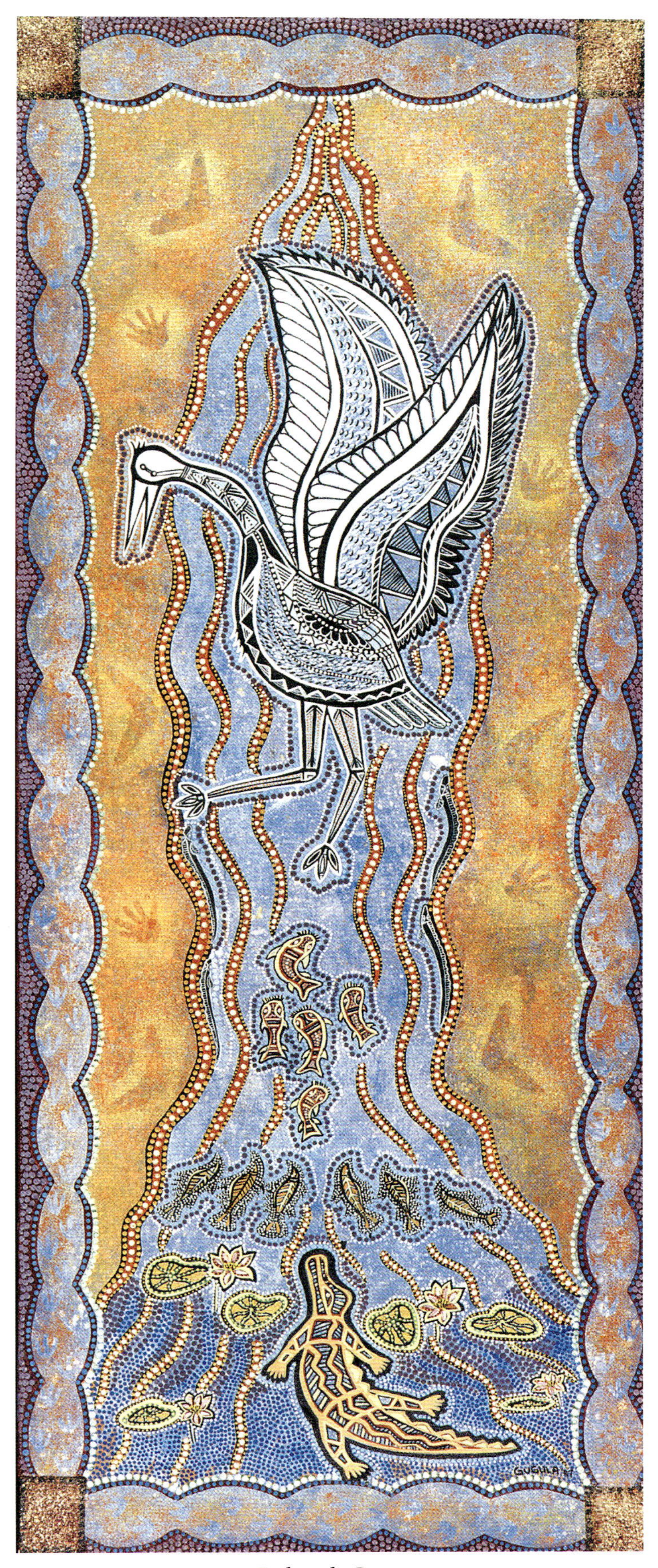

Deborah Cotter
Gurruru - Brolga Dance

FISH POT

HARRY NONA

Unglazed, incised and sgraffito slip decoration - stoneware glaze.
22 x 29cm
1989
Private Collection

Although Harry is known more for his paintings, when the series of ceramic sculptures, including *Fish Pot*, which was based on sea creatures from the tropical waters that surround Badu Island, was exhibited in Cairns in 1989, the response to these beautiful pieces was immediate and every piece was sold on opening night.

The natural carving ability of the Torres Strait Islander student artists, which had manifested itself with such immediate results in the medium of linocuts, saw Harry's basic clay forms incised, decorated and glazed to bring to life each marine creature depicted in the ceramic sculptures.

The photo of *Fish Pot* (based on the coral trout) can only suggest the design on the back - a mantle of carved shapes using an overlapping pattern resembling fish scales - which cascades down from the head of the trout, across the back of the swelling clay form to embrace the bottom of the sculpture like a shining blue glazed cloak.

Reproduced courtesy of Cairns Regional Gallery, Cairns.
Photography: David Campbell

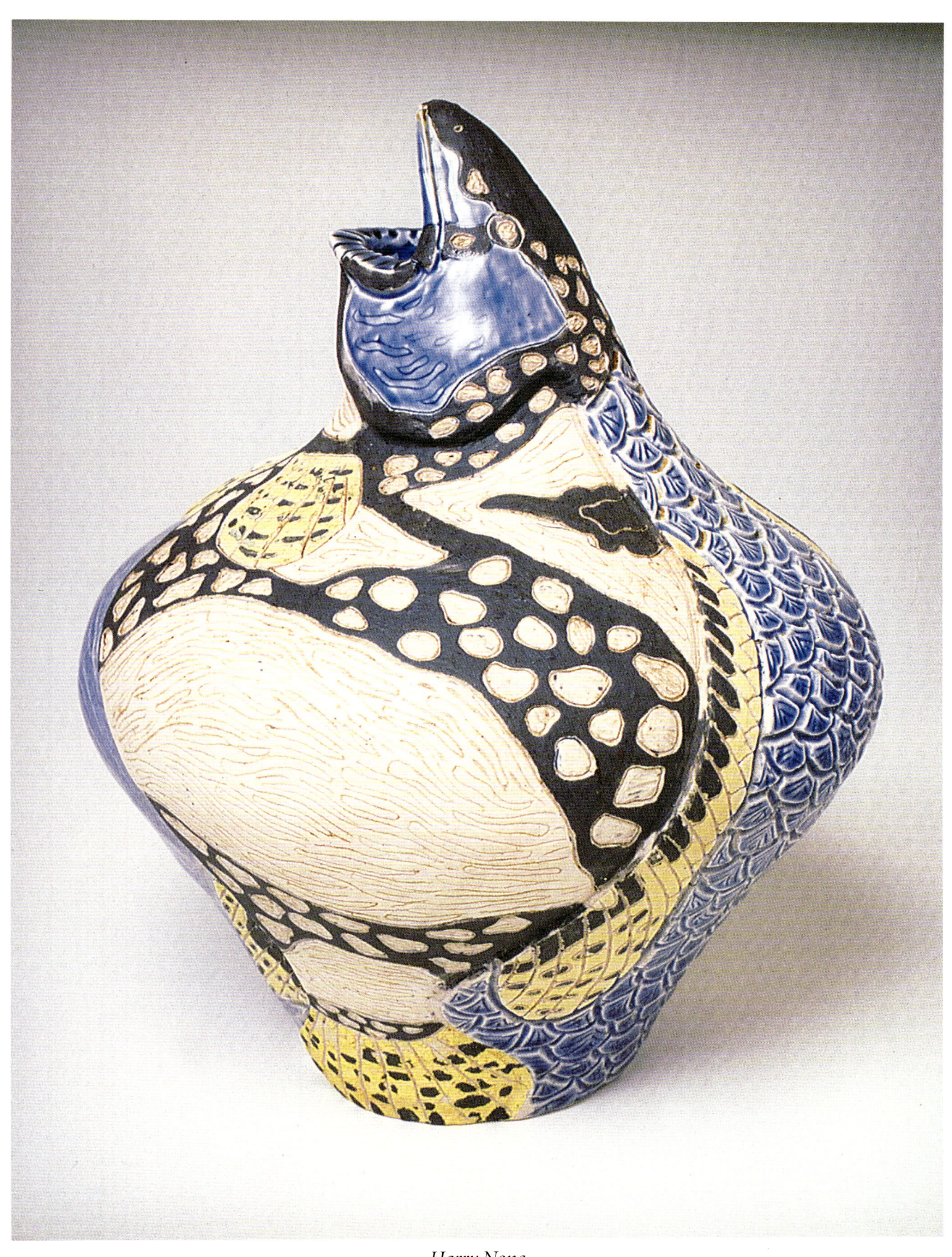

Harry Nona
Fish Pot

THE COMING OF THE LIGHT

KATHRYN NORRIS

1997
Pastel on Paper
56 x 76cm
National Museum of Australia Collection

The Coming of the Light refers to a time when my ancestors were told what to do, with little regard for their own religious beliefs and little regard for the prior established connections between the Australian mainland and Papua New Guinea.

The male figure is shown in chains with his mouth shut, signifying the way my ancestors were not allowed to speak in their native tongue after this time. This meant the Europeans silenced the sounds of our drums, and many of the our culture's songs and our language. Our ancestors were forced to assimilate to a different culture.

The sailing ship represents the actual arrival of the Europeans. After landing, the Europeans made it clear they did not approve of our Island ways, so they built churches with four walls and claimed that there was only one religion.

I guess the moral to the story is that there is more to life than history recorded by Europeans and that a picture is worth a thousand words.

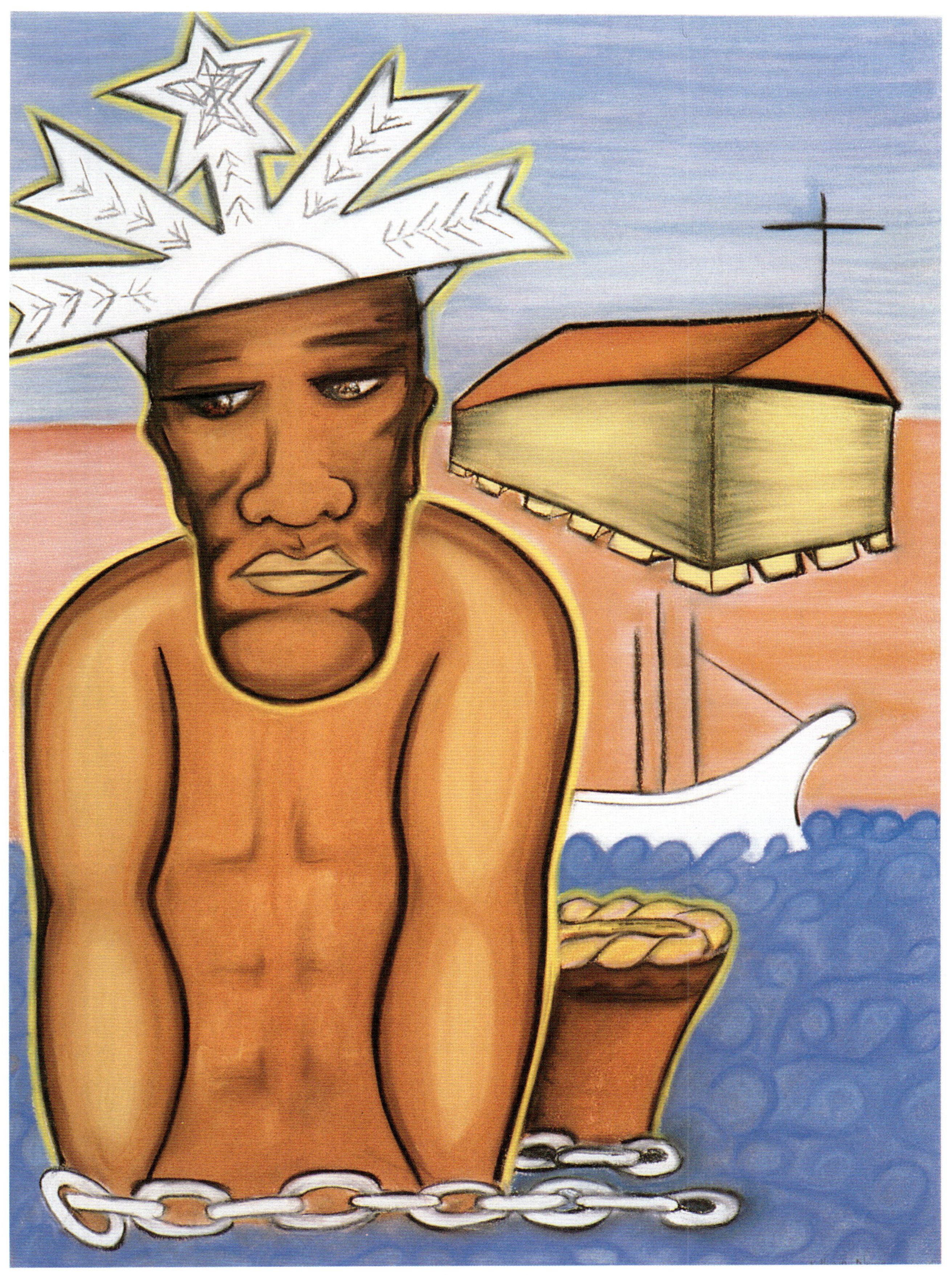

Kathryn Norris
The Coming of the Light

THE OLD TIMES - DORMITORY TIMES

Samantha Meeks

Installation - mixed media

"This installation represents the people of the dormitory times in the Yarrabah settlement. Both of my grandparents lived in the dormitory at Yarrabah. Through listening to my grandparents' stories of the old days, I began to feel it was necessary to reflect on their stories.

The drawing is of my grandparents, now deceased. They lived in a period where the living conditions and food were inadequate, dominated by the strict dormitory rules and lifestyle. The children looked after each other and their family members as one big family.

Christianity played a big part in the dormitory lifestyle. They had three church masses a day, and it was also taught in school. They had allocated chores to do, which were based around cleaning, cooking, sewing and collecting fire wood. The poem that is emerging through the drawing represents the sadness and hard times they went through:

One morning I stood wailing under the dormitory
held back only by wire netting.
While my parents also crying,
they vanished into the bush.
Heading back home.
Why do we have to stay,
we want to come home with you.
We don't like it here.
We want to be where we belong,
with our family.
Do not walk beyond this point.
Do not walk beyond this point.
Do not walk beyond this point.
Do not walk beyond this point.
Do not enter.
Do not enter.
Do not enter.

The figures represent the people and the system of the church. The red and black figure hanging on the right hand side is made of latex rubber. It represents the people with leprosy that were confined away from the Yarrabah Reserve so that they would not be seen. It also represents the heartache and pain they suffered from being separated and alienated from their people. The figure featured in the centre made of cards with crosses on them represents the church. The church's aim in those days was to try to breed out the indigenous culture and so a ban was placed on tribal language, as it was seen as evil. The yellow ochre colored figure on the left represents the separation of the half-caste children, and the sad times they faced away from their parents. The red eyes painted on the two black pieces of wood, appearing through the leaves, represents the story of the red-eyed man, told to us by my grandparents when we were kids."

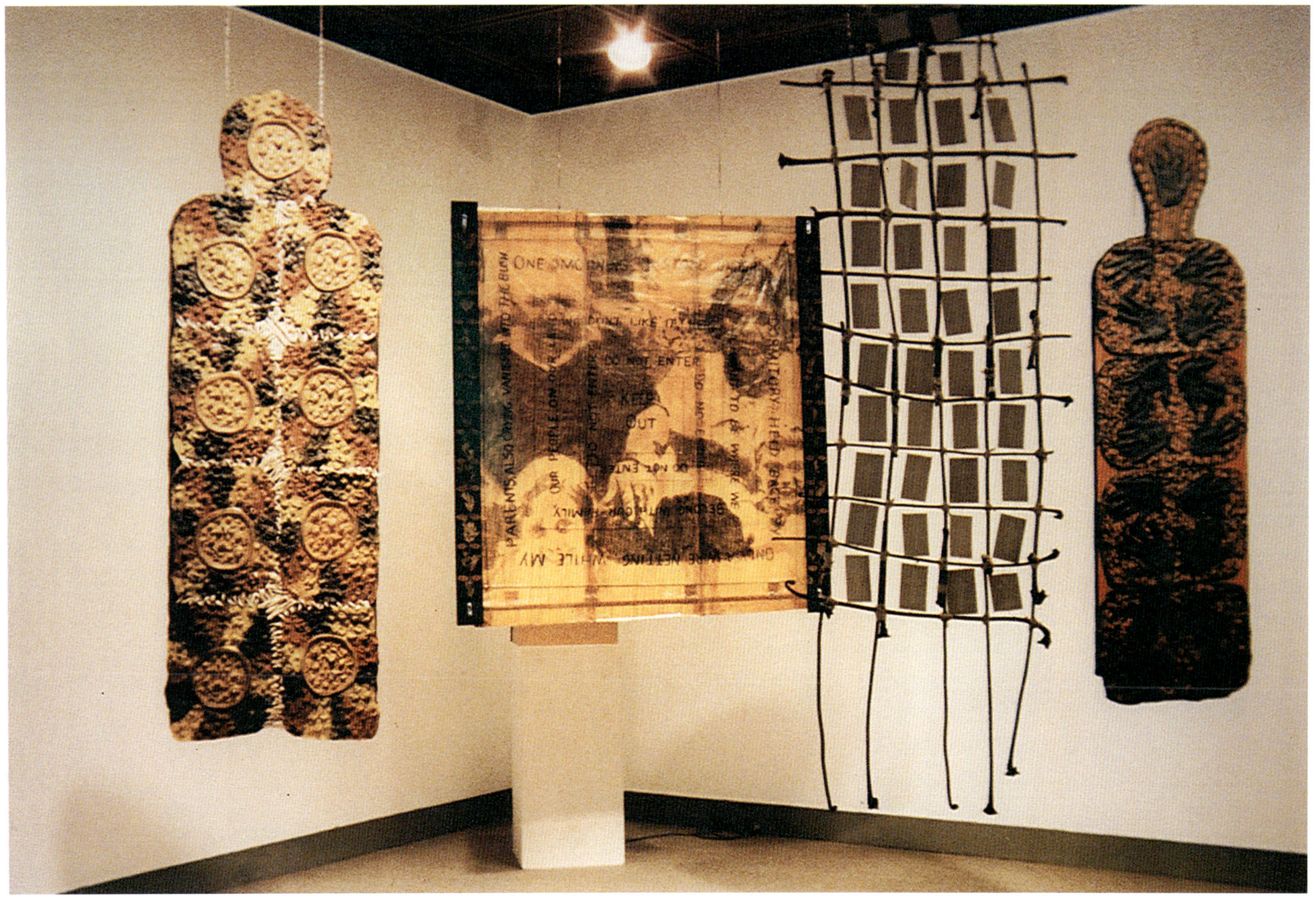

Samantha Meeks
THE OLD TIMES - DORMITORY TIMES

Mura Uruiau Danaka

Alick Tipoti

1995
Linocut
54.5 x 100cm
Centre Culturel Jean-Marie Tjibaou Collection, Noumea.

Mura Uruiau Danaka represents the thudding noise which resonates from the impact of the *Gabagab* (stone head-club) against the living form of a warrior.

Because of the spiritual kinship the head warrior has with the sea and land, his death brings sadness to all living creatures.

The figures in the linocut that are climbing, are making their way up to join all the warriors who lost their lives to headhunters in the past. These warriors' skulls were displayed on the Death Rack and were kept by well known and successful headhunters of the Torres Strait.

When a village learns of the death of a leader, sacrifices are made during a traditional death dance ceremony. These sacrifices are represented by the traditional whips, over the village, shown above the death rack.

In the old days, when a well known leader or headhunter died, his loss was heard, felt and seen spiritually by many creatures of the world.

Courtesy of the artist.
Reproduced courtesy of Cairns Regional Gallery, Cairns.
Photography: David Campbell

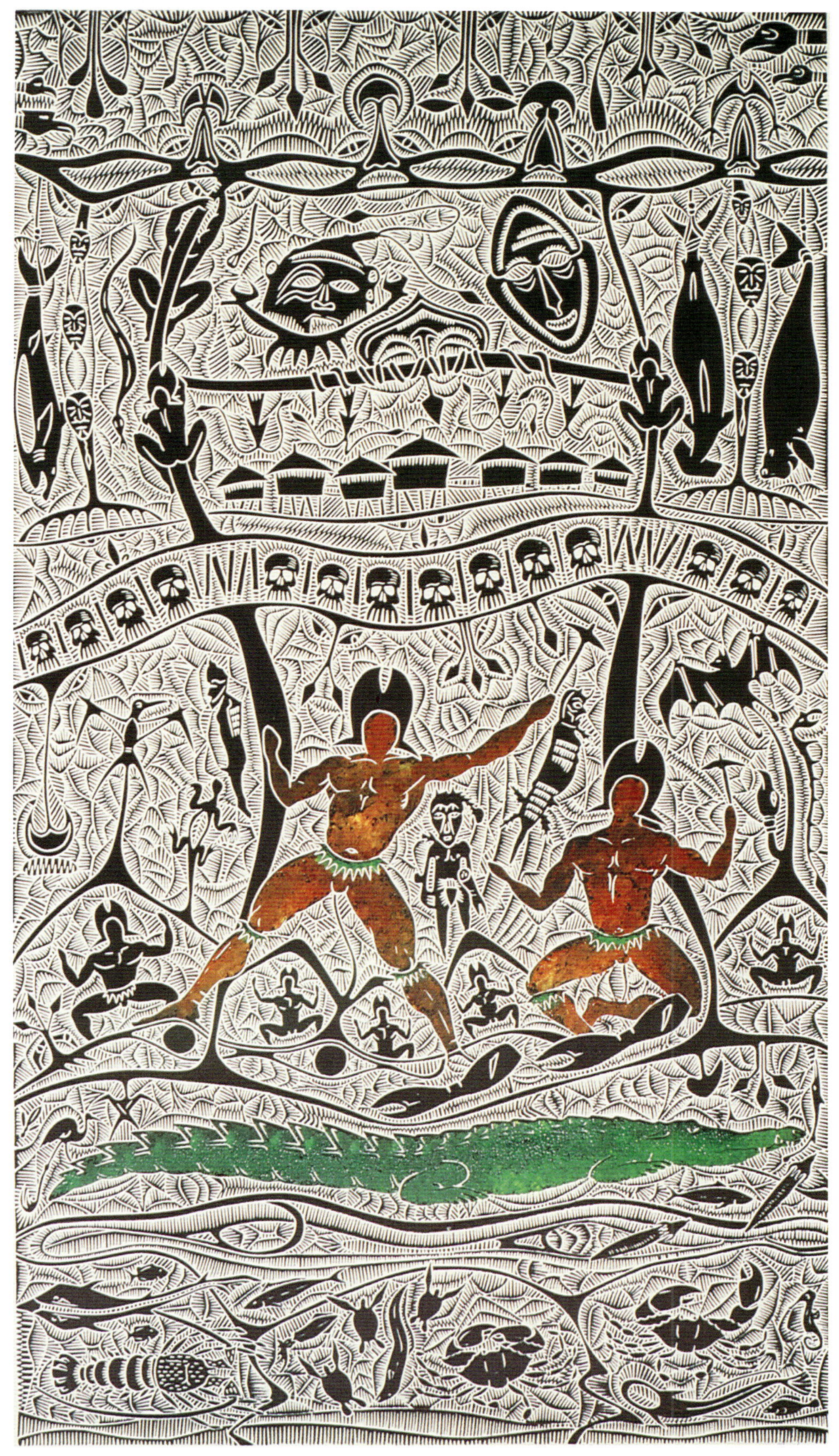

Alick Tipoti
MURA URUIAU DANAKA

SEARCHING FOR FOOD

JOSEPH McIVOR

1994
Acrylic on Canvas
Private collection - New York

Joseph tells of visiting the cave paintings of the Quinkan-Laura area on Cape York with a local elder who told him that in the past Aboriginal people from Bloomfield, Mossman, Laura and Cooktown all "put a bit of their own paintings there". Studying the paintings there helped him to express his own ideas using a symbolic language that was a direct cultural continuation of his ancestor's visual language.

Speaking of this painting, Joseph says:

"When I was a young fellow, about nine or ten year old, I started to have a lot of time and patience for making spears with my Grandfathers. One of my Grandfathers made a couple of special spears for me knowing that I loved, and excelled at, hunting.

This painting was inspired by those traditional events which I hold special, for myself that is taking time to spend with the Elders.

During the Christmas period, a lot of the bush trees/ shrubs from the Cooktown area bloom, and this indicates to us that it is time for hunting and gathering of certain foods.

The spear is mainly used for the hunting of fish. Also depending what plants are in bloom, we then gather whatever fruit/vegetable is in the pathway, as we head off for fish."

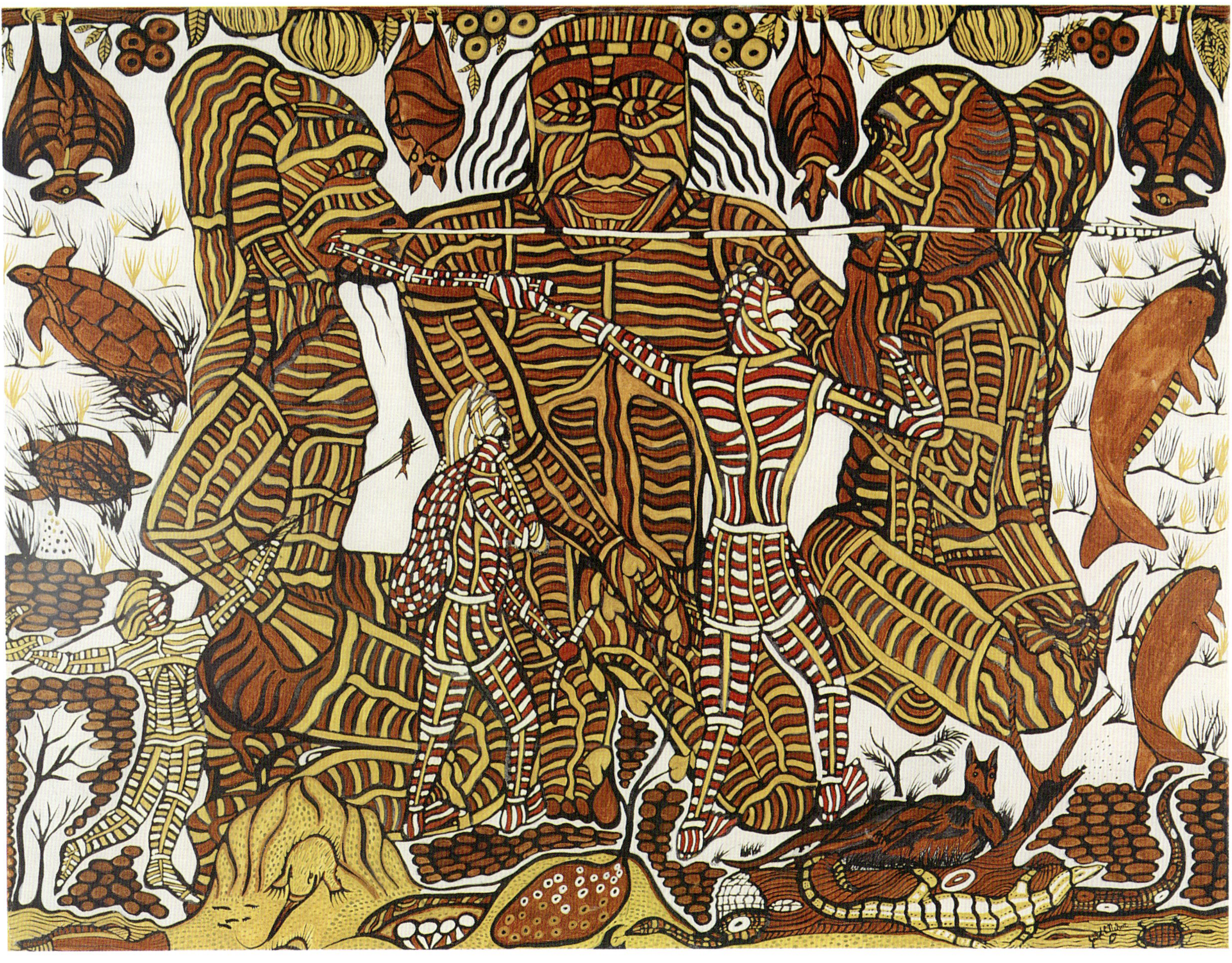

Joseph McIvor
SEARCHING FOR FOOD

DUNGAL AU BIBER - R
(THE POWER OF THE DUGONG)

JOEY LAIFOO

1997
Linocut Print
35 x 73cm
Private collection

Out of all the seasons in the Torres Strait, the *Kuku Gub* (North Westerly wind) brings the roughest weather, a time when waves measuring up to two metres flow through the waters of the Strait.

Dugong are seen swimming through these waters. Being very powerful creatures they swim across the tides, easily making their way towards their feeding grounds.

In the linocut print, the background designs behind the dugong represent the two diverse characteristics of the dugongs. Firstly, there is a feeling of calmness and physical grace of its beautiful round image as the dugongs dive into the blue waters, feeding on turtle grass in the shallows. Then there is the other side of the dugong - the power of the dugong - its aggressiveness when disturbed.

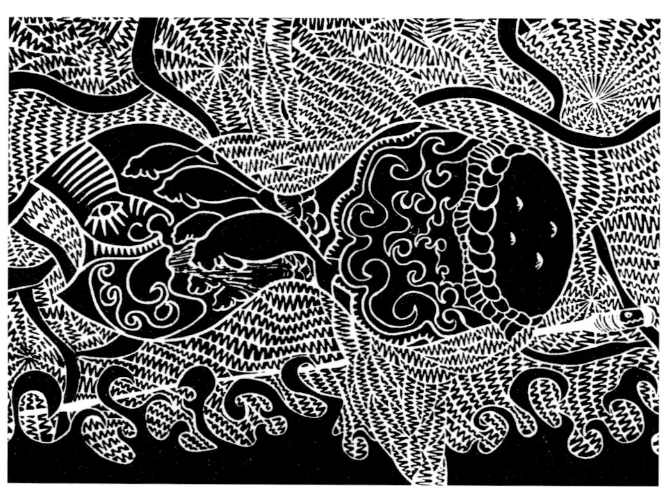

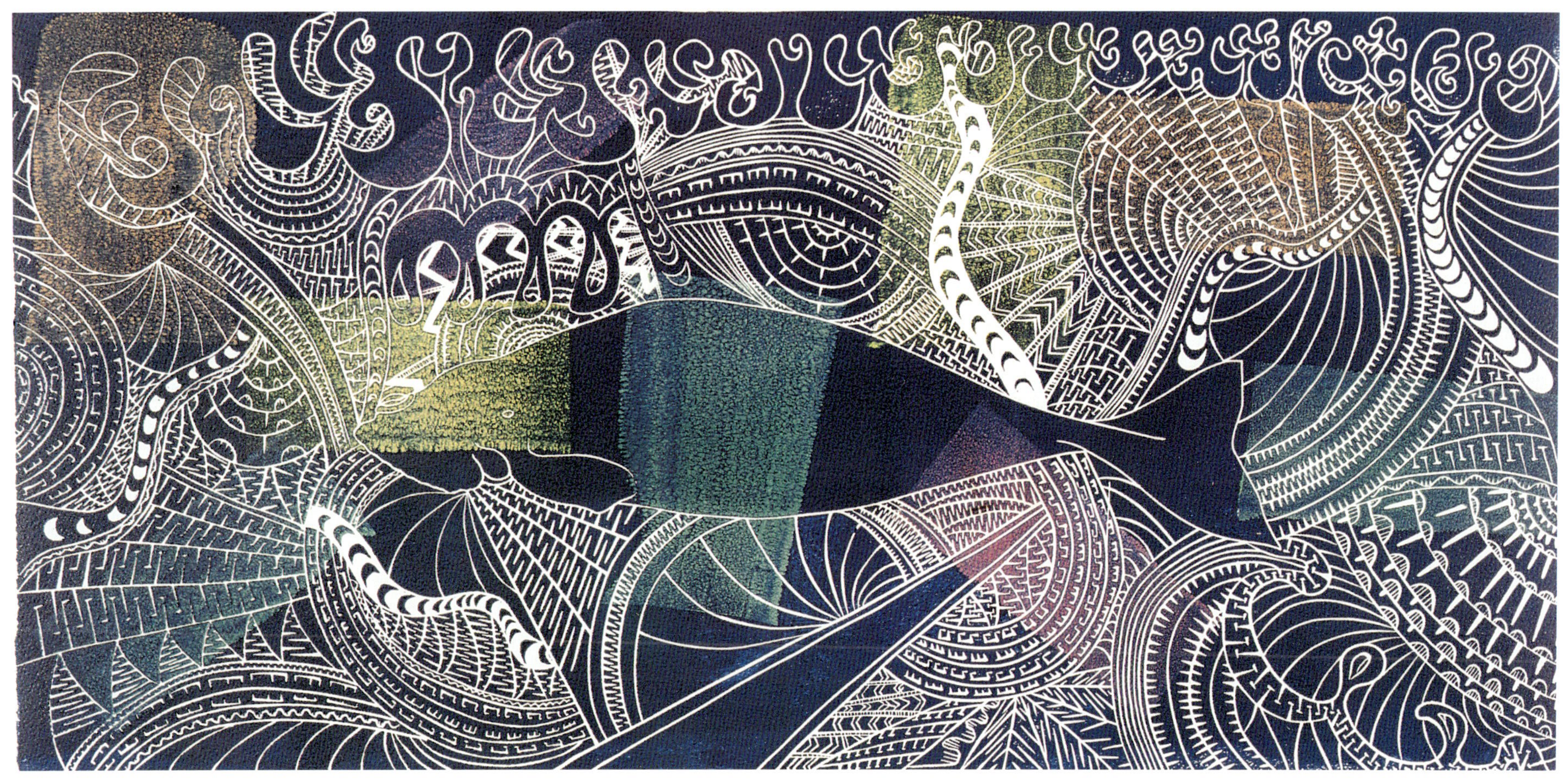

Joey Laifoo

DUNGAL AU BIBER - *R* (THE POWER OF THE DUGONG)

THE HUNTERS

Colin Higgins

Wall Mural
1999

This is an early morning hunting scene. The sun is rising in the East and the tide is coming in to shore, flooding around the mangroves. The fish are feeding, making them vulnerable to the hunting skills of both man and crocodile.

The setting is Yarrabah Bay. Represented in the background is Baldy Mountain, a significant and well known landmark for the Yarrabah Aboriginal Community in North Queensland

Photo courtesy of the Training Centre for Youth Services (Yarrabah Community)

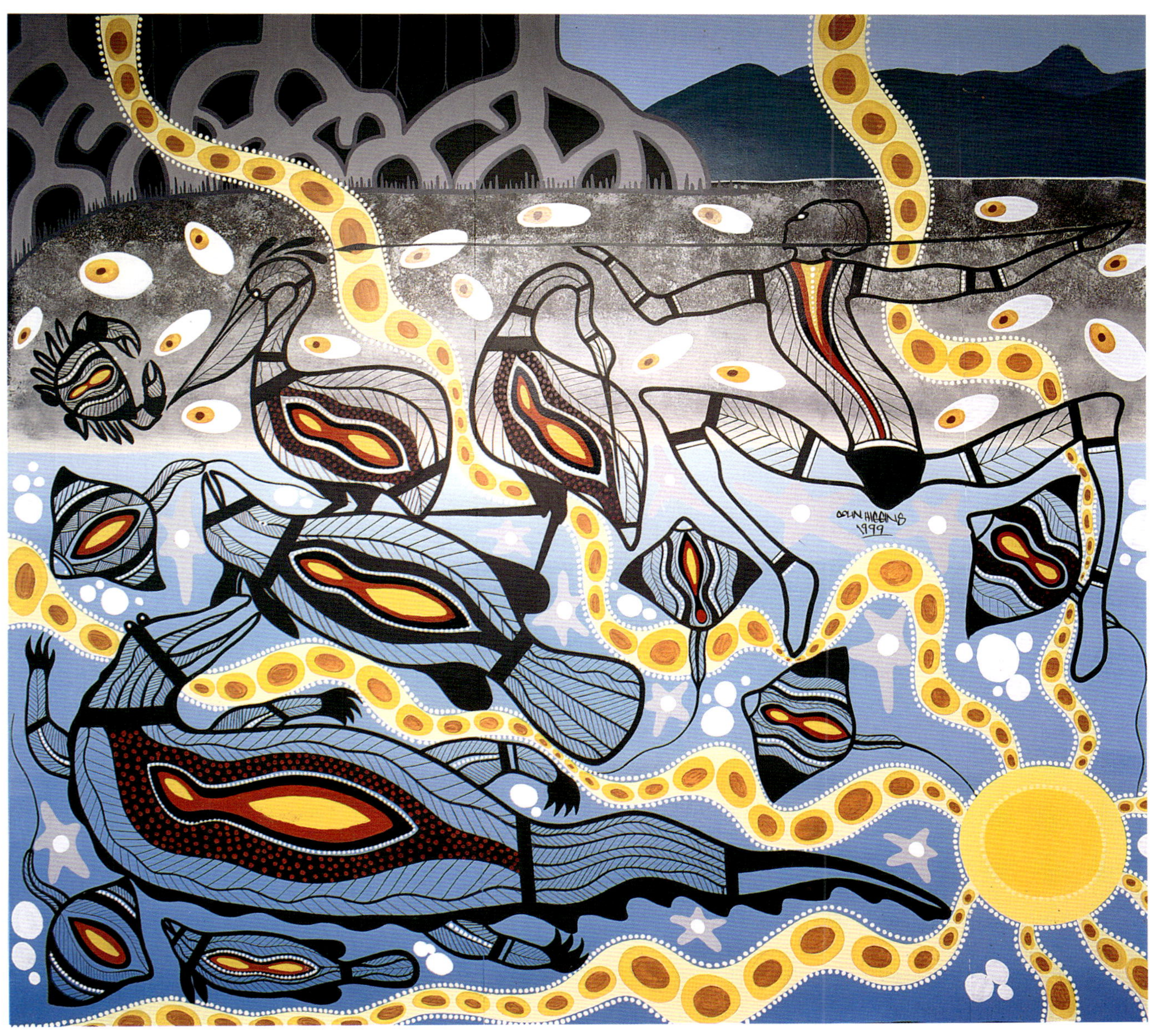

Colin Higgins
THE HUNTERS

MAL LAG AR DAPPARR-AW WHURAL AR IDAL
(SEA, LAND AND AIR CREATURES-*KALA LAGAW-YA* LANGUAGE)

DENNIS NONA

Linocut Print
56 x 76cm
Centre Culturel Jean-Marie Tjibaou Collection, Noumea

This image depicts the intimate connection between sea, land and air creatures in the Torres Strait Islands and shows that humans are but one element in the eternal pattern of life, death and rebirth. The image is illustrated in three sections: the lower section depicting the sea, the middle section is the land and the upper section the air.

The sea creatures include a pregnant dugong (*Dangal*), a sting ray, a turtle, a swordfish, an x-ray image of a sea snake with a fish inside and a speared octopus. A figure wearing a shark devil mask (*Markai*), used in funeral ceremonies, holds the stingray's tail with one hand and the flipper of the turtle in the other. Coconut palm fronds hang between its legs. This figure symbolises the connection to the sea and sea creatures for all Torres Strait Islander people.

The middle ground depicts the muddy mangroves inhabited by crocodiles (*kodol*), waiting to catch wild pigs (*Burom*), which come at low tide to crush shell fish with their powerful teeth. The geese represented inhabit the big swamps on Badu Island.

Above the crocodile are wild berries which are found along the beaches. The fruit bats are eating wild mango and bananas (*Catham*) and other fruits. Sweet potato, shown here, and bat (*Sapourr*) are very good to eat together. At top right is an orange Cesre, a bird which is similar in appearance to a Willie Wag Tail. On each vertical side of the image are the hunting tools used: on the right is a harpoon used for catching turtle and dugong: on the left is a spear.

The detailed line patterns surrounding the animals are traditional Torres Strait Islander designs which are often carved onto turtle shells. The characteristic jagged tooth shapes of the shark, dog, crocodile, swordfish and parrot fish form the basis for these patterns. Throughout the image, mask-like faces (*Purr*) appear and disappear from the mass of lines. To the left of the Cesre an upside-down spirit figure (*Mari*) intervenes in the life cycle.

Reproduced courtesy of Cairns Regional Gallery, Cairns.
Photography: David Campbell

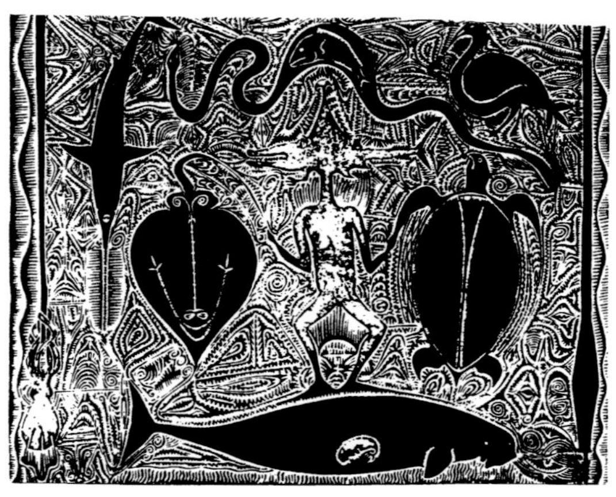

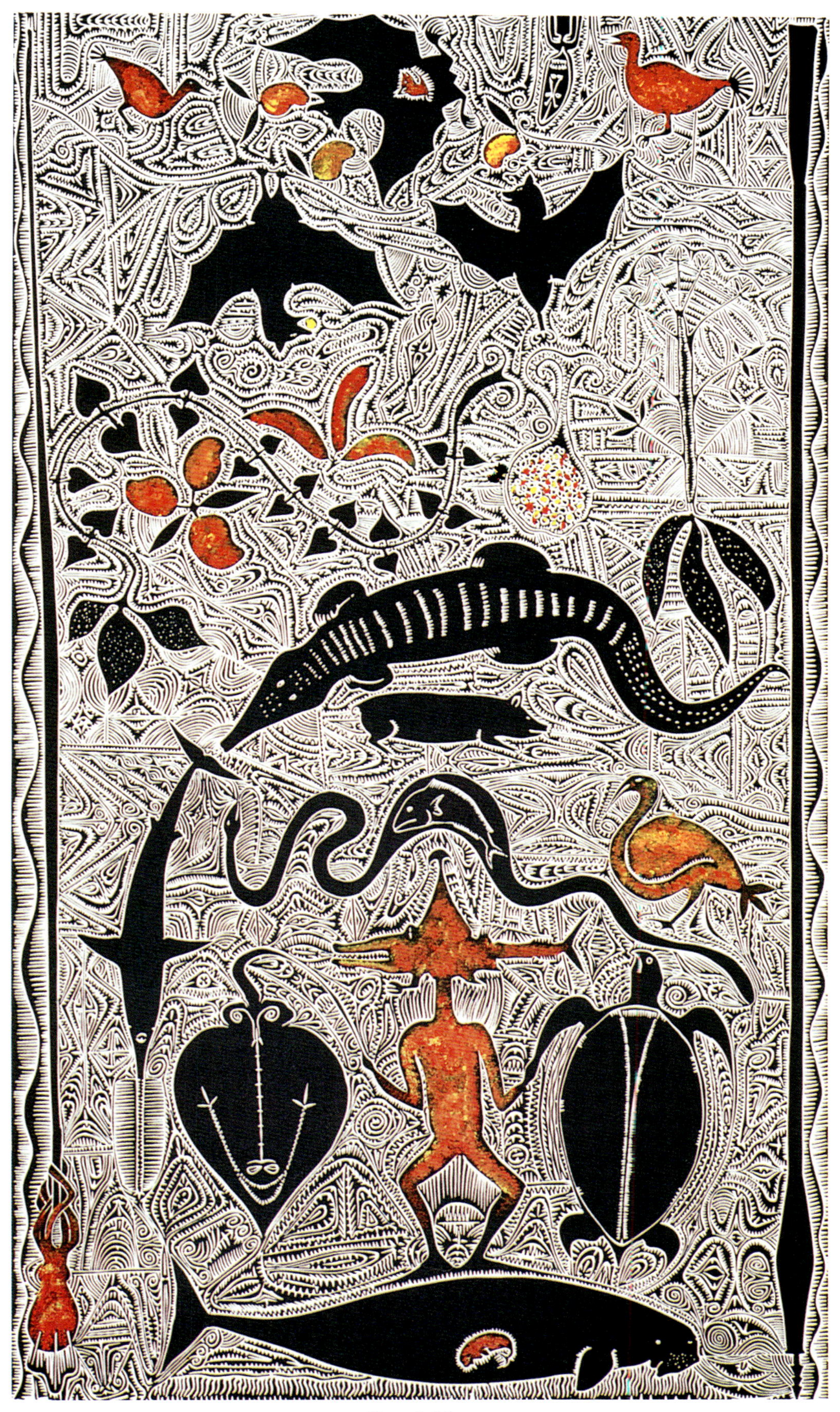

Dennis Nona
Mal Lag Ar Dapparr-Aw Whural Ar Idal

THE WOMEN'S SHIELD

SHANNON SHAW

1997
Linocut Print
30.5 x 41cm

The women are sitting around a campfire and there are waterholes situated behind them. The tracks are those made by the women when gathering water; and the animal tracks leading to them are made by kangaroos and possums.

Four men are sitting on the outside and they want the women; however they are unable to get them because the women are protected by the shield.

That is why it is called *The Women's Shield.*

Courtesy of the artist.

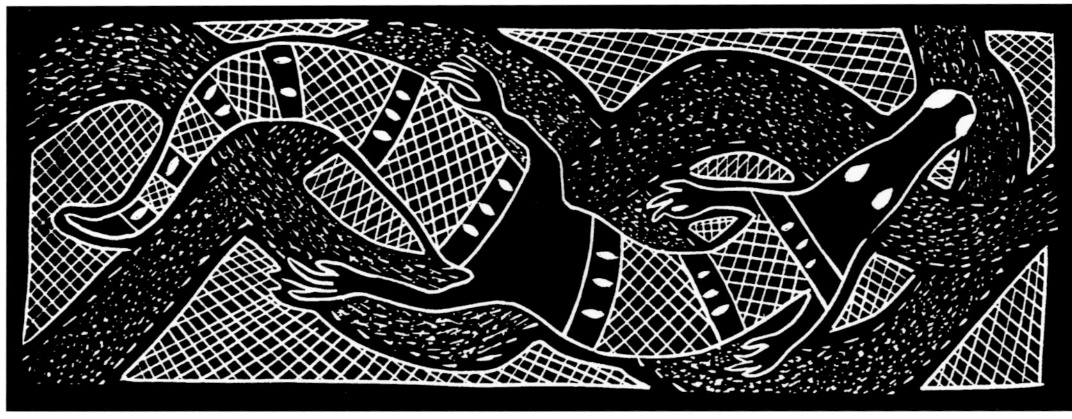

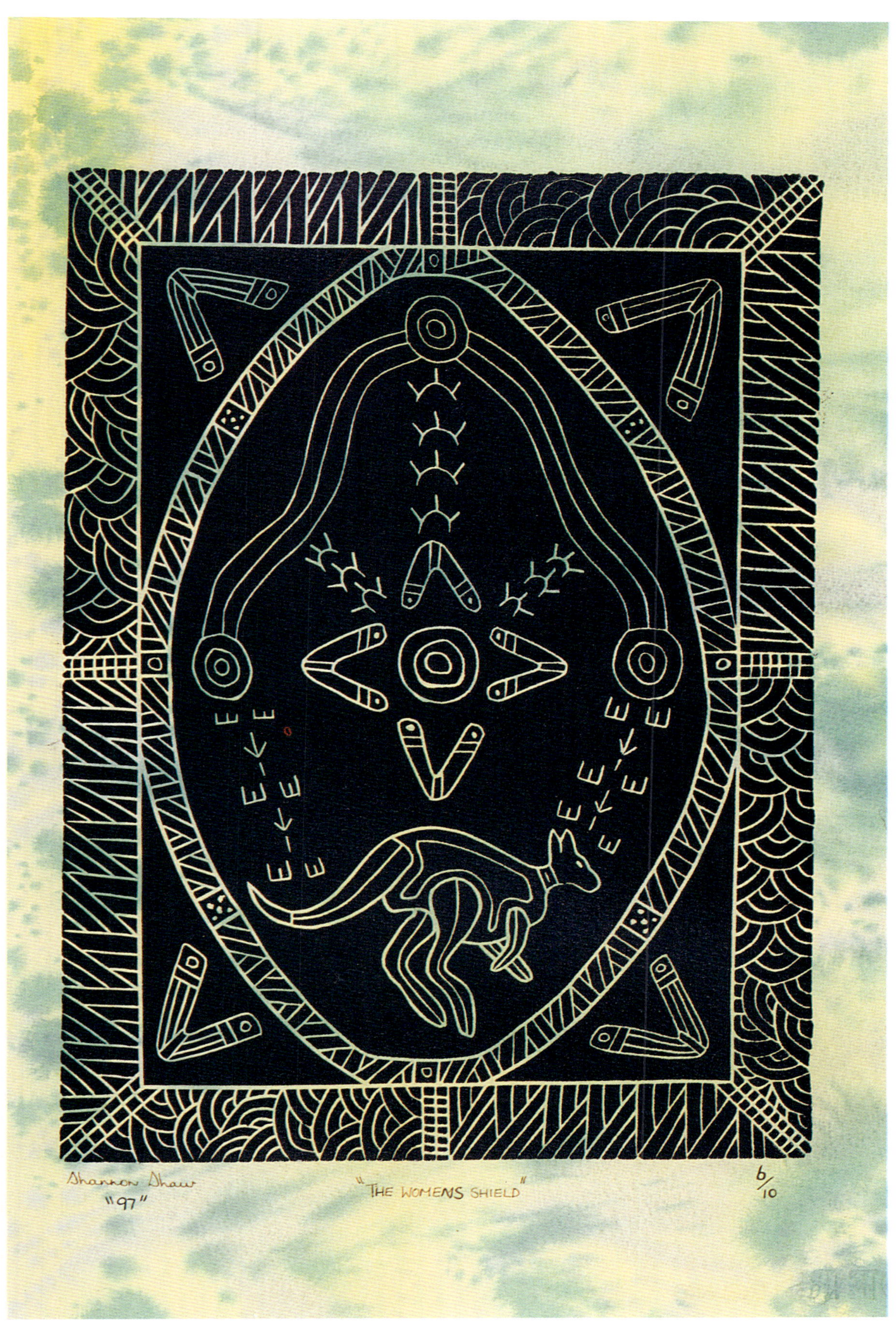

Shannon Shaw
The Women's Shield

ABORIGINAL CROATIANS

Helena Loncaric

1992
Screenprint on Cotton
Screen size: 74cm x 90cm

The artist's mother is Aboriginal and her father Croatian. Her Aboriginal ancestors originated from the Butchulla (*Batjala*) Tribe of Fraser Island and the Gungganyji Tribe in Yarrabah. Her artwork is mainly influenced by her Aboriginal ancestry; however, it is not taken from age-old stories and traditions, but deals directly with her own life experiences. The designs largely consist of land and sea animals together with patterns and decorative designs which sometimes reflect the plants and waterholes found in the areas surrounding Cairns.

Although the artist's Croatian heritage does not play a major part in her art, there are similar motifs to those of Croatian needlework, and motifs which seem to appear on their own. The two techniques blend together to form the artist's own individual art style, affectionately known by the artist's family and friends as "Wogarigine".

This screenprint consists of emus, kangaroos, turtles, scrub turkeys and lyre birds. There is no specific storyline in this piece, but the animals seem to be walking around searching for something, some might say food, land, or just 'sticky beaking'. The patterns surrounding the animals could resemble eggs, plants, and land formations; the jagged line in the middle of the piece could symbolise the heartline, the relationship between Murris and their environment.

Photo courtesy of the artist.

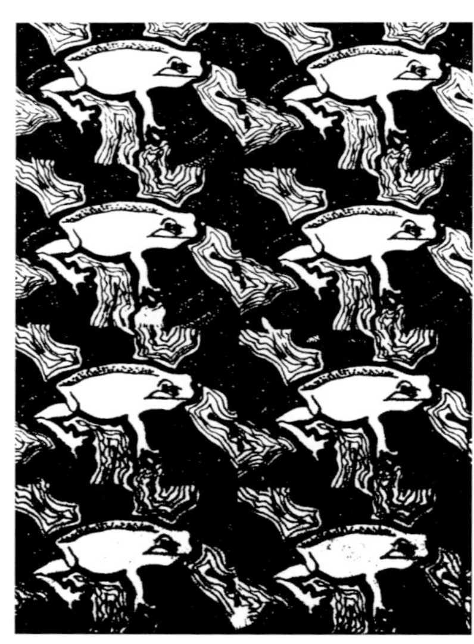

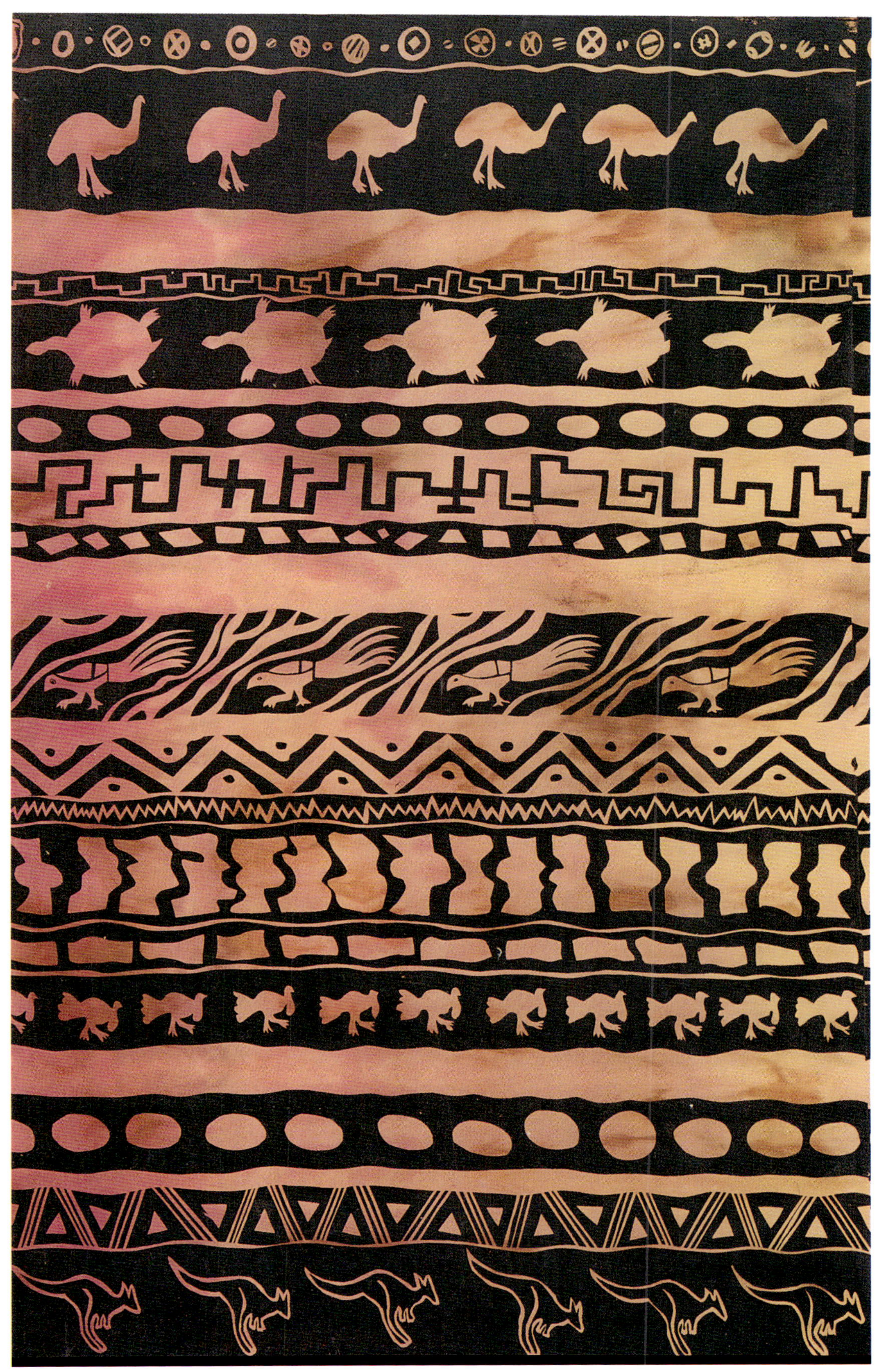

Helena Loncaric
ABORIGINAL CROATIANS

LE-OP
(FACE OF MAN)

JOSEPH DORANTE

Synthetic Polymer - Paint on Canvas
91 x 152cm
1998

"Torres Strait masks are the most distinctive form of Torres Strait art in existence today. These masks, which were used in various mortuary, increase, initiation and cult practices, may be divided into two distinct types: wood and turtle shell. The most spectacular are the turtle-shell masks, made from the carapace of the hawksbill turtle. These masks are seen as one of the outstanding art forms of the primitive world.

The possible development and refinement of turtle-shell as the raw material for art production may lie in the scarcity of suitable wood in the Torres Strait, which led to a search for a local, workable material. The inter-generational passing of knowledge allowed the artist to refine his techniques to such an extent that objects in institutional collections today only hint at the variety of form that would have once existed.

Turtle-shell masks were generally manufactured using the following method:

Flakes were detached from the carapace, cleaned and shaped by rubbing edge ways on sedimentary stone. Sometimes they were cut by scoring deeply and snapping off a section. If a concave, convex or compound curve was required, the flake was heated in wet sand beneath a cooking fire or dipped in boiling water. While pliable, it was formed into the desired shape, then cooled. Shaped pieces would be assembled on the ground and marked at intervals along the edge for drilling. This was [traditionally] done with a pump-drill or [later, when wire and iron pieces were obtained from wrecks] by heating the end of a piece of wire and burning the holes through. Plate edges would be overlapped, holes matched, and bound at intervals with sennit. Occasionally, the joins were covered with strips of cane. Rods of cane or bamboo were sometimes bound into the structure to stiffen it.

Following the completion of the form, decorative elements would then be added. Composite material included shells, seeds, feathers, natural fibres, leaves and human hair. Alternatively, inscribed designs could be added which were then highlighted by the addition of earth pigments or lime."

Reproduced with permission from: Mosby, Tom. 1998 "Torres Strait Island Art and Artists", in Ilan Pasin (This is our way): Torres Strait Art, Cairns Regional Gallery, Cairns.
Photography: David Cambell

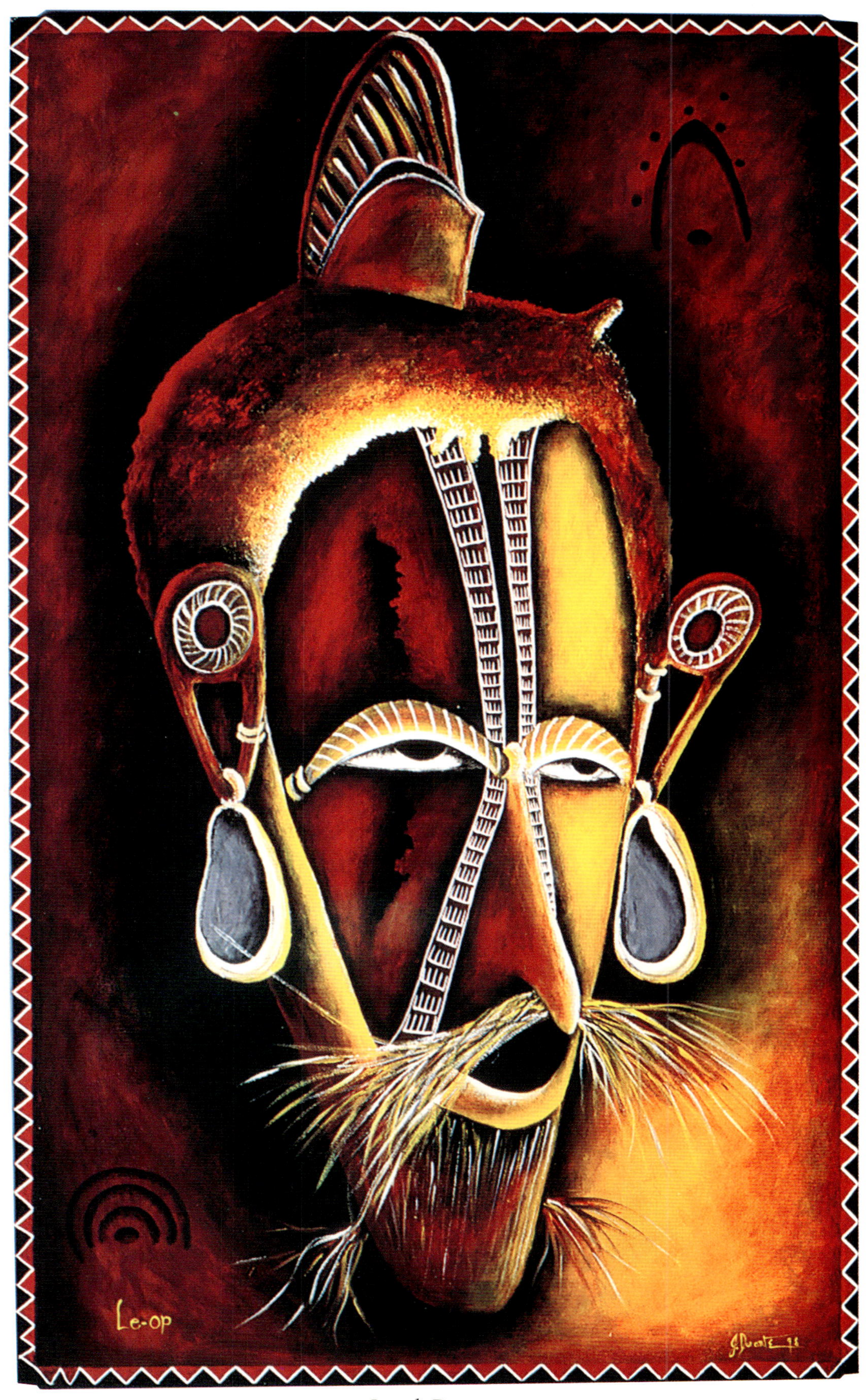

Joseph Dorante
Le-Op (Face of Man)

Self Portrait

Jakki Skeen

Mixed Media on paper
56 x 76cm

The use of the photographic image in one form or another reflects the increasing appearance of the photographic image in a fine art context. New approaches to the visual arts have seen artists using diverse mediums to make individual statements.

In Jakki's 'Self Portrait' she has collaged photographs of herself onto the surface of the painting. Surrounding these photographs are images relating to her cultural background, heightening the viewer's awareness of the underlying themes of identity Jakki is seeking to portray in this work.

Jakki is a young Aboriginal woman artist seeking cultural strength from her family, and through her art studies. She writes:

"I would like to pass my art and my stories on to our younger people so our culture grows stronger. I feel more young people should become involved in the arts, as it is our traditional form of teaching."

Courtesy of the artist.

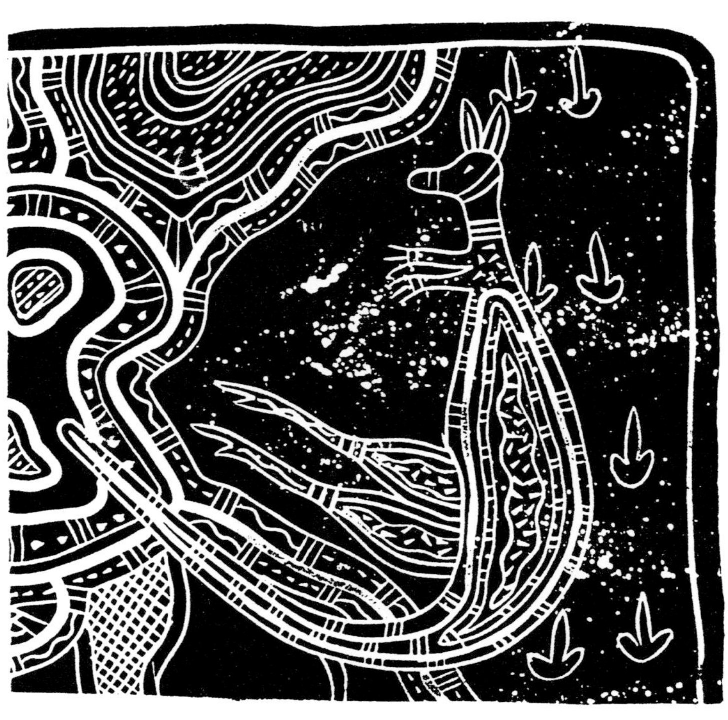

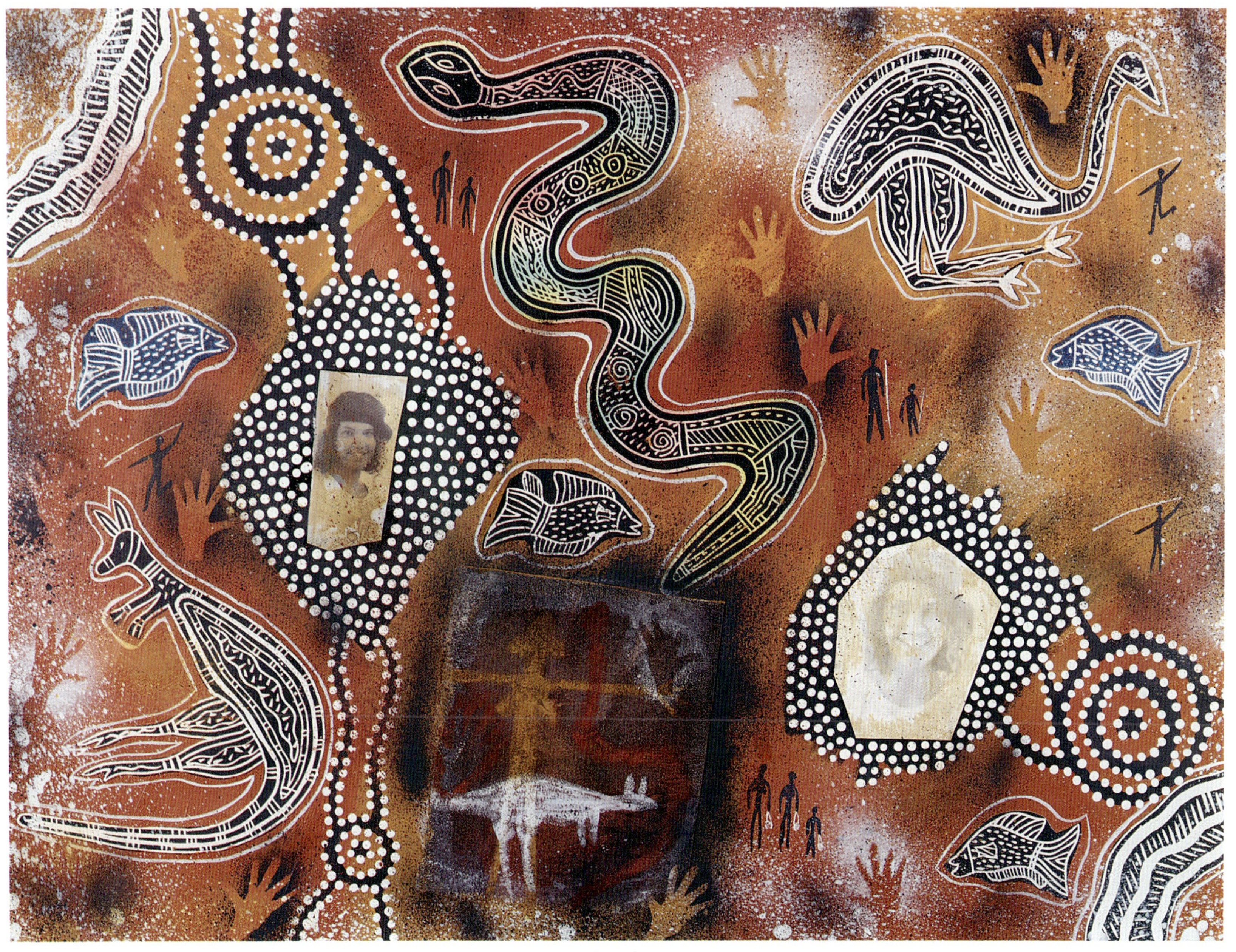

Jakki Skeen
SELF-PORTRAIT

GOANNA HUNTING TURTLE EGGS

Warren Brim

Acrylic on Canvas
Private Collection
60 x 75 cm

This painting is about the way the goanna, if he has the chance, will dig his way through sand in order to steal fresh turtle eggs.

Warren's people, the Djabugay people of Kuranda on the tablelands above Cairns, are rainforest people. Bush tucker was always plentiful in the past. Some favourite sources of bush tucker enjoyed by the Djabugay people were goanna, scrub turkey, wallaby, quandongs, sour plums and wild honey. From the rivers his people caught yabbies, freshwater turtle and local fish such as black bream and catfish.

Warren uses traditional colours in his artwork, mostly ochre colours. His subject matter always refers to the survival of the Aboriginal people and Aboriginal culture.

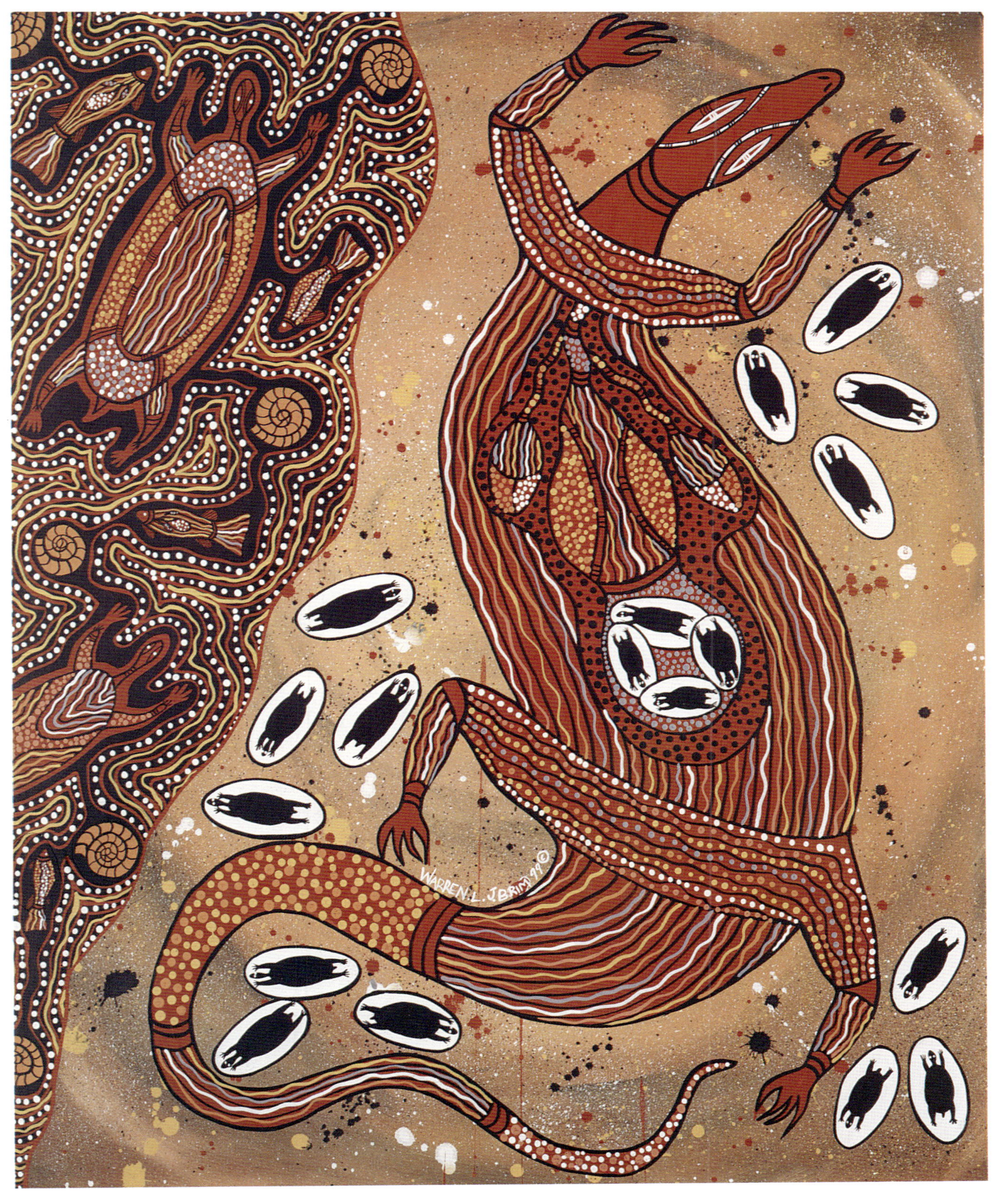

Warren Brim
Goanna Hunting Turtle Eggs

ON THE LUGGER

ANDREW WILLIAMS

1997
Screenprint on paper
23cm x 26.5cm

Andrew writes:

"This is a silk screen print which was created to reflect upon my own family's history and connection to the Torres Straits. The main image of the work is actually taken from a family photograph of the deck of one of the luggers my Grandfather worked on. My Grandfather worked many jobs to support his family, with pearling, trochus shell and bêche-de-mer being among them. He followed his own father's footsteps working on luggers and diving, eventually working his way to skipper and achieving his pilot's licence. He was proud to be Torres Strait Islander and never forgot his own country, which was the small Eastern island of Ugar (Stephen Island) till the day he passed on.

The selection of this image shows how I personally as a Torres Strait Islander born on the Mainland have had to turn to photographic images like the one in this print to look at my personal family history. It is not to say that this was the only means for myself to gather this information, as I would often talk and listen to my Grandfather discuss our family heritage. However, to have photographs of the past showing various events and family members was irreplaceable. Despite my living and growing up away from this aspect of culture, these photographs re-enforced that I did actually belong to something special. In fact these family photos were my link to a past and heritage strong and rich in culture.

The art piece was intended to resonate an image of a part of history of the Torres Straits, by showing one of the prominent industries for Torres Strait Islander men. Depicting how they laboured and struggled in the pursuit of wealth for others, and in some instances at personal risk for little or less than the normal wage set for white workers. However, it is also intended to show that despite this, these men, through their work on the luggers, felt proud and were able to keep their own connection to their culture and heritage alive.

I have tried to show this by using small icons which I have overprinted upon the photographic image, to re-inforce the idea of the strength of the culture of the Torres Strait people."

Reproduced courtesy of the Cairns Regional Gallery.
Photography: David Campbell

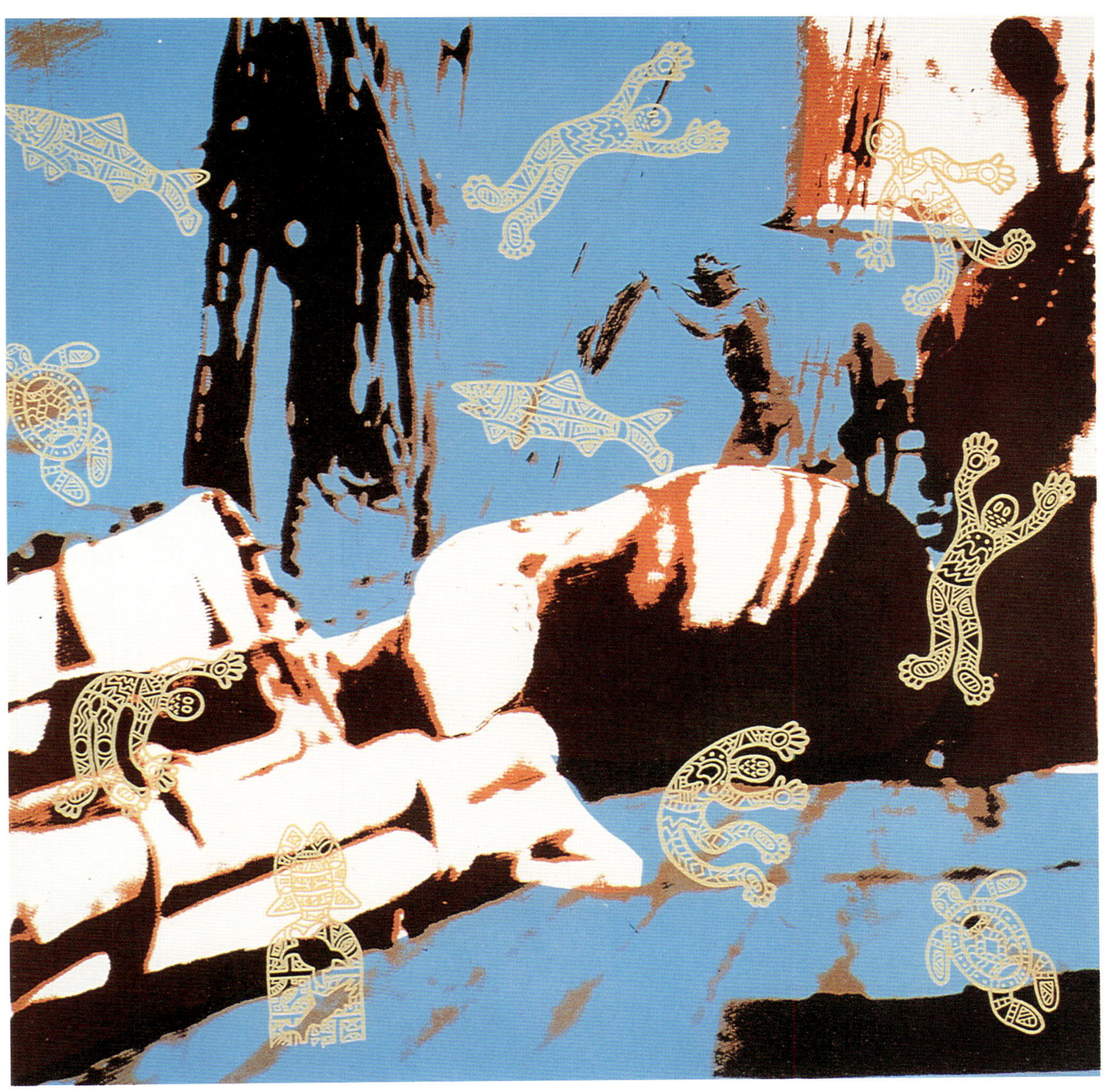

Andrew Williams
On the Lugger

GIVING YOUR HEART TO THE LORD

Joseph Cummins

Linocut
40 x 45cm
1997
Collection: National Gallery of Australia

Joseph writes:

"I was deeply moved when only a couple of years ago I went to the Hopevale Aboriginal Community near Cooktown, and met with an Aunty I had never seen before. She was very religious and had a great love for her family. She told me to give my heart to the Lord, and direct my life through his teachings.

So, I did what she said and when I returned to Cairns, where I was then studying at the TAFE, I started going to church.

I am now a Born Again Christian and with the Lord's help I will work with him for the rest of my life.

In my print, I have depicted both the traditional old people and today's urban Aboriginal people. The two circles in the image represent towns and communities and the small handprints represent the many people (both black and white) who have given their hearts to the Lord.

The angels on either side of the cross are the Guardian Angels, who are there to look after their flock.

The large hands are the hands of God, who gave us his only son and the dove above the cross represents the Holy Spirit.

The angels on either side at the top of the print are praising the Lord.

Christ was crucified and died on the cross for the sins of the world."

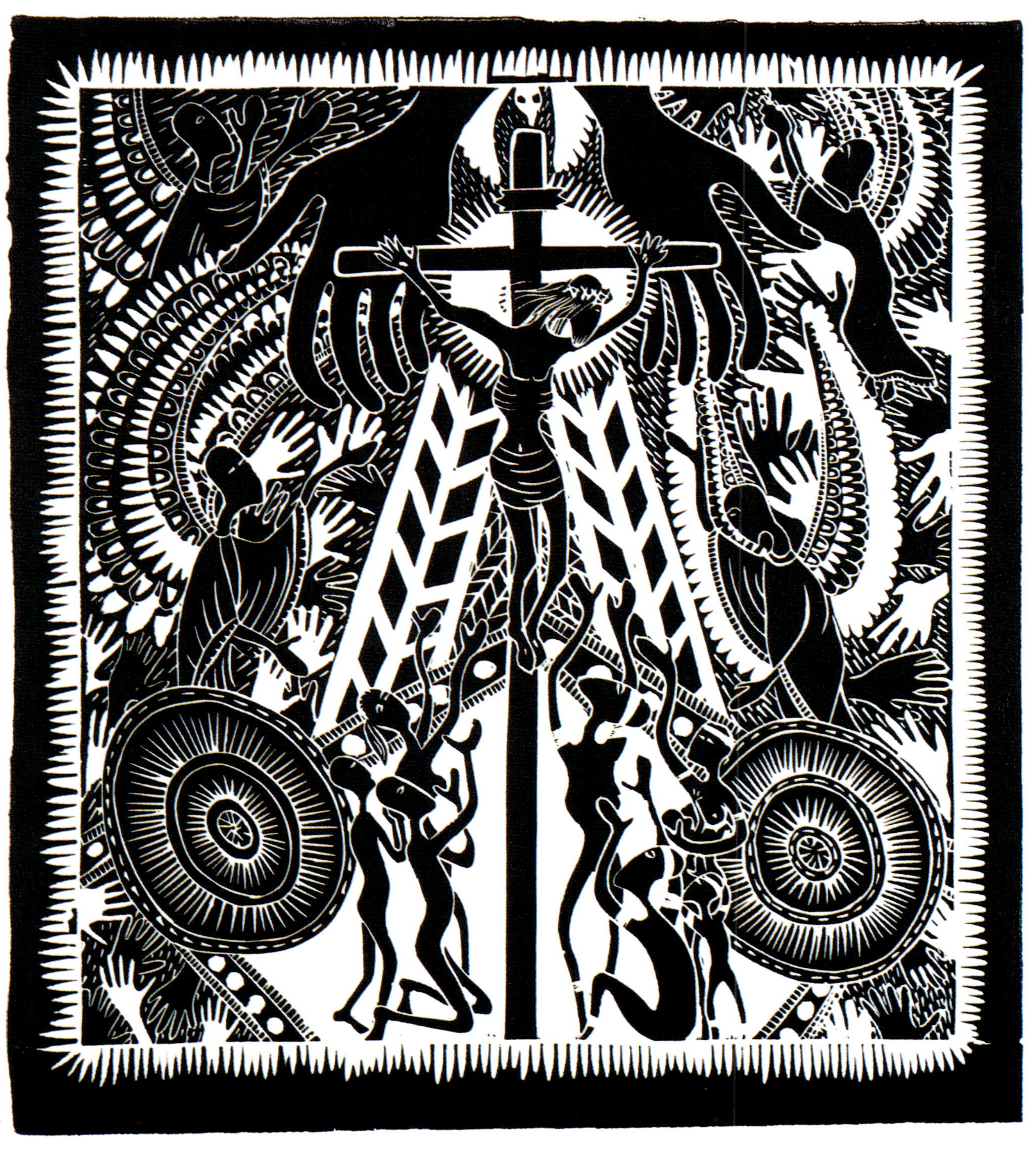

Joseph Cummins
Giving Your Heart to the Lord

HEADDRESS

Sophie Buli (nee Jacobs)

Batik on Cotton
1997
90 x 200cm
National Gallery of Victoria Collection

This artwork features a Torres Strait Island headdress. Known in Torres Strait culture as the *deri*, *dari*, or *dhoeri*, the headdress can be found in both the Eastern and Western Islands.

Sometimes standing as high as 600mm, the headdress is made using the feathers of white seabirds, the Torres Strait pigeon (*Gainau*) and the Egret (*Sear*). The feathers were tied into a cane frame with a fine string and sometimes cassowary feathers were bound into the lower part of the headdress. Occasionally, the tuft of a Bird of Paradise was also used. The frame was painted red, white and blue. These colours signified the colours of the islands within the Torres Strait.

The shapes and images portrayed in the batik also represent nature's bounty, as does the headdress itself. The long feather in the middle was used for the weather, the end-tips of the feathers represent fish tails and particular patterns represent both the natural and cultural aspects of Island life. The six round circles at the top of the artwork represent pearl shells with carved patterns.

Three of the patterns at the bottom of the artwork represent dance ornaments (*getau za*) from the Western islands of the Strait. *Sik* is the name of the dance ornaments referred to by other islands. These ornaments feature a sucker-fish motif in the centre of a wooden disc, tied with bamboo to a cane ring. Feathers are fixed around the perimeter and the ornament is painted red, black and white. Sometimes a turtleshell cut into a circle is used. The wooden block has a pearlshell in the centre and the bottom edge is mock lace.

The *Dari* was, and is still worn in ceremonial dances today and is most commonly featured during the dance with bow and arrow. Murray Island Dancers used it for a dance called the *Kabar*. The men of the Murray Islands wore the headdresses as they performed traditional dancing at Parramatta Park in Cairns for Her Royal Highness Queen Elizabeth the Second.

Headdress is part of the National Gallery of Victoria's travelling exhibition "Raiki Wara: Long Cloth from Aboriginal Australia and the Torres Strait".

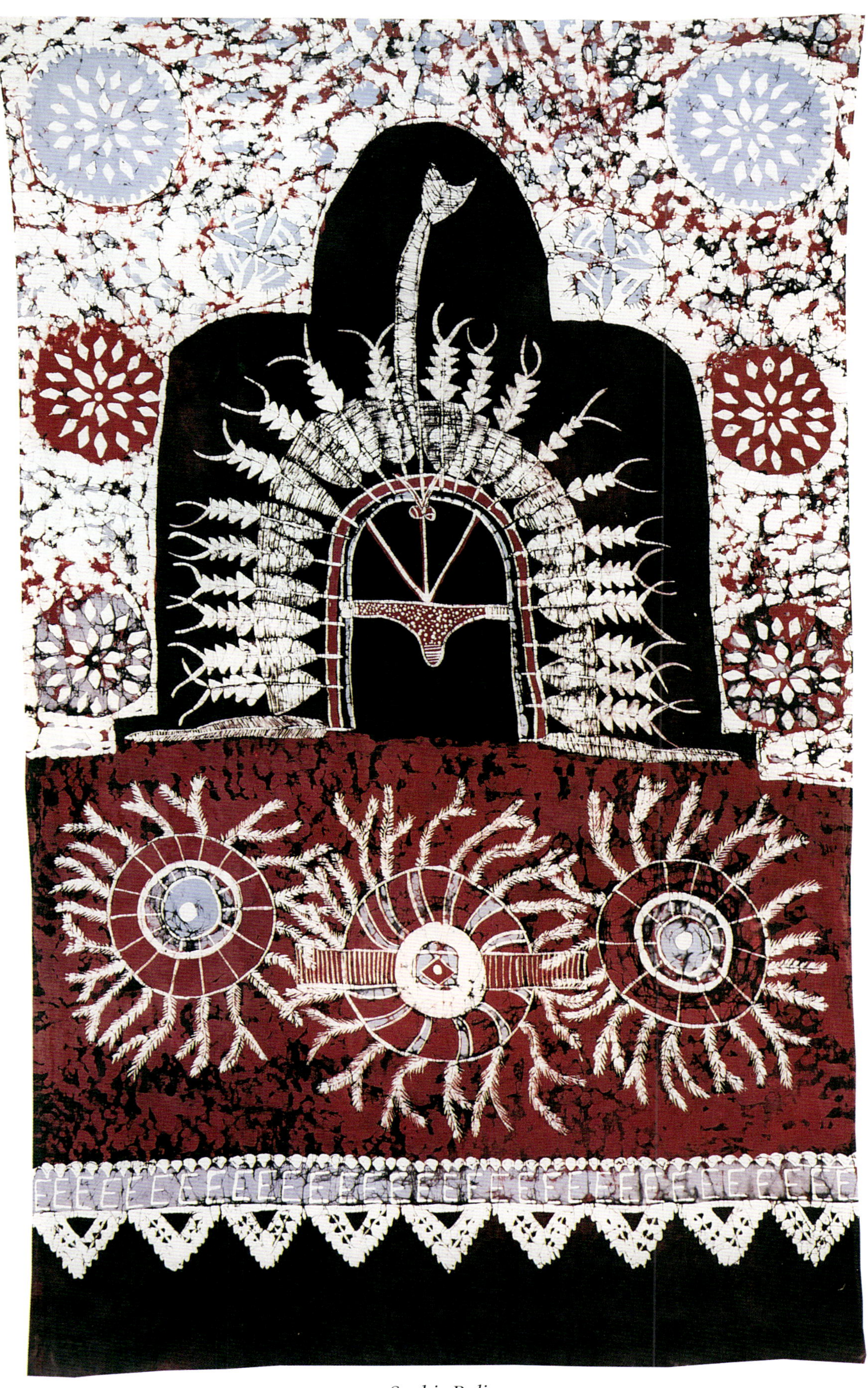

Sophie Buli
HEADDRESS

THE RAINFOREST 1

Felicia Andy

1999
Linocut print
20 x 29cm
Private Collection

Felicia writes about her work:

"At Downey Creek, about thirty kilometres from Innisfail, the place I was born, is a beautiful area of tropical low-altitude rainforest. It is a relatively rare example of this type of rainforest, and its scientific name is *Complex Mesophyll Vine Forest*.

This forest is made up of giant trees, some with trunks three metres in diameter, standing up to forty-five metres high. Below the canopy created by these trees are many layers of other trees, each layer filtering out more and more of the sunlight. Walking on the sun-flecked ground beneath these trees is a mystical experience.

Since European settlement of North Queensland began in the 1860s, the rainforest has been consistently cleared for agriculture, grazing, mining and logging. Today, more and more people are moving into North Queensland from other states, seeking a lifestyle away from the noise and pollution of the cities, making the clearing of more rainforest area for residential development yet another threat.

In my linocut, I celebrate the beauty of the rainforest near my home and hope that people seeing my print will understand how important it is to stop exploitation of these areas of ancient rainforest,

Deep in the forests, somewhere, I believe the spirits still live."

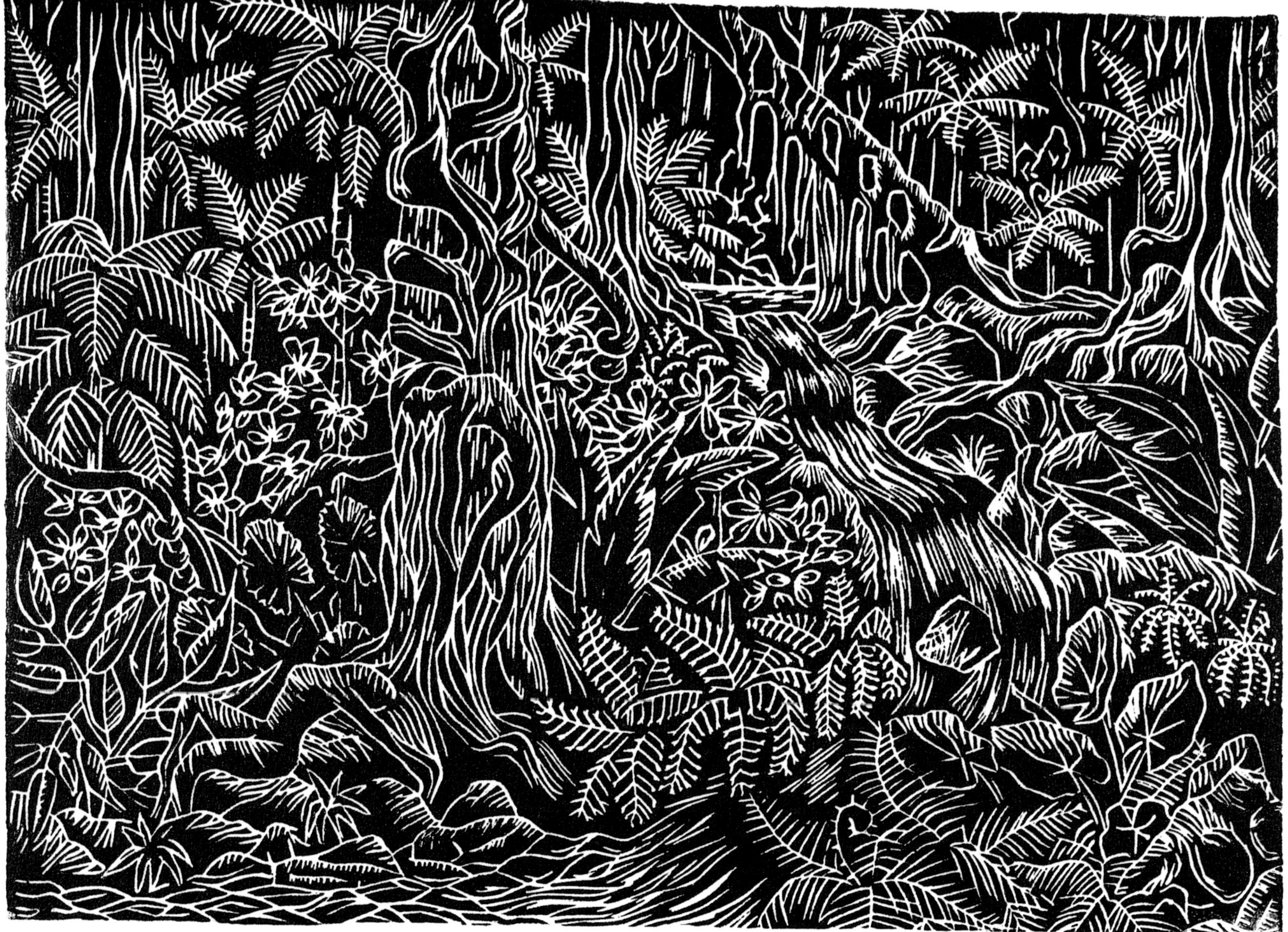

Felicia Andy
THE RAINFOREST 1

Crayfish on the Reef

Lorraine Iboai

1999
Acrylic on Canvas

Lorraine writes:

"The painting 'Crayfish (Kaiar) on the Reef' portrays a crayfish sitting on a coral outcrop, while the small reef fish glide past to the rhythm and motion of the sea current.

The crayfish in its natural environment has an array of brilliant colours. The diversity of these brilliant colours and its physical features enable the crayfish to camouflage itself into the uniquely beautiful and fascinating natural surroundings of the tropical reef, hiding it from the dangers of its lurking predators that inhabit the domain beneath the waves.

Various elements provided inspiration for the painting. Firstly, the vivid colours of the crayfish, and how well they blended together, along with its other physical features were befitting to the style of my painting.

Most importantly, however, is the inspiration gathered from my cultural ties and cultural identity as a Torres Strait Islander. The crayfish, more commonly known as 'kaiar' by the Western and Central islanders of the Torres Strait, is one of the major sources of income for the Torres Strait islanders. Not only is it a source of income, the 'kaiar' of the Torres Strait is no doubt one of the most tasty and delicious lobsters. The 'kaiar' is exported to the gourmet markets of Japan, France, USA, Singapore and Malaysia. This recognition makes me very proud to be a Torres Strait Islander!

The use of vibrant colours and contemporary indigenous designs that I have utilised reflect and represent the natural colours and characteristics of the 'kaiar' in the domain beneath the waves of the Coral Sea."

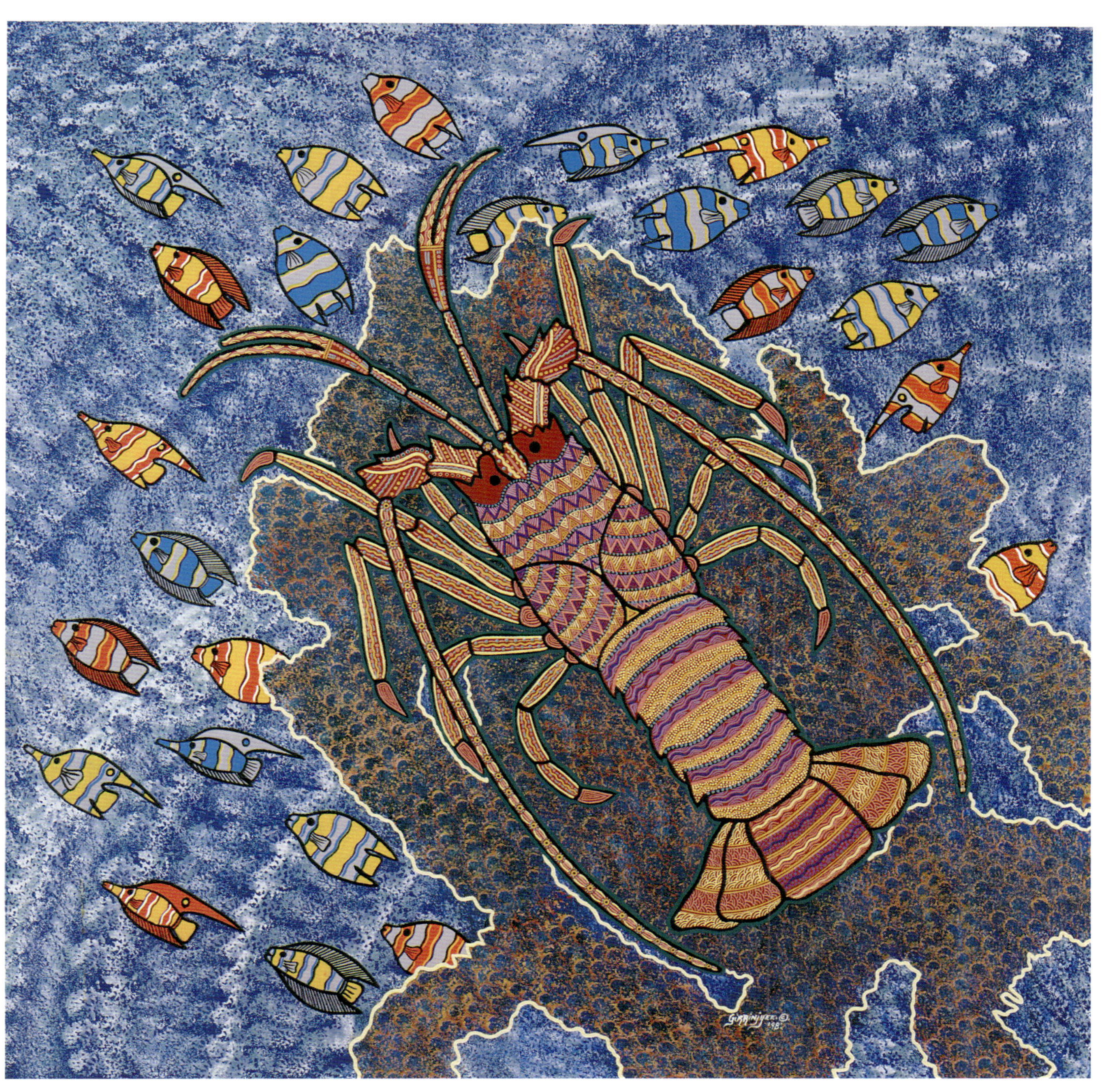

Lorraine Iboai
CRAYFISH ON THE REEF

STINGRAYS

Tatipai Barsa

Linocut
44cm x 47cm
Private Collection

Tatipai is from Mer (Murray Island) situated on the eastern side of the Torres Strait. In many of his paintings and prints he draws on images from his island home. The sea life, the reefs and the currents and powerful tides of the seas of the Torres Strait provide never-ending inspiration for his images.

Tatipai's patterns also reflect the traditional carving and plaiting of his people, his colours are those of the tropical sea, the corals and the exotic flowers of the islands.

In his works, based on the sea, the patterns echo the movement of the sea grasses, the shifting sands and the strong lines of the currents.

"Stingrays" was first shown in Sydney at the Aboriginal and Tribal Art Center in a group exhibition in 1997, one of the many group shows he has been involved in over the last few years. They include "Now Days-Early Days" at the Cairns Regional Gallery in 1995, and the year before in an exhibition of Indigenous art from Australia titled "Epama Epam: Everything Has Meaning" held in Canada.

Tatipai is represented in many national and private collections in Australia and overseas.

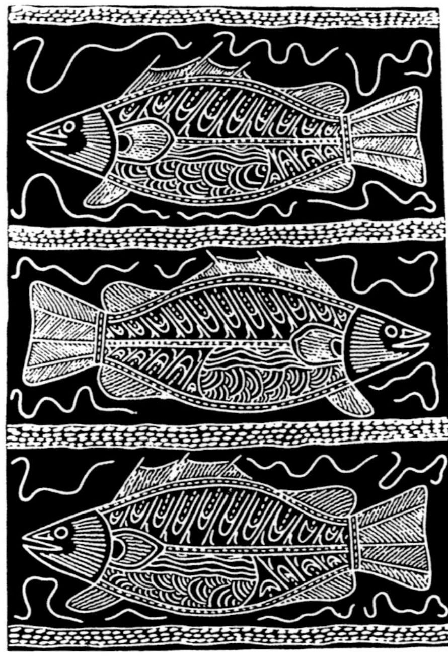

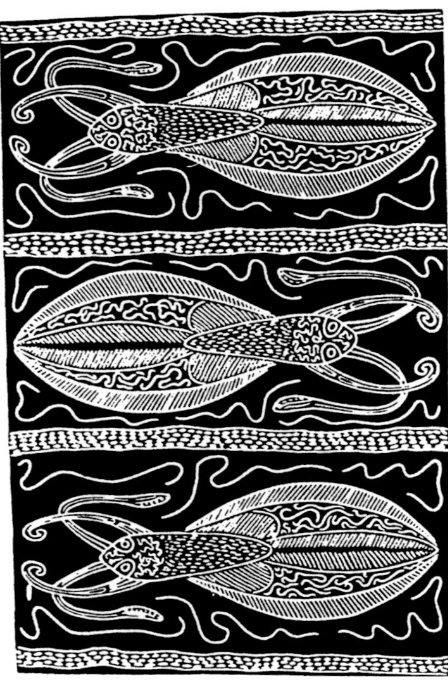

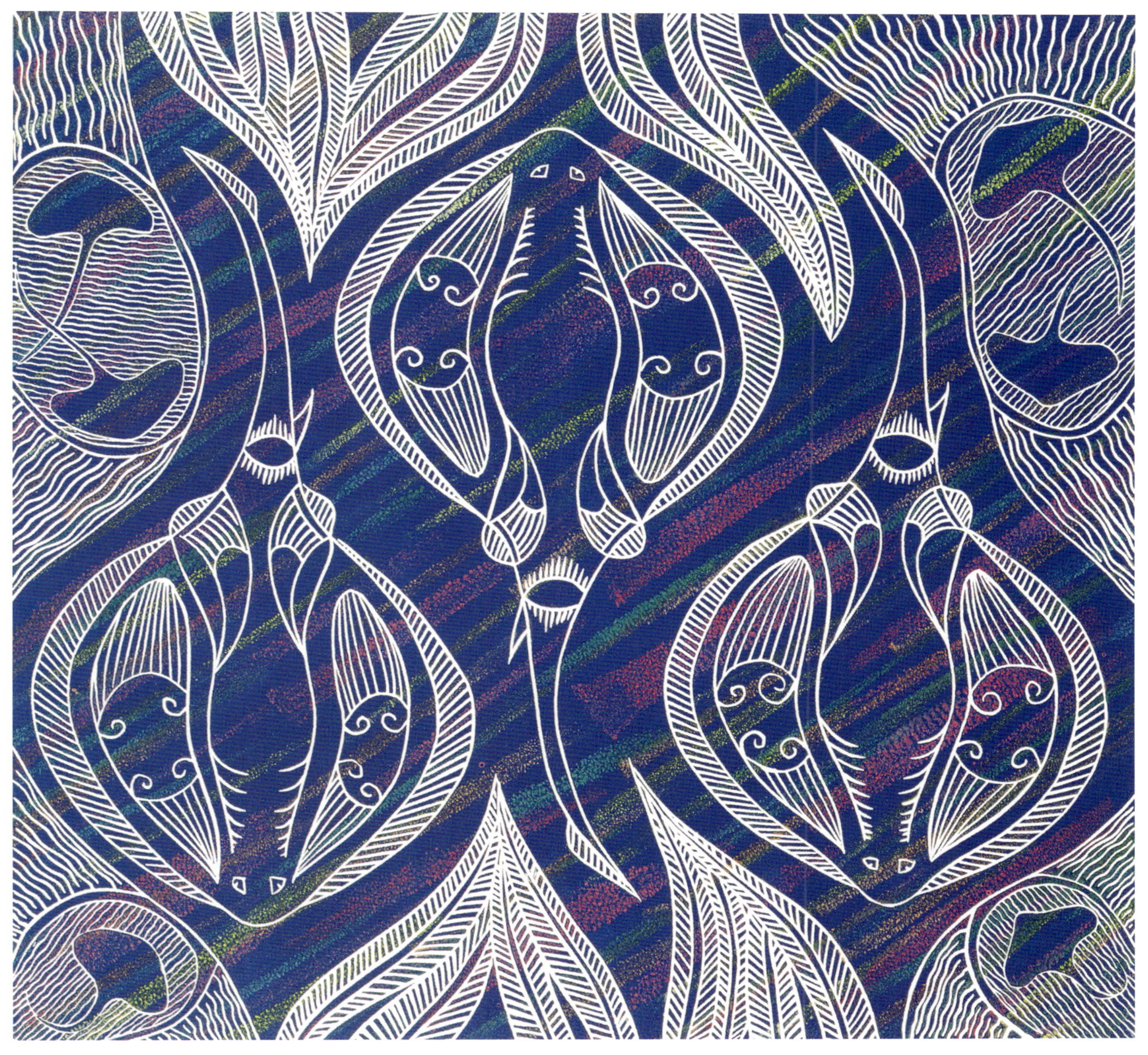

Tatipai Barsa
Stingrays

THE COMING OF THE LIGHT

Ken Thaiday

1998
Pencils on cartridge paper.
155cm x 210cm

Ken writes:

"This is the celebration of the coming of the LMS (London Missionary Society) missionaries to Darnley Island in 1871. The light of the Gospel of Jesus Christ was shared among the Torres Strait Islander people from this time. Before this, these people had been cannibals and had lived in warfare with others, but on hearing the message they broke their arrows and spears and became Christians by accepting the word of God.

In the art work the central Christ figure is reaching out to the people. The Greek cross is superimposed over the figure and the rays of light flow out from him to the people who have begun to change from their darkness into the light.

The missionaries are there telling the people to turn from their wicked ways and repent. For many this is an instant and welcome change.

On the right hand, the fish (a symbol of the Torres Strait Islanders dependence on the sea for a living) are drawn to the Christ figure, a reference here to the disciples being 'fishers of men', is also significant."

A preliminary sketch for a proposed series of stained glass windows for the baptistery, St Monica's Cathedral, Cairns.

Courtesy of the Artist.

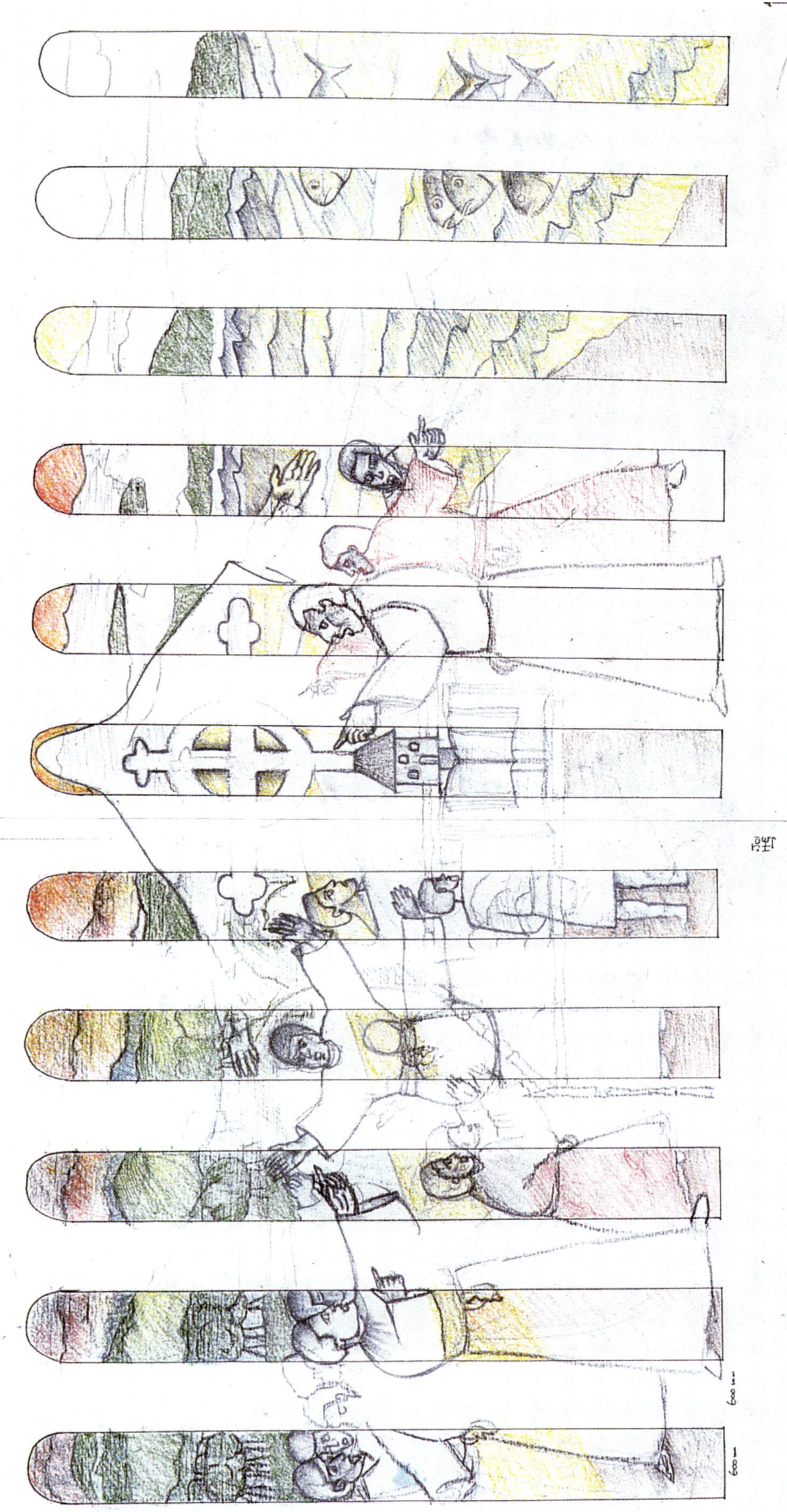

Ken Thaiday
The Coming of the Light

TWERET SPIRITS, NJOORLUM SPIRITS AND ANTHROPOMORPHS OF ABORIGINAL LIFE

POOARAAR (BEVAN HAYWARD)

1990
Etching
28cm x 48.2cm
1990

The existence of the Aboriginal people of Australia began when nature first forged together life-sustaining properties to produce fleshless creatures which Aboriginal people called spirits. Those spirits were brought to life by nature under specific climatic conditions within different areas of Australia. Consequently, every area produced a different type of spirit.

Although these structures were fleshless, they still possessed the same five senses as we know them today.

When some great earthly upheaval disintegrated those spirits, some of their life-sustaining properties were metamorphosed by nature into other life-forms. Those life-forms then produced the anthropomorphs.

The anthropomorphs were the first fleshly forms to initiate rules for their particular socio-cultures, that were also entwined within the spiritual realm of that particular locality.

To make a statute as a document of land ownership and rules to live by, they painted and/or engraved their own images on the rocks near to their place of origin.

In this etching I have tried to express the importance of the spirits and the anthropomorphic statutes to the lives of the various tribal groups of Australian Aboriginal people.

Courtesy of the Artist.

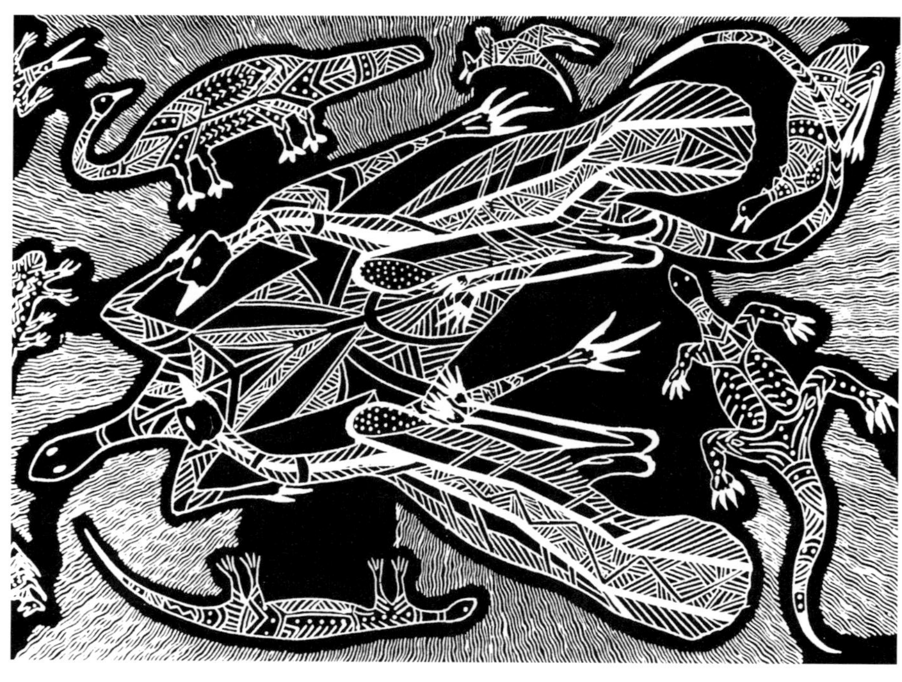

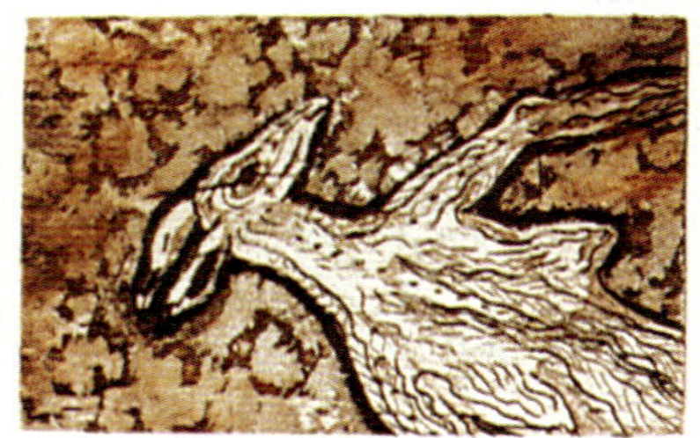

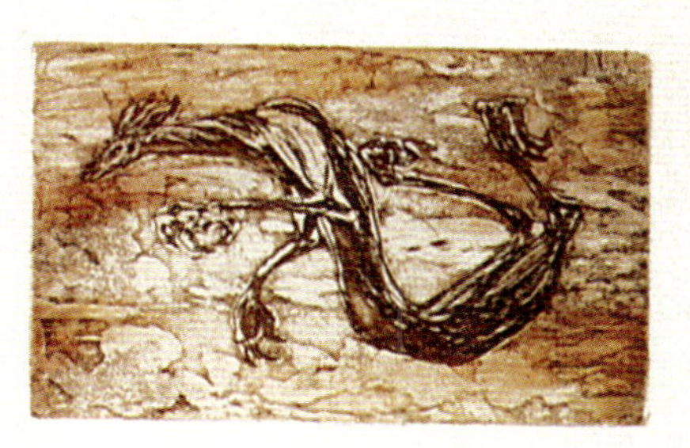

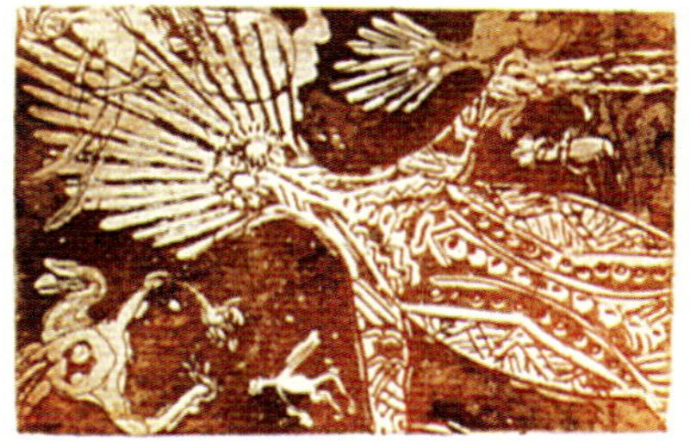

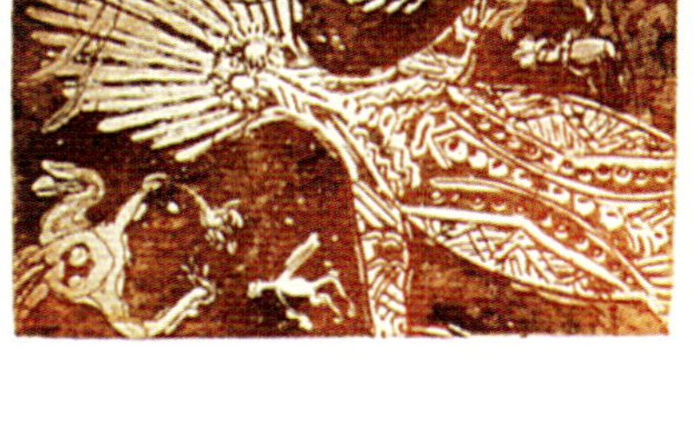

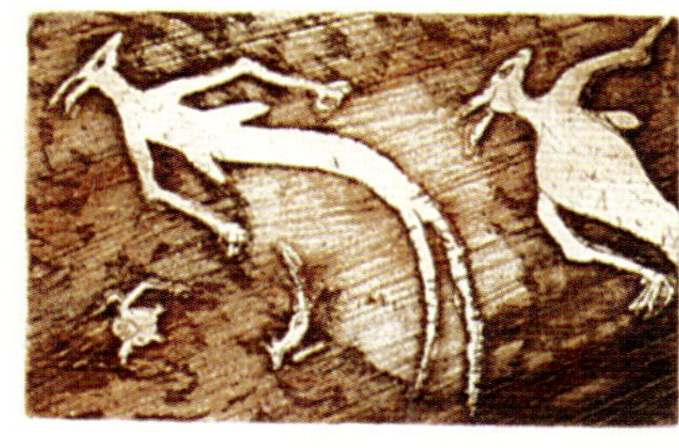

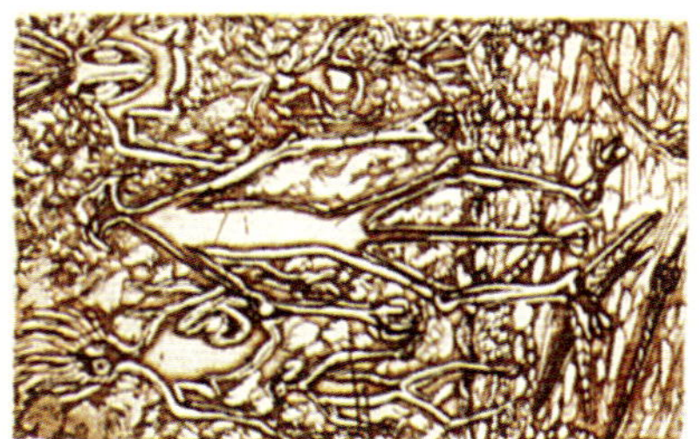

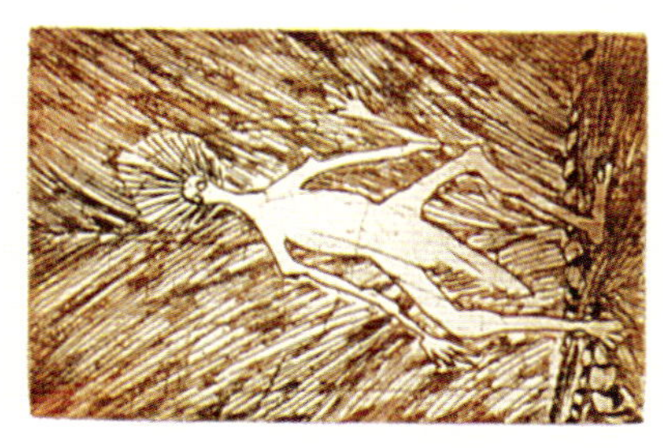

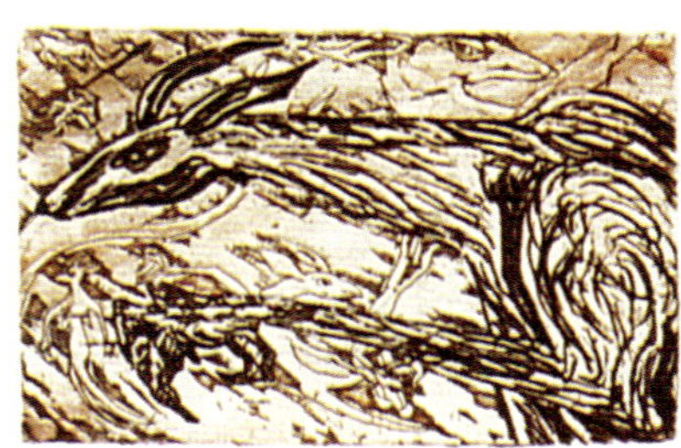

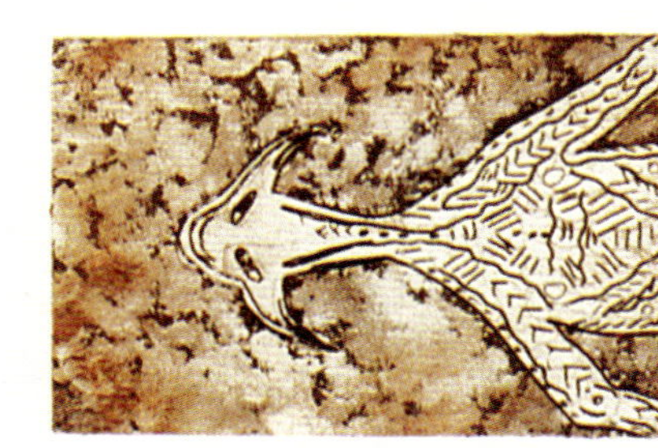

Pooaraar (Bevan Hayward)
TWERET SPIRITS, NJOORLUM SPIRITS
AND ANTHROPOMORPHS OF ABORIGINAL LIFE

PAST AND THE PRESENT

Frederick Baira

Linocut
40cm x 60cm

This print shows the ways that the old culture of the Torres Strait is slowly changing, the old ways eroded by the new (modern) culture of today.

The centre of the design features the images of traditional island homes situated beside a suburban house, the likes of which can be seen all over Australia. Above the dwellings island warriors wearing traditional Dhari (head-dress) are depicted beside today's island men wearing modern hats.

In the foreground, a dugong is being prepared for a feast as was done in the old days. It still remains a favourite food for the Torres Strait Islanders today.

The repeating pattern that forms a background linking the main images is the *Bu* or trumpet shell. The *Bu* was used in the old days to summon people for special occasions like weddings, feasts and dancing. It was also used to summon people to church after the missionaries came, because there were no bells in the early days.

The sound of the *Bu* is still used today in island dance performances. The print depicts this tradition with the dancers shown at the top of the picture. Below the dancers, two women can also be seen beating the traditional warups (drums).

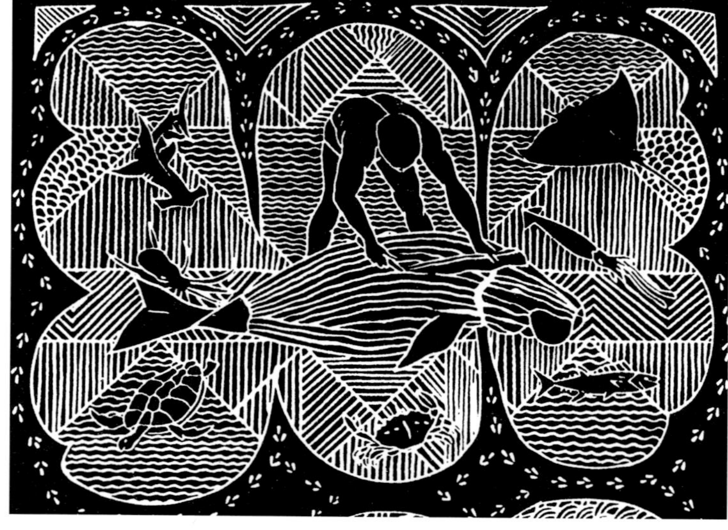

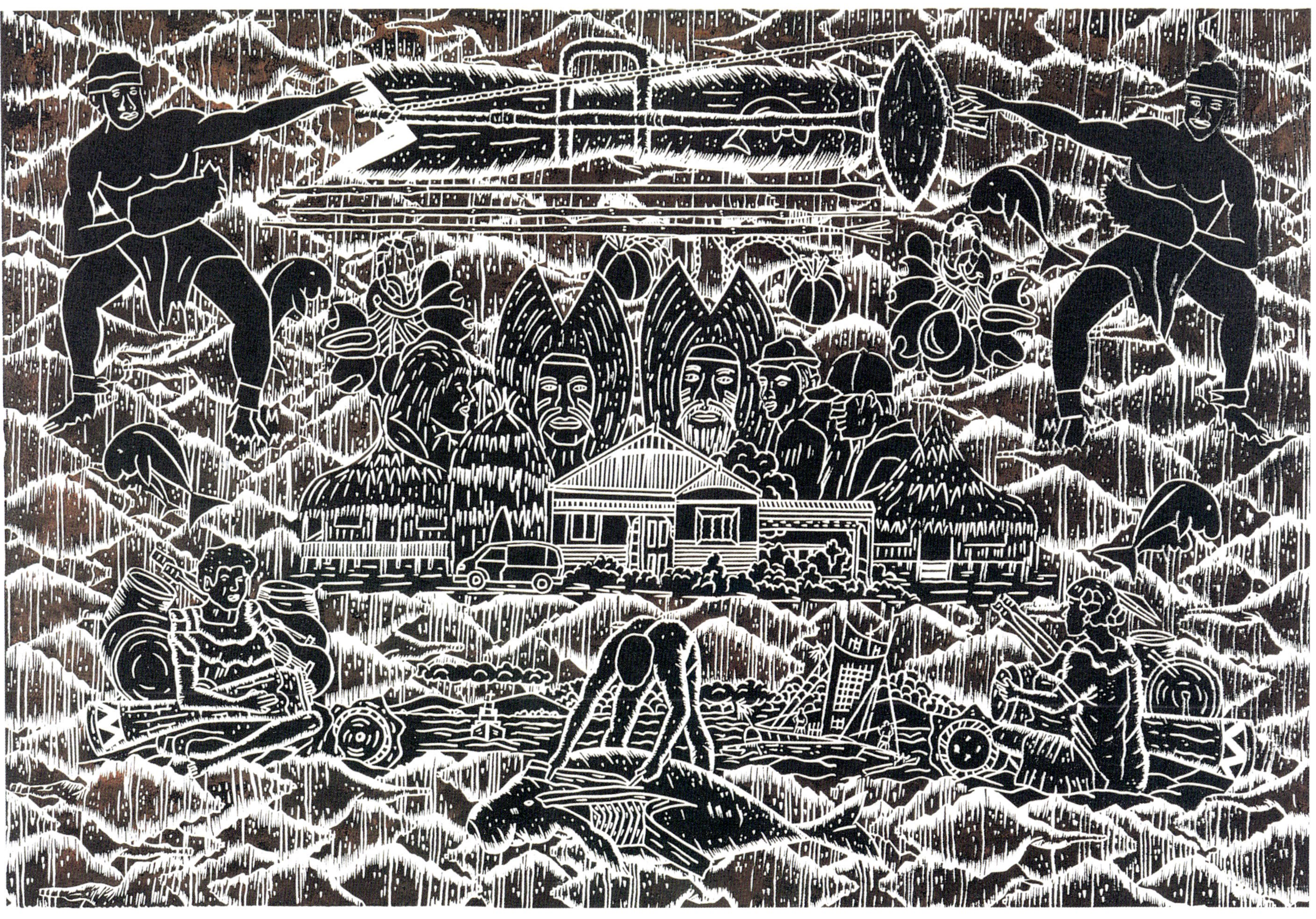

Frederick Baira
Past and the Present

THE ZUGUTIAM - THE SHARK OF ZUGU

Matatia Andrew Warrior

1998
Reduction Woodcut
28cm x 62cm

The *Zugutiam Warriors*, or *Zugabal*, are a group of fierce fighting warriors of Mabuiag renowned throughout the western islands of the Torres Strait. They were formed from the cult of *Kuiam*, a legendary and historical warrior hero of the same island.

The two leaders of the warriors wore sacred *gugu* (googoo) or owl masks, and the two sacred sand crab emblems of Kuiam.

The first of the two wore *kutibu*, the larger emblem of the two on his chest, while the second wore *giribu*, the smaller emblem on his back. These sacred emblems protected and gave strength to the warriors. The sacred emblems were so important they were kept in a sacred cave on a separate island just off Mabuiag.

Courtesy of the artist.

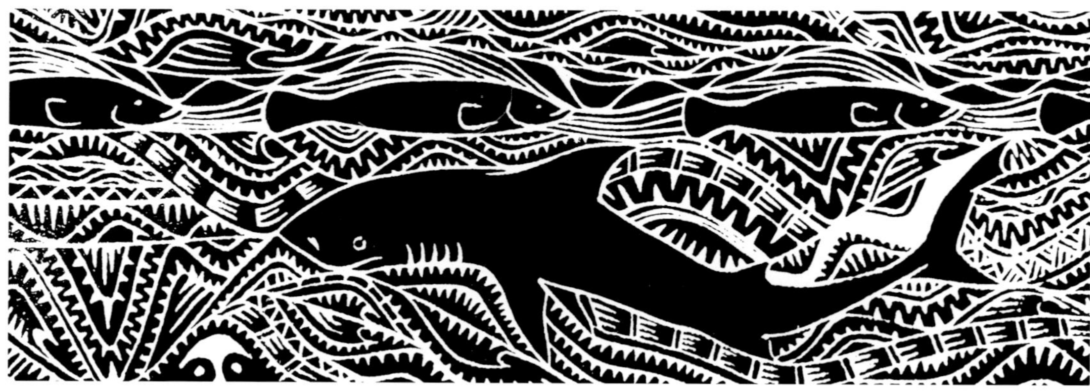

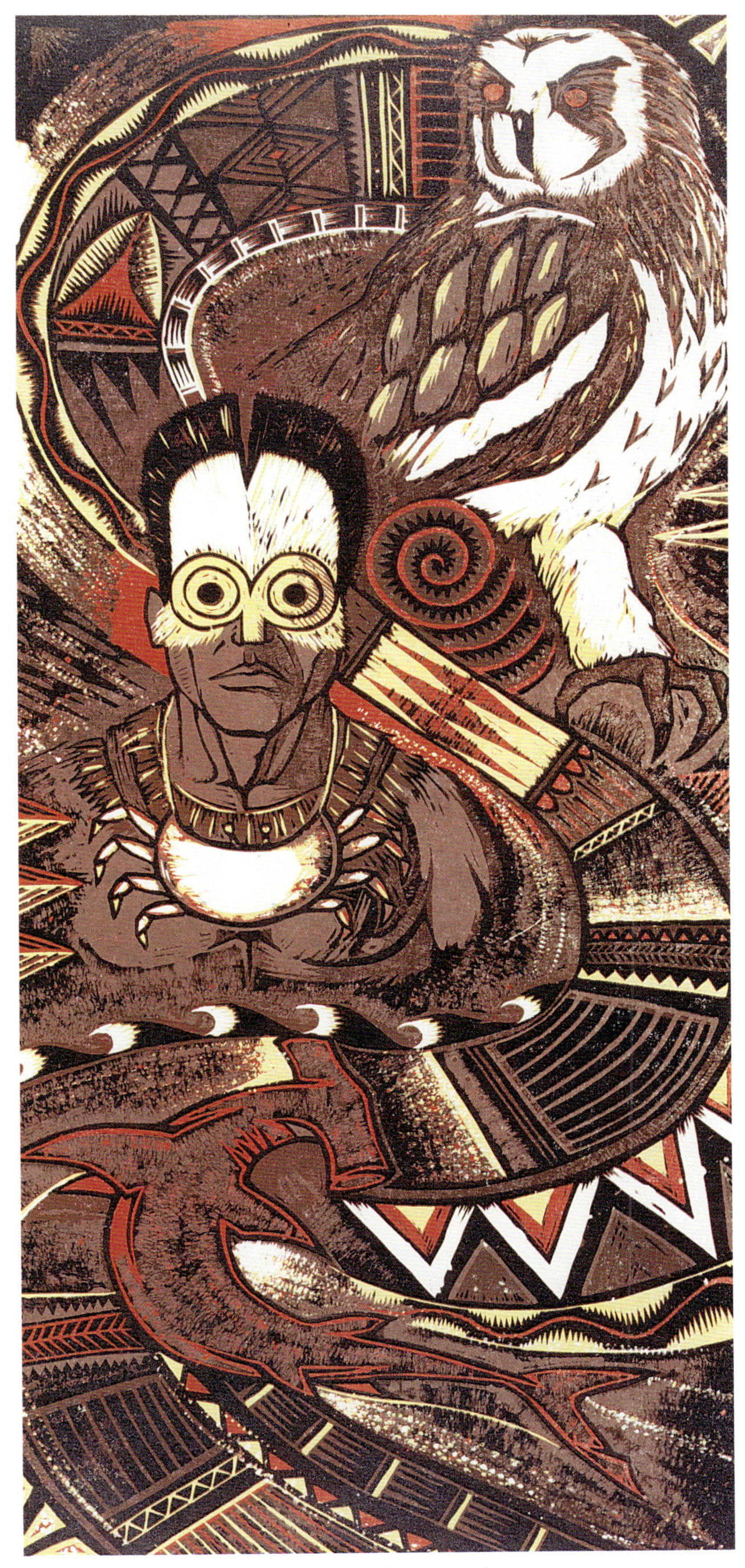

Matatia Andrew Warrior
The Zugutiam - The Shark of Zugu

THE SEA GODS HAVE AWOKEN

Brian Robinson

Plywood, synthetic polymer paint, screws, woven palm fronds, wooden dowelling, varnish.
100 x 200 x 30cm
1998
Cairns Regional Gallery Collection

The Islander's knowledge of the habits of the many forms of marine life in the waters of the Straits and their highly developed hunting and fishing skills have always assured them of a ready supply of seafood.

Turtles were hunted throughout the Straits and females were preferred. Sometimes they were caught on the beaches, after having laid their eggs in the sand. Generally, however, they were hunted from canoes. The hunters used either harpoons (mainly in the Western and Central islands) or single pronged spears (in the Eastern islands). The best time for turtle hunting was towards the end of the year, during the mating season when turtles were often found floating lazily near the surface of the water, well above the reefs.

Dugong were found mainly in the more shallow seas in the Western part of the Straits. They were hunted from canoes, or harpooned from wooden platforms built above their feeding grounds of seagrass. At low tide, the hunters could see where the dugong had been feeding by the marks left in the soft silt or mud of the seaweed patches. The men would quickly build a platform over this spot. One hunter would then wait until night, with his harpoon tied to the platform by a neatly coiled length of rope, sometimes 200-350 metres long. At night, during the high tide, the dugong would surface for air and the hunter could collect his prey.

Fishing from the shore or around the reefs was done either by using fishing lines made from vine or vegetable fibres (with hooks fashioned from turtleshell), or with spears. In the Eastern islands, where large schools of sardine are found along the shores, a bamboo scoop (weres) was used. Also in the Eastern islands, large rock-walled fish traps were built in the shallows. Fish were trapped in these at low tide, becoming easy prey for spear-armed hunters.

Traditional methods of hunting and fishing have changed little from early times to present, although nowadays dinghies and motor-boats are used in place of canoes, and modern fishing equipment has replaced the bamboo spears and turtleshell fish hooks.

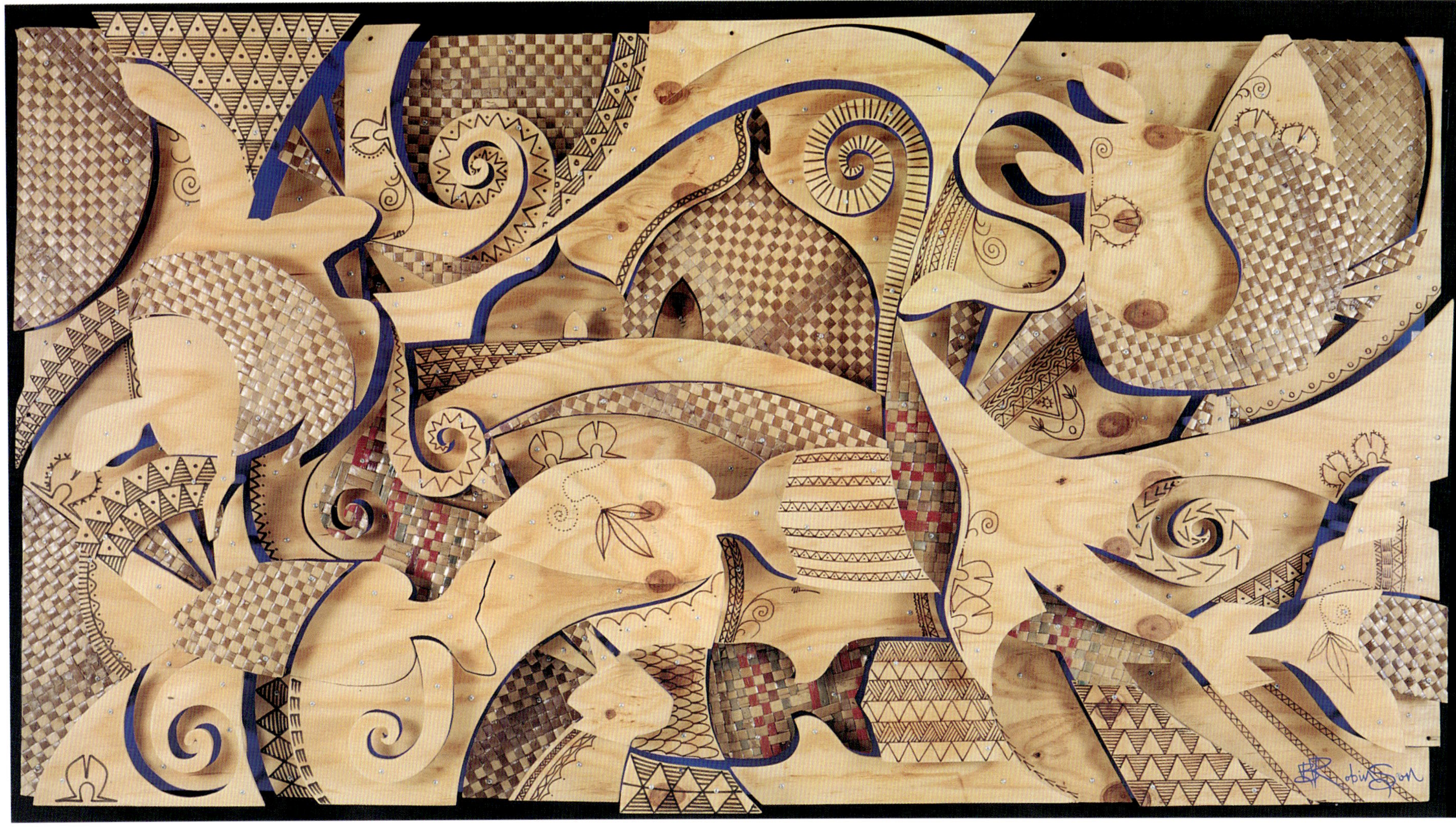

Brian Robinson
The Sea Gods Have Awoken

GIANT BARRACUDA

Daniel Geia

1999
Acrylic on Paper
38cm x 56cm

The Giant Barracuda is a story fish from Palm Island.

The story tells of two men: one old man and one young man who both go fishing around Palm Island in their small boat. The young man speared a giant barracuda and the old man told him to let it go because it was too big. The giant barracuda was longer than the boat.

The young man did not listen to the old man and consequently the giant barracuda tipped the boat right over. The old man and the young man were both drowned that day and became reefs surrounding Palm Island.

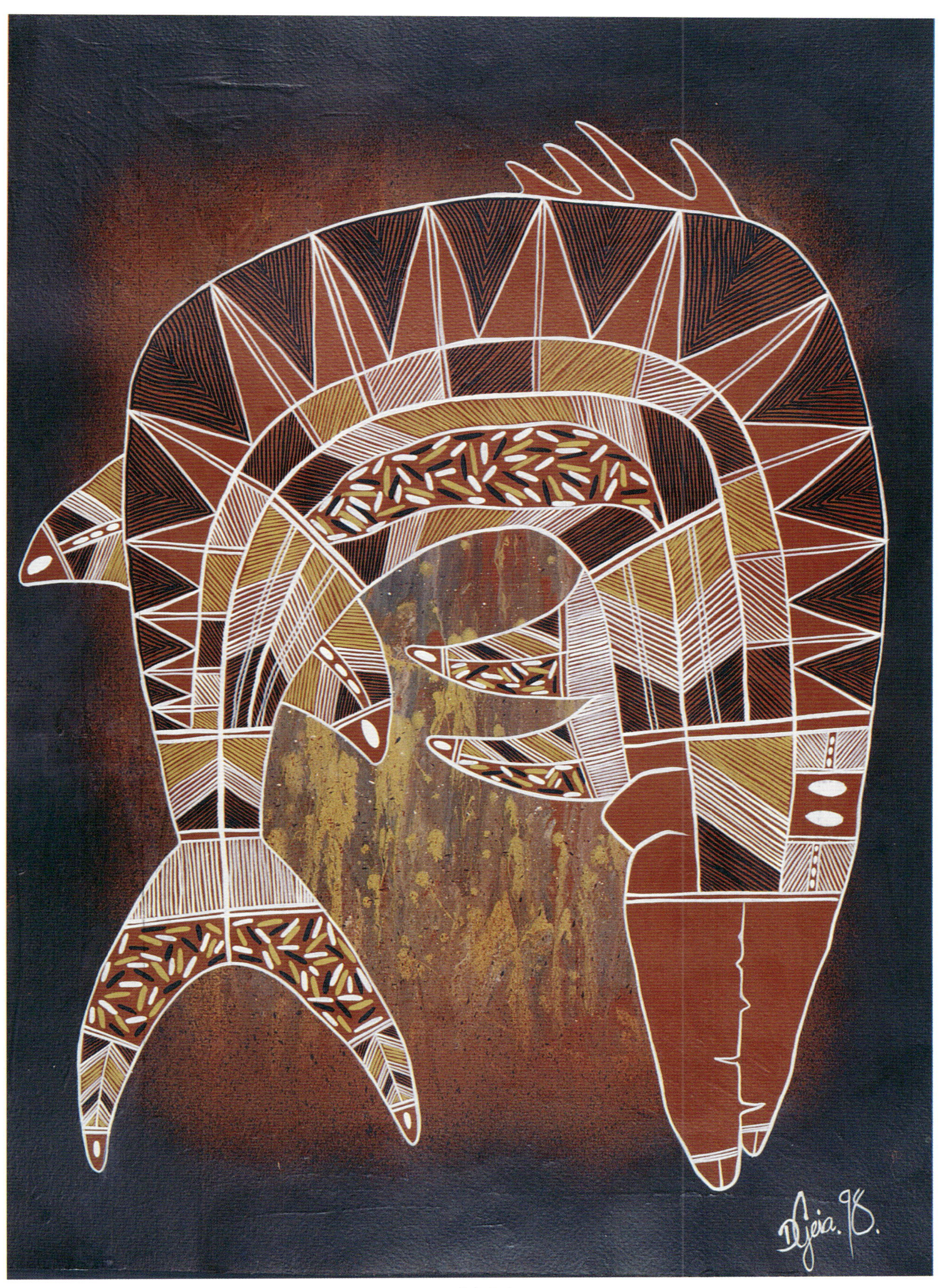

Daniel Geia
GIANT BARRACUDA

WE WERE NEVER PART OF THE INDUSTRIAL REVOLUTION

ELAINE LAMPTON

1995
Acrylic on Canvas
Private collection
125 x 135 cm

By "We" I mean the indigenous peoples of this country. We already had a vast educational system in place before the invasion of the British. This system involved being educated in life skills, while actually living life.

With the start of the Industrial Revolution, schools as we now know them were founded, and indigenous people are now required by law to attend these institutions to "learn" about life.

The painting depicts an industrial scene on top of images of a culture that has largely been buried or engulfed by progress and education. It is interesting to note that the last thing of the indigenous people of Australia being exploited today is their visual ART.

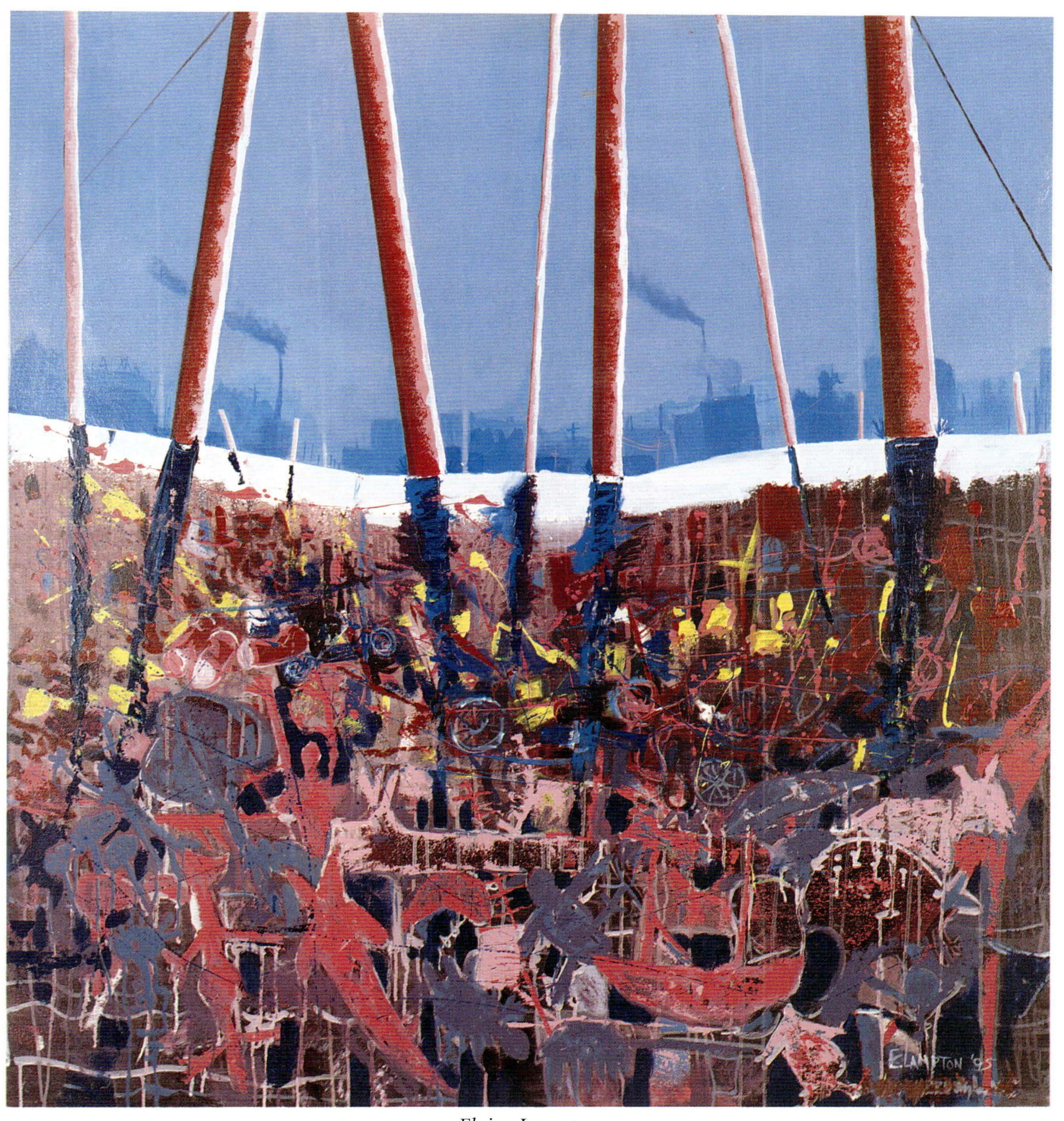

Elaine Lampton

We Were Never Part of the Industrial Revolution

TWO LOBSTERS
(MANBARRA)

ALLAN PALM ISLAND

Linocut Print
42.6 x 46cm
1998
Perc Tucker Regional Gallery Collection - Townsville

Many of Allan's prints are based on the sea creatures that provide the traditional foods of his Palm Island people. Amongst these are of course the lobsters he has presented in this print. There are many different sea creatures living in the waters around the artist's home. They include: dugong, turtles, crabs, stingrays and many species of edible fish. These creatures provide both a stable source of food for the Palm Island people, as well as being the subjects of important ancestral significance.

The 'Two Lobsters' is a reduction linocut print. In the print, Allan is expressing the movement of the tropical sea using the colours and patterns surrounding the lobsters.

Photography: Robert Parsons

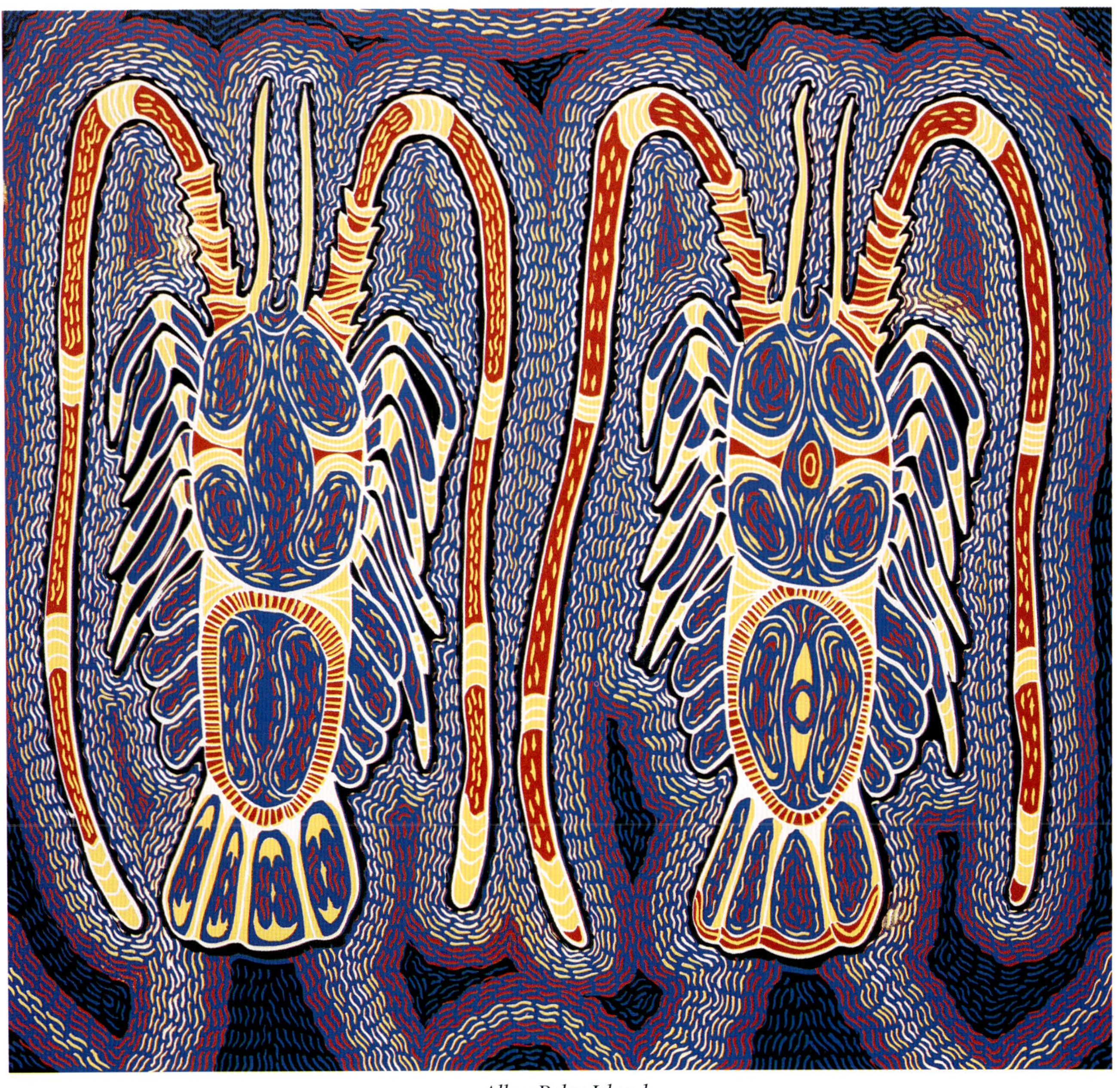

Allan Palm Island
Two Lobsters (Manbarra)

LINKING CULTURES

JENUARRIE

Low fired terracotta water bottle

This work makes reference to both the land and the sea.

The low-fired terracotta water bottle is working with extremes that have evolved through adaptation from the "Lappita" style pottery-making techniques.

The chains represent the links we all have with family, and our cultural heritage - the continued links we carry in our everyday lives - then and now.

The work captures the calming influence of waves and water.

Incorporating other mixed mediums (inlay) represents compatibility and reconciliation.

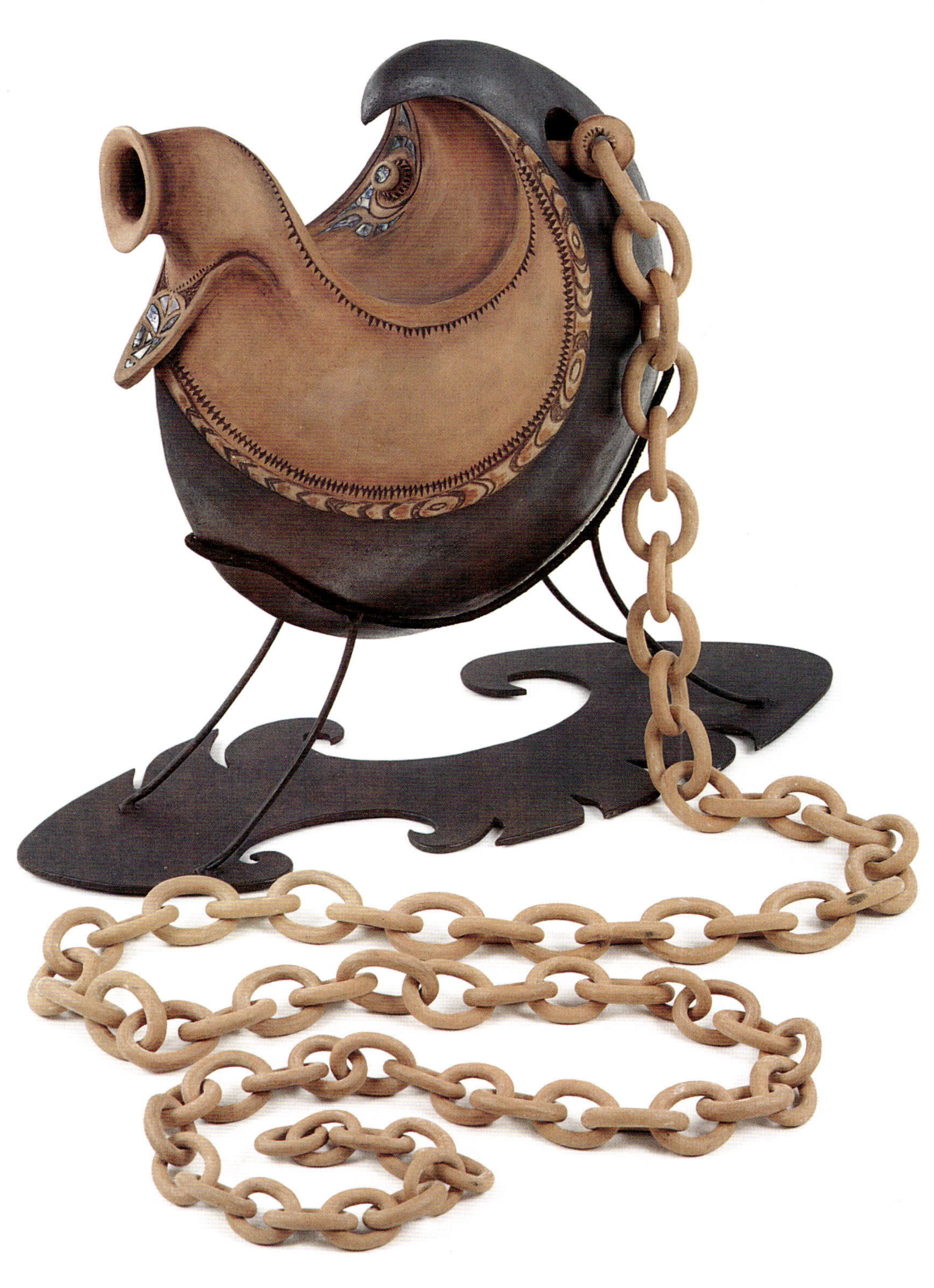

Jenuarrie
LINKING CULTURES

SEA GOD

Ceferino Garcia Sabatino

Mixed Media - Clay, cassowary feathers, shells, paint & raffia.
1997
Private collection.

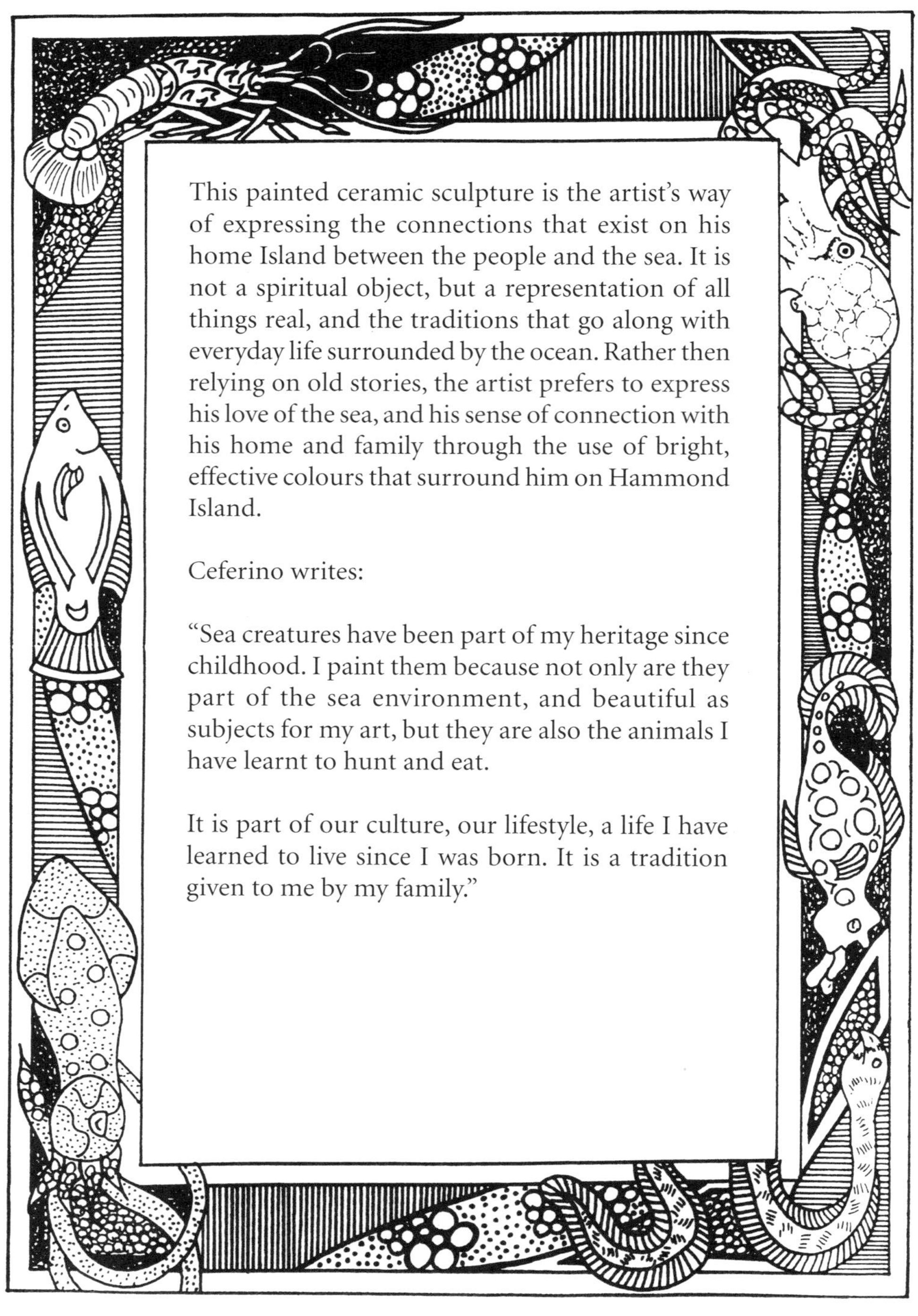

This painted ceramic sculpture is the artist's way of expressing the connections that exist on his home Island between the people and the sea. It is not a spiritual object, but a representation of all things real, and the traditions that go along with everyday life surrounded by the ocean. Rather then relying on old stories, the artist prefers to express his love of the sea, and his sense of connection with his home and family through the use of bright, effective colours that surround him on Hammond Island.

Ceferino writes:

"Sea creatures have been part of my heritage since childhood. I paint them because not only are they part of the sea environment, and beautiful as subjects for my art, but they are also the animals I have learnt to hunt and eat.

It is part of our culture, our lifestyle, a life I have learned to live since I was born. It is a tradition given to me by my family."

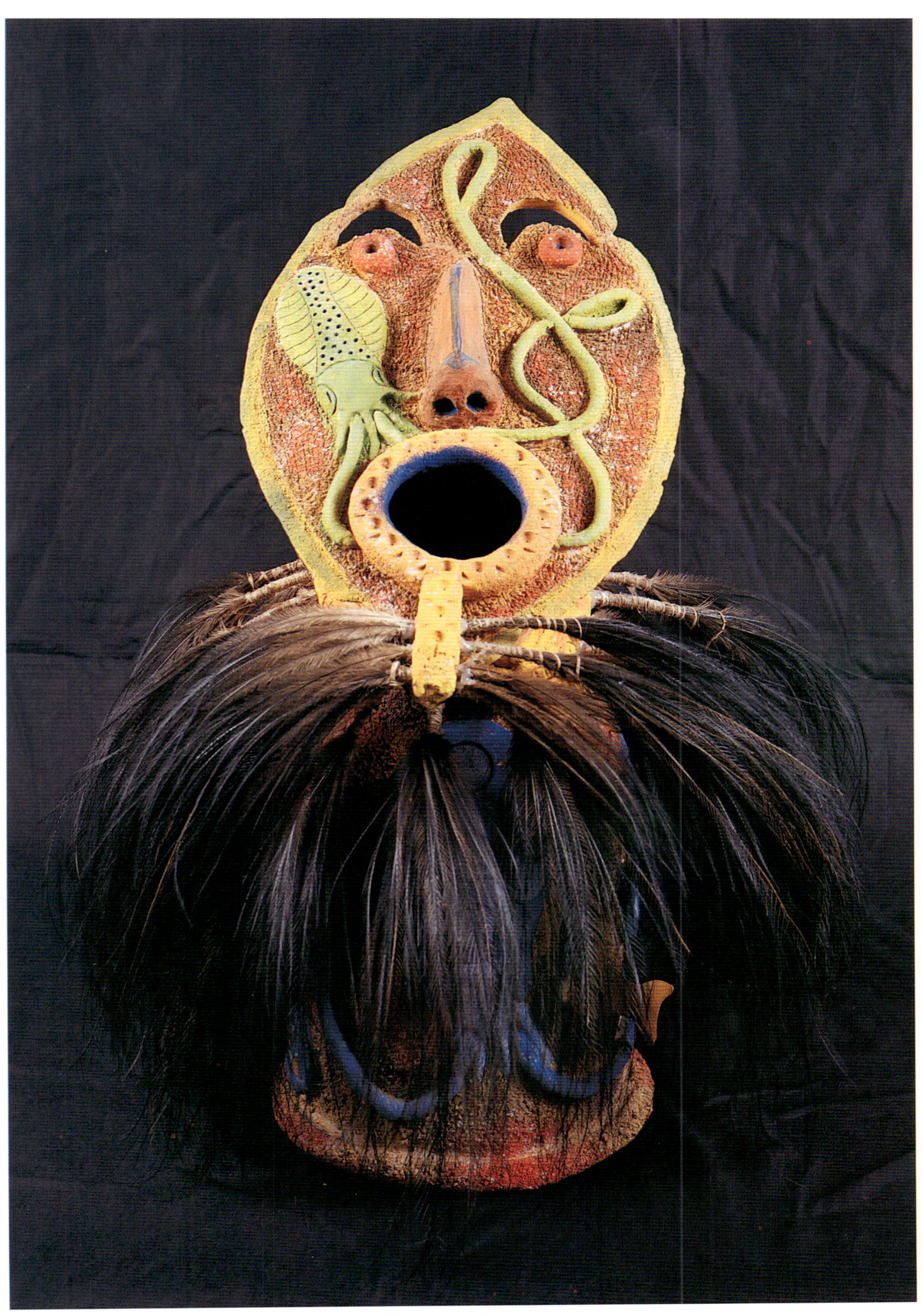

Ceferino Garcia Sabatino
Sea God

SHORT BIOGRAPHICAL SKETCHES OF THE ARTISTS

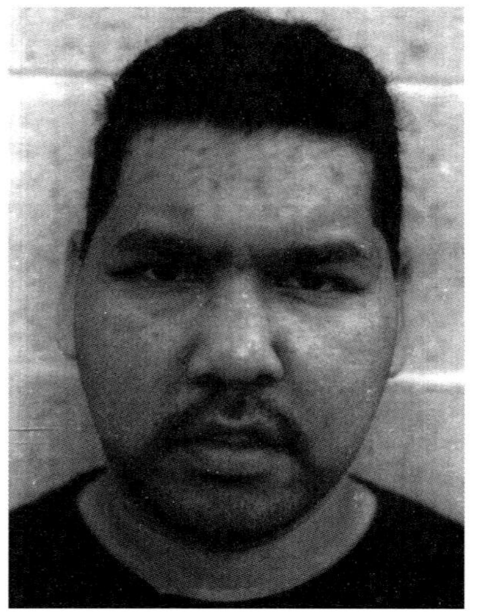

Vernon Ah Kee
Self Portrait
Born and raised in Innisfail Queensland, Vernon spent his childhood fishing, swimming in rivers, and playing cricket and football with his cousins. His family moved to Cairns when he was in grade nine, where he completed High School and later went on to attend the Cairns College of TAFE in 1995-96. Vernon now lives in Brisbane Queensland with his wife Leesa, and their three young sons, Eddie, Gavin, and Michael.

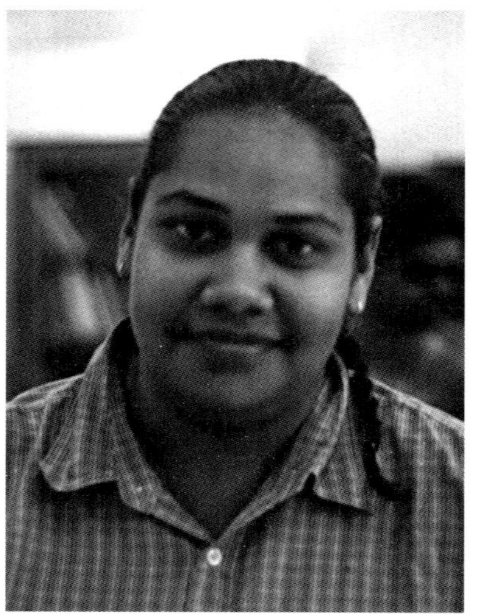

Felicia Andy
The Rainforest 1
Felicia was born in Innisfail, North Queensland on April 2nd, 1980. She moved to Cairns to study for the Diploma in Visual Art at the TAFE in 1999 after completing the Certificate in Visual Art at Johnstone College the year before. In her work, she seeks to explore subjects that have a personal meaning, calling on subjects about her emotional feelings, her background, places she has travelled to and identified with. Moreover, the beautiful rainforest that surrounds Innisfail always appears in her images.

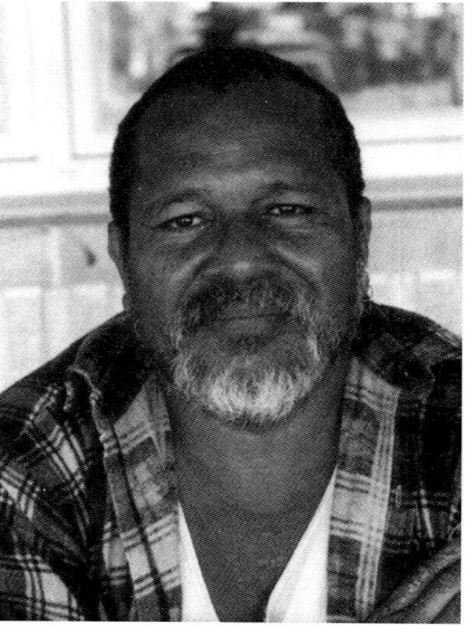

Frederick Baira
Past and the Present
Frederick completed a Diploma in Visual Arts (Aboriginal and Torres Strait Islander) studies at Cairns TAFE College in 1997, and is currently studying at James Cook University, Townsville for his Bachelor of Visual Arts. With family and friends living on many of the Islands in the Straits, Frederick feels he has a strong cultural link with the Torres Straits, and in the future intends working with young Torres Strait Islanders, to help them regain knowledge of their culture. His print 'The Past and the Present' is being purchased by the National Gallery, and will be presented as part of the National Print Collection in Canberra.

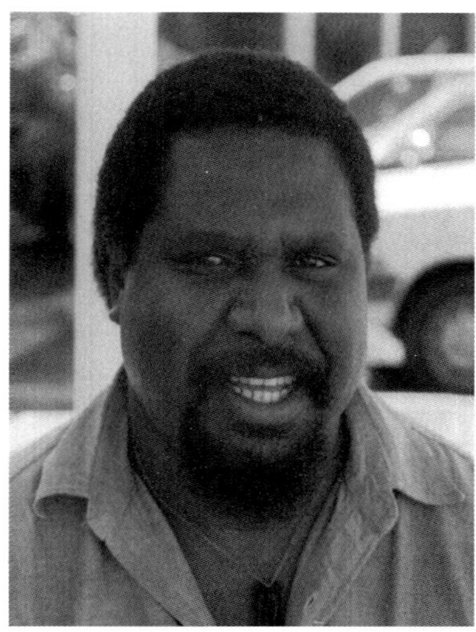

Tatipai Barsa

STINGRAYS

Tatipai originates from Mer (Murray Island), which is situated on the Eastern side of the Torres Strait. His art draws heavily on the beauty of his tropical surrounds; colours, shapes, animals, sea creatures and the traditional pastimes of the Torres Strait Islanders. Tatipai has been involved in numerous group exhibitions, both within Australia, and overseas. His works are represented in important National, overseas, and private collections.

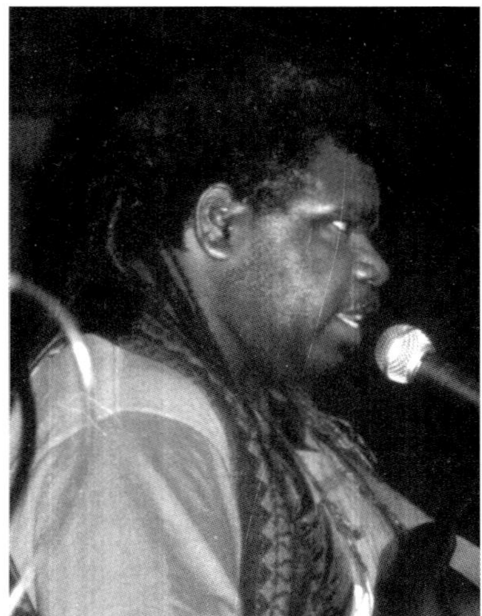

Thomas Bosen

THE BROLGAS AND THE ANIMALS

Thomas is a descendent of mixed parentage, both Torres Strait Islander and Aboriginal Australian. His father is a descendent of the Thaniquwith Clan group of the Gulf of Carpentaria, which is about eight kilometres North of Weipa. His mother is a descendent of the Kudal (crocodile) Clan group of Mabuiag (Javis) Island. As an artist, Thomas calls upon stories from both of his parent's clan groups. All of his paintings are based on traditional stories that have been handed down from generation to generation. He finds these stories help maintain, and identify one's own cultural identity, and also helps to identify one within a cultural society. He hopes these stories will also help the younger generation to understand their cultural identity.

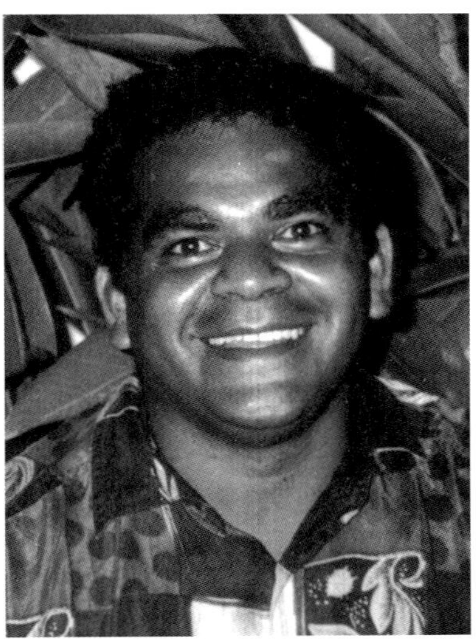

Bindur Bullin {Paul David Bong}

THE LEGEND OF THE BOULDERS

Named after a great warrior, Bindur Bullin is a member of the Indinji Tribe. The Indinji Tribe occupied the fertile rainforest lands from Cairns in the North to Babinda in the South, and West into the Atherton Tablelands as far as Kairi. Bindur Bullin incorporates traditional design with modern techniques in his paintings, and says "...each design has spiritual meaning. This is the only visual art recording of my unique Tribe". Bindur Bullin and his uncle Karlumbul were commissioned in 1995 to create an installation for the Departures Concourse at the International Terminal, Brisbane Airport, Queensland. The installation recreates the rainforest shields of the Indinji people. Carved fig root by Karlumbul and painted by Bindur Bullin in the totemic patterns of his forebears, these are displayed in the International Terminal along with the photographs of tribal members taken a century ago, with shields decorated in the same patterns.

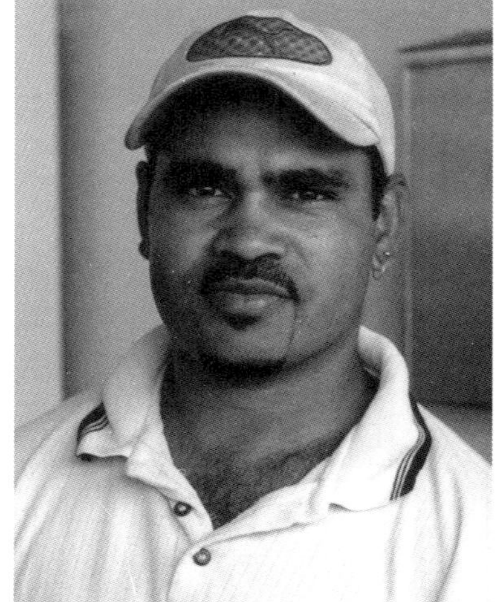

Warren Brim

Goanna Hunting for Turtle Eggs

23 year old Warren is currently undergoing a Visual Arts Course at Cairns TAFE. Born in Cairns, Warren grew up in Kuranda where his family remains today. A member of the Djabugay Tribe, Warren bases his art on living off the land, and the animals the Tribe traditionally hunted for. His paintings also depict Dreamtime stories.

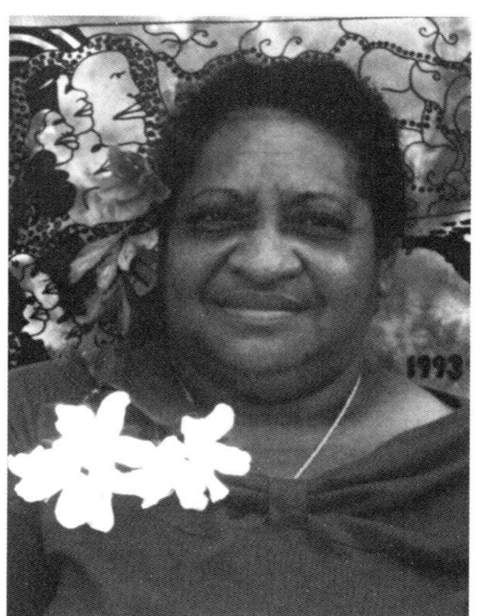

Sophie Buli (nee Jacobs)

Headdress

Daughter of Darnley Island (Eastern Island in the Torres Straits) parents, Sophie Buli was born in 1940 in Cairns. She attended the Aboriginal and Torres Strait Islander Visual Arts Course in 1988, during which she became interested in batik, pottery, lino printing and painting techniques. Sophie's most current commercial work is the Centrelink poster she created in 1998 : Tell Centrelink when kids come into or leave your care. During the week-ends and holidays, children from the neighbourhood and family come to Sophie's house to paint. They have even painted designs on the the cement posts under Sophie's house. Sophie acknowledges God's guidance, as part of her inspiration.

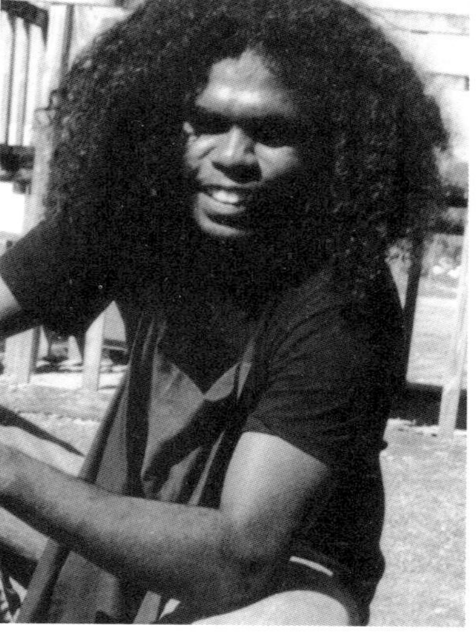

Leon Burchill

Goodi (The Ancient Barramundi)

Leon calls Cairns, in Far North Queensland, his home. It is the place in which he grew up as a traditional dancer, and creative artist. It is also where he completed a Certificate in Visual Arts at the local TAFE College in 1995. Leon is currently extending his creative pursuits after moving to Melbourne in 1996 to study drama. He is undertaking a Diploma of Indigenous Performing Arts Course, and hopes to get the chance to act professionally in the future.

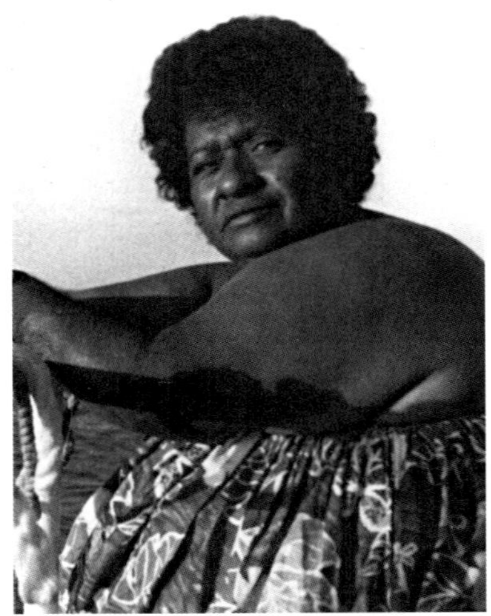

Shirley Christian
The Hole in the Sky
Shirley was born in 1934 to Torres Strait Islander parents Bill and Mary Savage in the small country town of Mossman, North Queensland. In 1938 her mother, sister, and Shirley left Cairns to live on Thursday Island until Shirley and her sister were involved in the World War II evacuation of Torres Strait families. They were taken without their mother to a small town called Cooyar, where they were placed in the care of the Sisters of Mercy Catholic Mission of the Sacred Heart Convent. When the war ended, Shirley and her sister were reunited with their mother in Cairns where they met many relatives they had not known previously. They also met their grandparents for the first time. Married in 1956, Shirley had ten children, five boys and five girls. In 1984, finally having found some time to pursue and develop her artistic skills at the age of fifty, Shirley studied for the Associate Diploma of Art at the Cairns TAFE in its foundation year.

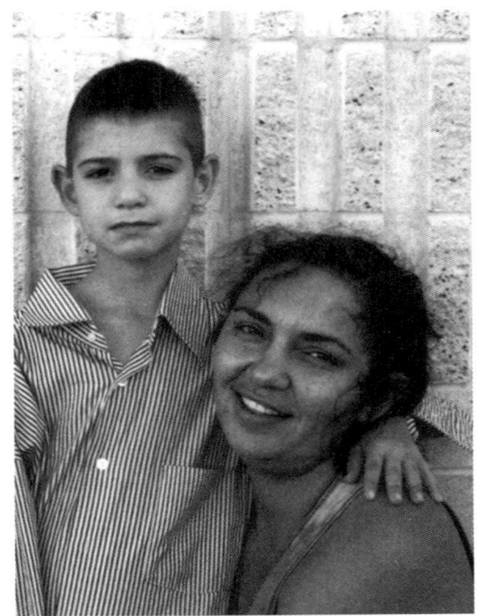

Mary Cummins
Serpent Creation
Being an Aboriginal artist is important to Mary. She has found art allows her to express her culture in the most beautiful way imaginable. A descendant of the stolen generation, Mary grew up around Townsville and Palm Island after her family had been sent to Phantom Island. Her Mother's people are : Ji-Man (Taroom), Noonuccal (Stradbroke Island), Western Yulangi (Maytown), and Nuri-Kingari (Bollon). She not only has a love for Murri art, but loves the concept of Western art as well. Her main mediums are batik and lino printing.

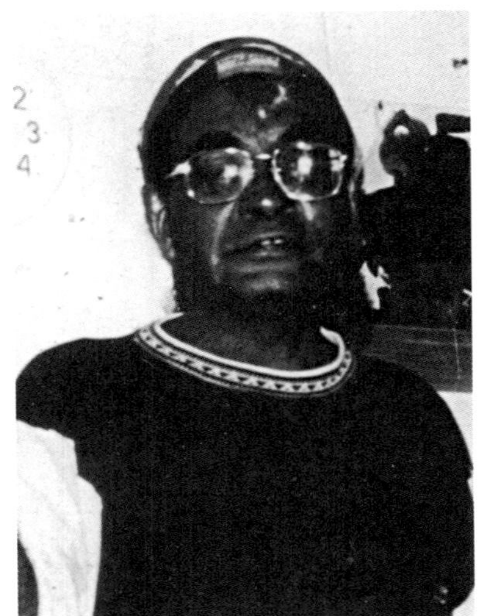

Joseph Cummins
Giving your Heart to the Lord
Joseph was born on Palm Island in 1957. His family moved to Townsville when he was six years old. It was at this early age it was apparent that he had a certain talent for painting and drawing. He was inspired by watching his cousin Vincent Serico paint, and the techniques he used, and so started to paint at a very early age. He sold his first painting "Industries of Townsville" at the age of fifteen, to a tourist. Shortly after, he sold eight or nine paintings to souvenir shops in the Townsville area. When the local Aborigines saw his paintings , he was commissioned to paint for several organisations. Joseph was shown traditional art and Dreamtime stories in Laura, Hopevale and Palm Island. He has developed his own techniques and style over the years in both contemporary and traditional work. Living on the coast, he feels that he should paint the sea and surrounding sea-life. He works in diverse mediums including: batik, ceramics, computer graphics, screenprinting, and lino cuts.

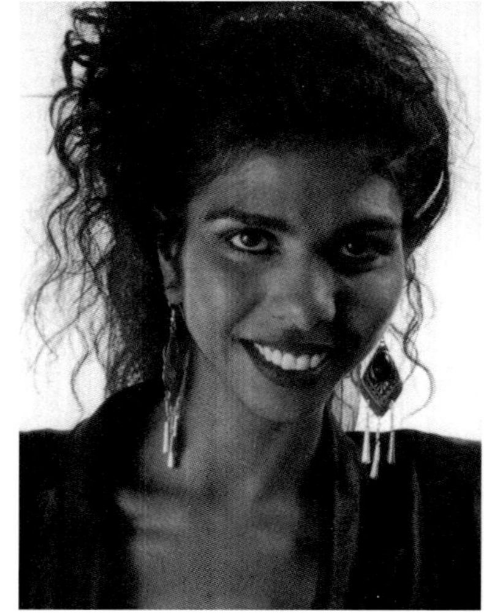

Deborah Cotter
Gurruru (Brolga Dance)
Also known by her Aboriginal name Gugula, Deborah is the daughter of Doreen Braikenridge and Peter Kyle. Her ancestry lies with two Clans: the Jirrabul, and the Birri Gubba. Deborah was born in Ingham, Nth Queensland, where she spent her childhood and schooling years, eventually studying at the Tropical Far North Queensland TAFE in ATSI Art. Deborah now resides in Bunbury, Western Australia, where she continues to teach Aboriginal art to both children and adults at various institutions.

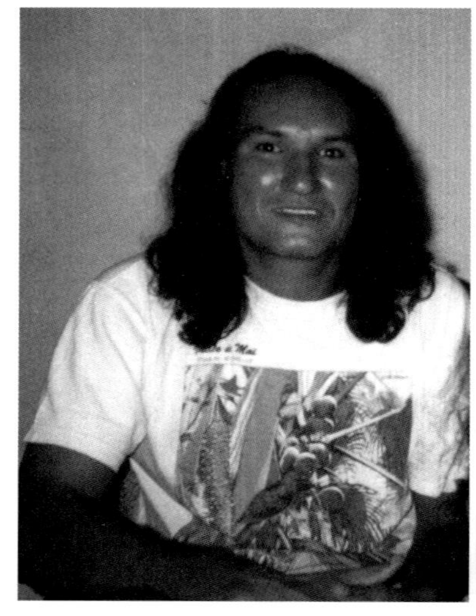

Joseph Dorante
Le-op (Face of Man)
Joseph was born on Thursday Island in 1965. His family originally came from Malaysia. His mother is a Torres Strait Islander, and his father is of German heritage. Joseph attended the Thursday Island Catholic School, and completed secondary school to year 12 level at Bamaga State High School. In 1990 he commenced studies with the visual arts courses at the Cairns College of TAFE. During this time he developed a strong, individual style, basing his images on traditional symbols and ritual objects of the Torres Strait. His striking artworks can be seen at the Jardine Motel on Thursday Island and at the Maritime Museum in Sydney. His works are in many private collections, both in Australia and overseas. Any spare time is spent carving black coral and pearlshell jewellery depicting turtles, dugong, or Torres Strait artefacts such as the warup (drum) or dhari (headdress).

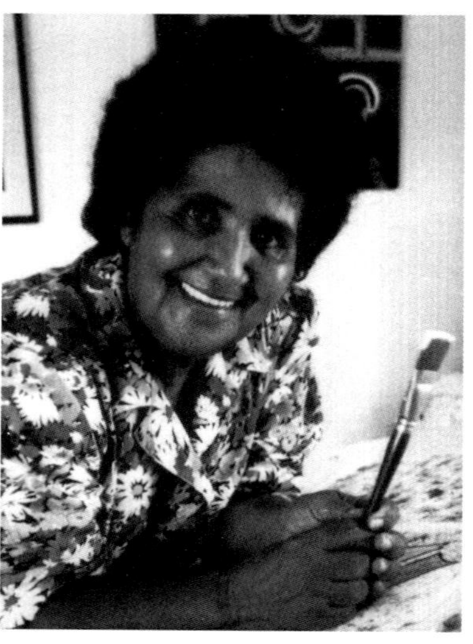

Mabel Edmund
Buutmaroo
Mabel Edmund was born in Rockhampton, Queensland. Her father was the son of a New Hebridian family who came to Queensland as an indentured labourer, and her mother was the daughter of a full-blood Aboriginal woman, and a Scottish father. After marrying in 1946, Mabel had three sons and three daughters. She was elected a Councillor on the Livingstone Shire Council and served the years 1970-1976. During this time, Mabel was appointed a Commissioner to the National Aboriginal Loans Commission, and served in this position from 1974 to 1980. In 1986, Mabel was appointed a member in the general division of the Order of Australia for her contribution to the betterment of her people. In the last decade her paintings have achieved national recognition. In 1992, Mabel published her memoir *No Regrets*; the book was highly commended in the David Unaipon Award. Mabel's second book *Hello Johnny*, published in 1996, was a series of humorous reminiscences. After suffering a stroke in 1994, Mabel still continues to paint, and has begun to write her third book.

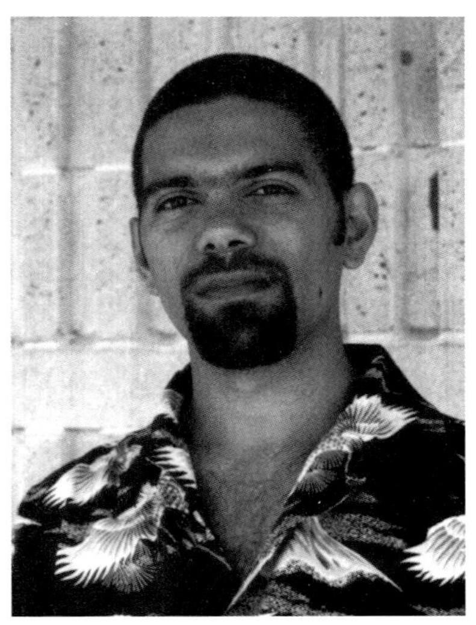

Shaun Kalk Edwards

Ma Rembeling

Shaun was born in 1975 to the Kokoberrin Kokonar language group of Inkerman Station, situated in the Staaten-Nassua River area on the West Coast Cape York Peninsula. After attending the Good Council Catholic School and Saint Augustine's College in Cairns, Shaun graduated in 1997 with a certificate in ATSI art, offered at the North Queensland Institute of TAFE Aboriginal and Islander Art Centre, now known as the Banggu Minjaany Centre. Committed to preserving cultural and environmental resources, Shaun is currently the head Ranger for the Kokoberrin Natural and Cultural Resource Management, and Chairman of the Kokoberrin Tribal Aboriginal Corporation for the last four years. Shaun and his family curated an exhibition entitled *The Art & Life of the Kokoberrin*, which will be shown at the Cairns Regional Gallery in March 2000. Shaun was employed in Normanton as Co-ordinator of the Karboyick Larkinjar Aboriginal Corporation for Health where he worked on improving health services.

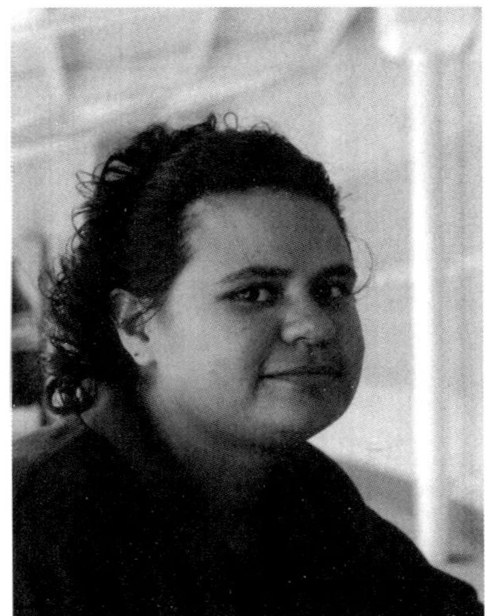

Janet Feildhouse

Mum and Dad's Pillow Talk

Janet was born in Cairns on the 29th May, 1971. Her background ancestry is Polynesian, Torres Strait Islander, and European. Her art studies have seen her graduate with an Associate Diploma in Visual Arts in 1991, and a Certificate in Survival Skills for Artists in 1992 from the Cairns TAFE. In 1993 Janet applied for the position of tutor with the Faculty of Aboriginal and Torres Strait Islander Studies at the TAFE. She was soon accepted for this position and has worked within the Visual Arts Department since then, completing further studies in Desktop publishing, computer skills, and gaining a teaching qualification through the Instructional Skills course. Janet now delivers all the ceramic modules with the ATSI visual Arts study areas.

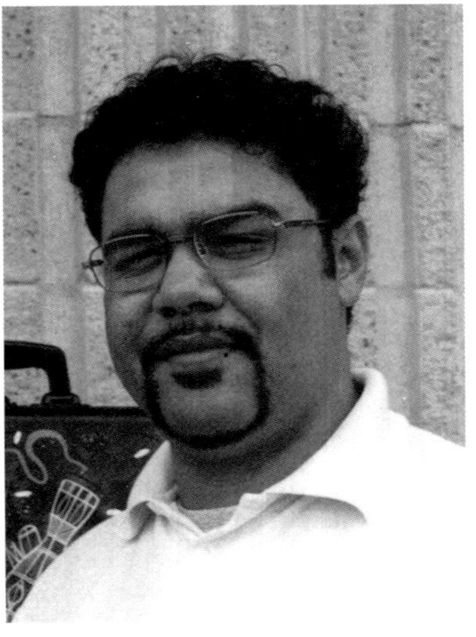

Daniel Geia

Giant Barracuda

Daniel was born in 1973 in Proserpine, North Queensland, but has spent most of his life on Palm Island where he attended school before moving to Charters Towers to finish his schooling. From there, he was accepted into the two year Associate Diploma Course [Art] at the Cairns TAFE. Daniel's mother Virginia Geia was born and educated on Palm Island where she worked until moving down south. This is where she met Daniel's father who was at the time an American tourist. Daniel's grandmother Betty Frog is from the Kalkadoon tribe. She was sent to Palm Island as a small girl where she lived all her life and met Daniel's grandfather Thomas Geia. Although Thomas was born on Palm Island, he is actually from the Torres Strait (Moa Island); however, in his time he did lots of jobs on Palm Island. These included community policing, building the community hall, becoming a council member, and acting as chairman of the Island.

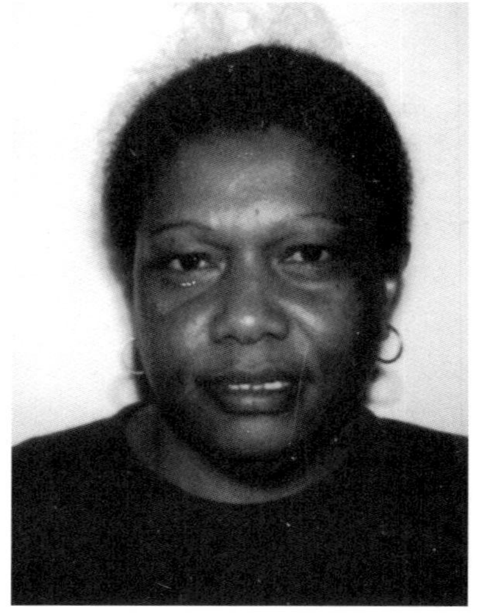

Anne Abednego Gela

Shark Dancer

Born Rachel Abednego on Thursday Island in 1953, Anne's family's totem is the Koedal, meaning crocodile. Anne was a founding member of the Saima Torres Strait Islanders' Corporation in Rockhampton, and is currently working as an Arts Coordinator for the corporation. She has exhibited her works in numerous shows, and curated the Shades of Malu exhibition, and co-curated the That's Women All Over exhibition with Joyce Watson. The first Torres Strait Islander artist to receive an Individual Arts Grant from Arts Queensland, Anne has used her art skills to communicate with, and help, others gain self esteem and enjoyment by holding workshops over the last four years. "Art to me is very healthy, a healer and the one great communicator".

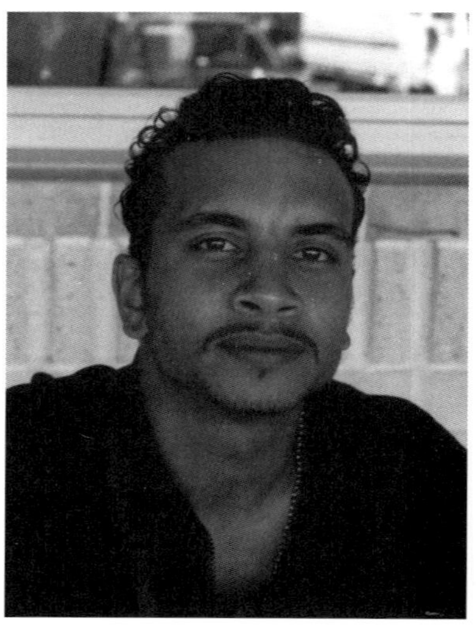

Colin Higgins

The Hunters

Colin was born in Cairns in May 1974. He is descended from the Yindinji Clan, the Guugu Yimithirr, and the Kuku Djumgan people. He has been painting and drawing most of his life, and over the last few years has been commissioned to paint many murals including one in the Yarrabah Council building, the new Wu Chopperen Cairns Hospital, and at the Lockhart River Community. Colin Higgins is a multi-talented man. He is an urban poet, musician, and artist. He and his friend Karl Fourmill head up a popular North Queensland indigenous band called Blek Affiliation. As young Elders for their clan, they use their music as a forum for serious indigenous issues specifically concerning young Aboriginal men living in Far North Queensland. They speak and sing of hope, Christianity, and Aboriginal spirituality.

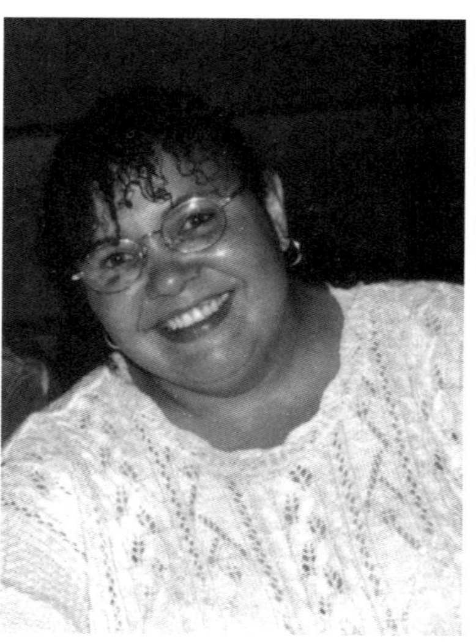

Lorraine Iboai

Crayfish on the Reef

My name is Lorraine Iboai (Girrinjyee). I am of Torres Strait Island and Aboriginal descent. My Torres Strait Islander identity is traced through my father, a Saibai Islander. My Aboriginality is traced through my mother, a descendant of the Yidinji people of the Goldsbrough Valley, Gordonvale, Atherton, and Cairns Region. As a child, I was given a traditional name by my mother. The name she gave me was Girrinjyee, which is a small eel that is found in the shallows of rivers and creeks. I have used my traditional name to acknowledge the authenticity of my artwork, which is of a contemporary style. The depiction of both flora and fauna in my art are a utilisation of life experiences that incorporate a combination of both traditional earthy colours and a mix of vibrant colours. Though I have been painting for the past fifteen years, my three years of study for the Advanced Diploma in Aboriginal and Torres Strait Islander Visual Arts at the Cairns TAFE has given me the opportunity to learn a variety of skills, such as textile screen printing, ceramics, and batik.

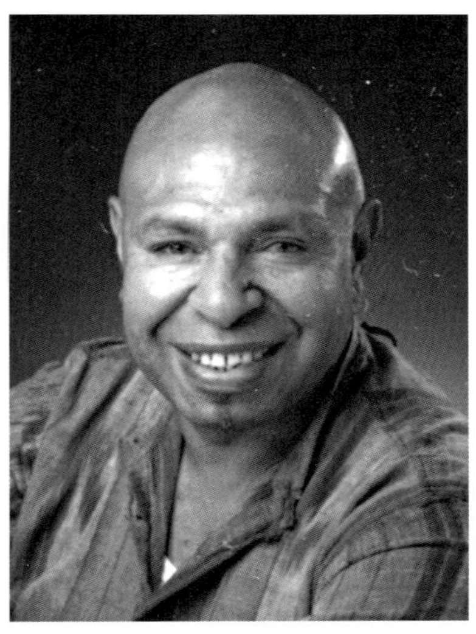

Ricardo Idagi

Torres Strait artefacts before the London Missionary Society's Arrival

Born in 1957 on Thursday Island, but now living in Melbourne, Ricardo Idagi has recently completed a small business course for Visual and Performing Artists and is currently in the early stages of establishing a business as an artist producing paintings, ceramics, and rock sculptures influenced and inspired by Torres Strait artefacts and culture. He is also planning an educational tour of Victorian schools promoting Torres Strait culture through dance and song. Ricardo still finds time to play in a band most weekends, and is compiling and recording songs he has written over the years for a CD to be released soon.

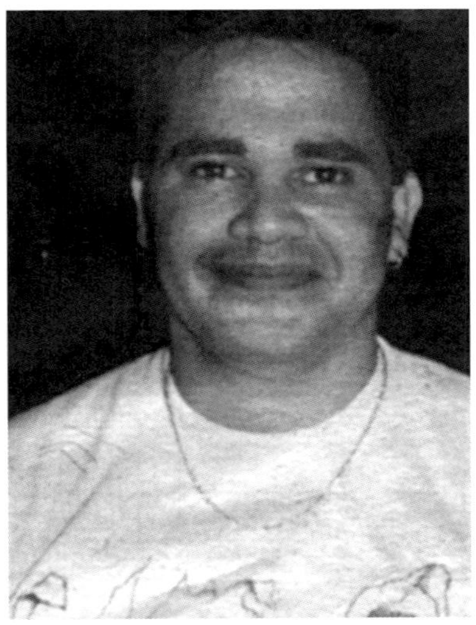

Ikanbala (Richard McLean)

Woree High Murals

Ikanbala is a descendant from the Yadhakana Clan of Cairns Crossing, Cape York. Influenced by his indigenous culture in personal life and extended family. Ikanbala states: "I am inspired by happenings of everyday life, and the effect it has on us, and events that effect society, whether they be political or otherwise."

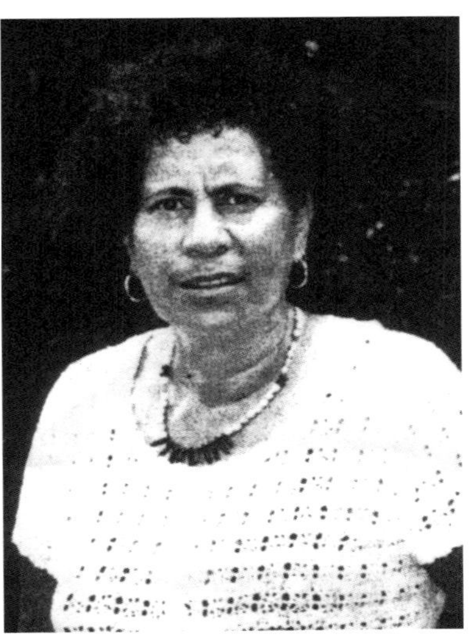

Jenuarrie

Linking Cultures

Jenuarrie grew up in Rockhampton, is one of seven children, and has six children of her own. She has Koinjamal heritage (Central Queensland) from her mother, and Kanaka (South Sea Islands) heritage from her father. Jenuarrie graduated from the Cairns ATSI Art Course in 1986, later establishing a pottery and printmaking studio at Lake Placid, with her sister Heather Walker. In the period 1987-1990, she became a chairperson on the Aboriginal and Torres Strait Islander Visual Arts panel of the Australia Council, and travelled overseas as an artist, consultant and lecturer on behalf of both the Australia Council and Arts Queensland. Jenuarrie returned to Cairns in 1998 to work as the Far North Queensland (FNQ) Aboriginal and Torres Strait Islander consultant for Arts Queensland, where she liaises with local and government bodies to assist the production and marketing of Indigenous art and culture.

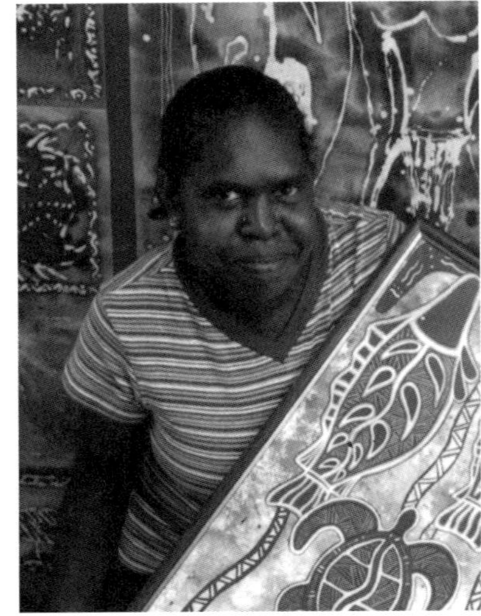

Marilyn Kepple

Minya

27 year old Marilyn knows the value of family. A mother of four herself, she is part of a family consisting of four sisters, four brothers, thirteen nephews, six nieces, and many aunts and uncles. Marilyn recognises and thanks her own mother for what she calls a 'great upbringing', as her mum was not only her mother, but her best friend as well. Marilyn attended and completed her senior years at school in Brisbane, where she excelled in sports like basketball, athletics, and touch football. She had many friends at high school, and says she was always treated with great respect. Her artwork is mostly concerned with animals from the bush, and sea creatures that represent the traditional foods of her people.

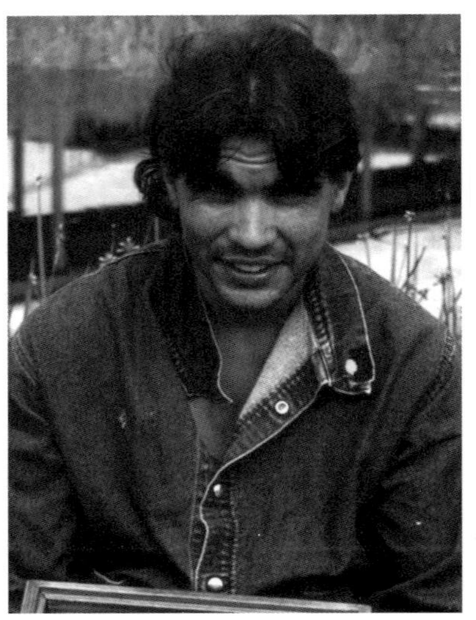

Wayne Kite

Staging Flame

Wayne Kite was born 24 years ago in Charleville, but his ancestral country lies in New South Wales, the home of the Waradjuri people. Every good artist draws on the subconscious mind for his/her creativity. Wayne describes the same process as painting from "Dreaming" experiences, tapping into not merely his own self, but into a deep, near-eternal connection with the land and its ancestral people. When commencing a work, he begins with a "truth-direction" which establishes a rhythm and background, like the throbbing undertones of the didgeridoo which Wayne plays expertly. There is another strain in the music from Wayne's didgeridoo, a dirge of pain. He is serving a life sentence in a North Queensland Correctional Centre. Working...and reworking...his pastels help him deal with confinement. And after a time and much soul searching, he will consider a work finished, as some day society...and he himself...will consider his "time" finished. Like the winged warrior, he believes he will rise from the ashes of his past, and renew himself as an Aborigine and as an artist.

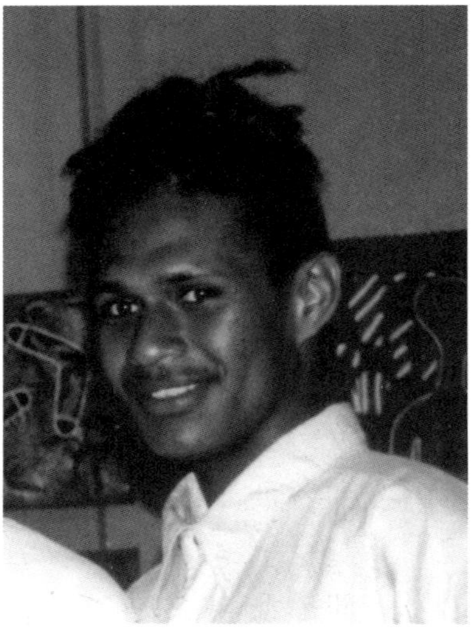

Joey Laifoo

The Power of the Dugong

Joey is a young artist from Badu Island in the Western Torres Strait. He was born in 1978, and finished secondary school at Charters Towers before commencing art studies in Cairns in 1996. Many of Joey's family are well known artists of the Torres Strait.

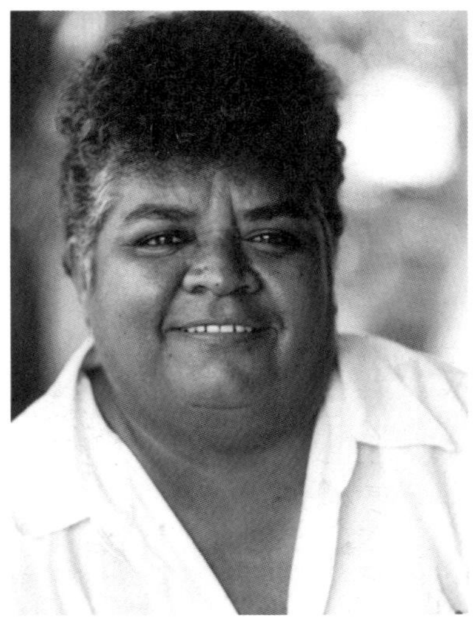

Elaine Lampton

WE WERE NEVER PART OF THE INDUSTRIAL REVOLUTION

Elaine was born in Townsville in 1950. She has worked previously as a professional nurse for about 14 years, mainly as an operating theatre nurse, which ultimately led her to settle in Cairns in 1975. She started formal art training in 1984 at the then newly established Aboriginal and Torres Strait Islander Arts Centre in the Cairns College of TAFE. It was at this time she developed the layered appearance of Laura rock art into her modern paintings and screenprints. In 1986 Elaine did two years training in graphic arts, and later studied pre-press procedures with the Department of Education Printery in Cairns. Having gained her Bachelor in Adult Education at Griffith University in 1991, she is currently a full time teacher at the Tropical North Queensland Institute of TAFE.

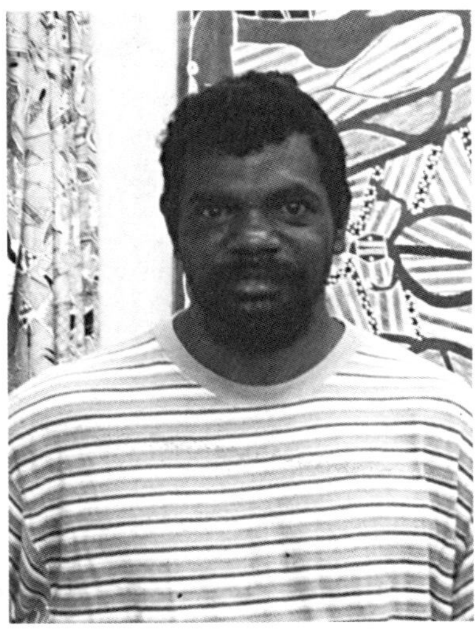

Gordon Landers

KAH (ECHIDNA MAN)

Gordon is the youngest son of the Landers' family which originates from Cherbourg. His clan is Wakka Wakka Gubbi Gubbi, and his Mother's people are Ma:linja:li. He has observed the transition from governmental suppression of his people to the more recent cultural revolution of indigenous peoples, which has enabled him to explore and express his identity. In 1998, Gordon and his wife were invited to exhibit in the Czech Republic, under the patronage of highly respected actor, Donucio. The well received exhibition was held at the Branek Theatre in Prague.

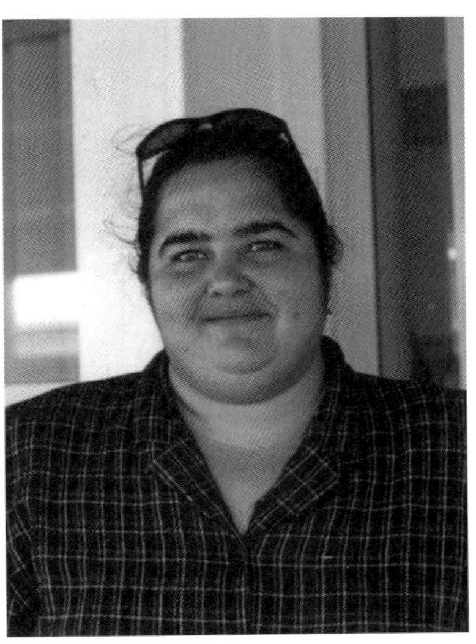

Helena Loncaric

ABORIGINAL CROATIANS

Helena was born in Cairns, Far North Queensland in 1973. She was born to an Aboriginal mother and a Croatian father. Her Aboriginal ancestry originates from the Butchulla Tribe of Fraser Island, and the Gungganyji Tribe in Yarrabah. Helena enrolled in the Aboriginal and Torres Strait Islander Visual Arts Course after high school in 1991. She moved to Brisbane in 1994. There, she studied for her B. Ed (QUT), majoring in Art, film and media, and she is now a qualified high school teacher. Helena moved back to Cairns in 1999, and is currently teaching art modules at TAFE (ATSI Arts Course). She is also involved in art workshops around the Cairns area, and hopes in the future to gain full-time art teaching, and to establish her own art production business.

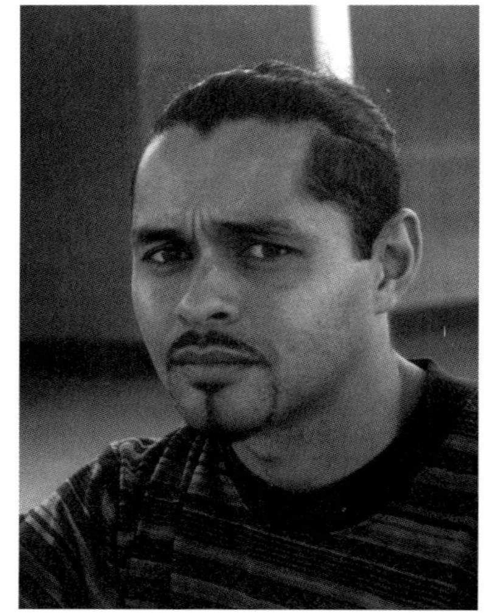

Walter Raymond Lui

Portrait of My Great-Great Grandfather

Walter, who was born in Mackay in 1972, comes from a long paternal line of Darnley Islander heritage. His father and his ancestors have lived on this Torres Strait Island for over four (4) generations. Before that, his ancestry has been traced back to the tiny island of Lifou in New Caledonia. On the maternal side his mother's heritage stems from Philippine, Spanish, and English (UK) culture, and is also connected to Darnley Island at some point in the past. Walter has been seriously involved in art since the age of fourteen, and has now completed several years of both TAFE and University study in the area. His most recent works have predominantly dealt with visual art research into historical events, in particular what is commonly referred to as 'The Coming of the Light' or 'July One'. This event pertains to the year 1871, when the London Missionary Society landed on Darnley Island after sailing from New Caledonia. One of Walter's ambitions is to exhibit his work in Noumea (New Caledonia).

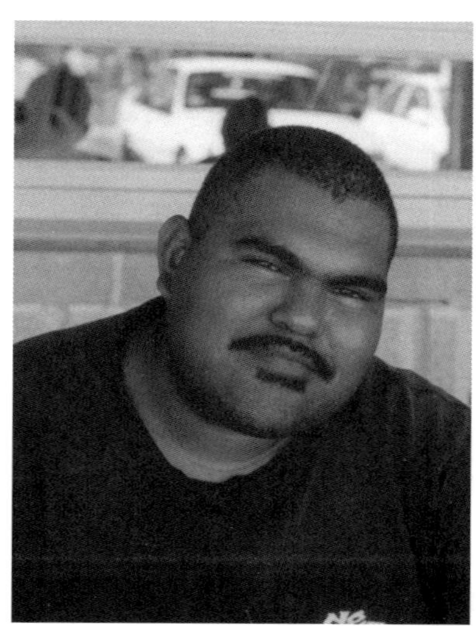

Glen Douglas Mackie

Four Brothers

Glen Mackie was born in 1975 on the Torres Strait Island of Yam (Iama). His heritage combines Aboriginal, Torres Strait Islander, Tongan, and American cultures. His father is Aboriginal, and his mother is a Torres Strait Islander; he draws on both of these cultures in his artwork. Glen enjoys painting Hammerhead sharks in particular, which are both his and his father's totem. His mother's totem is the Crocodile. He began painting at eight years of age, influenced and encouraged by the many family members who were themselves artists. He learnt to carve and paint, and enjoys painting, drawing and ceramics in particular. Glen left Yam to attend the Tropical North Queensland Institute of TAFE in Cairns to further his artistic education. In 1999, he completed a Certificate in Visual Arts, and is seeking to complete his second year diploma.

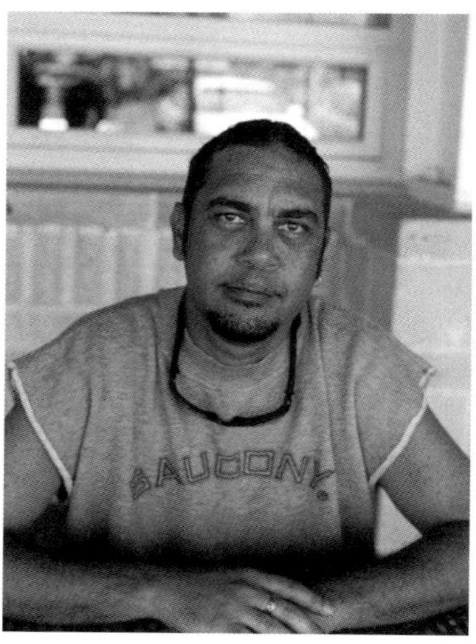

Blair Malthouse

Our Mu-yi Bub

Blair was born in Mareeba, Far North Queensland in 1964. Six years later his family moved to Cairns, and have lived there ever since. Blair has lived in Surfers Paradise, Brisbane, Fraser Island, Hervey Bay, Innisfail and other areas of Queensland during his lifetime. He describes himself as a contemporary indigenous artist. He is currently focusing on developing his own version of the x-ray style, and tries never to limit himself to one particular art style. Currently in his final year of the three year Advanced Diploma Course in Visual Arts at the Cairns TAFE, Blair would like to continue his artistic education by attending Griffith University's Art School .

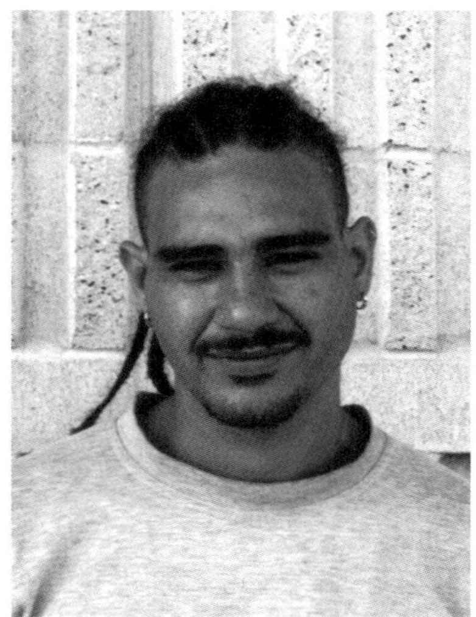

Robert Mast

BADULGAU DTHOERI

Robert was born on Thursday Island in 1976. He was brought up on Badu Island with his three older brothers and a younger sister, all of whom are artistically talented. He attended primary school on the island and secondary school at St. Augustine's College in Cairns. Robert studied the Access Course at James Cook University and then decided to study with the Aboriginal and Torres Strait Islander Visual Arts Course at the Cairns TAFE. After completing the two year course Robert went back home to Badu, and worked for a time on a pearling Lugger diving for crayfish. At night on the boat he would carve either dugong ivory, black coral, or wood. Robert is completing the Advanced Diploma in Visual Arts this year, 2000. He has exhibited widely over the last few years in Australia and in New Caledonia and he says that growing up on Badu with the native tongue - Kala Lagaw ya- and also the traditional beliefs, he has much to say through his art to the generations to come.

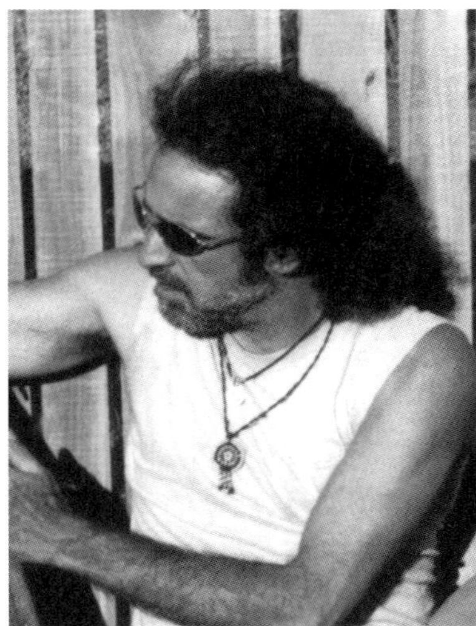

Matu (Brian O'Beirns)

DJUBBA (TREE GOANNA)

Matu (traditional language) was born in Port Douglas, North Queensland, and attended school in the nearby town of Mossman. His grandmother was born in Walpurra Country near Mt. Carbine in the Windsor Tablelands, and his grandfather's tribe is the Kuku Warra north of Laura. His youth was spent fishing and hunting in the rivers and nearby reefs of the North Queensland Coast. He has always loved wood, and used it to make spears and boomerangs for hunting. He has also made dugout canoes, bows and arrows, so woodcarving played an important part in his young life. Matu started to carve artefacts in his thirties.

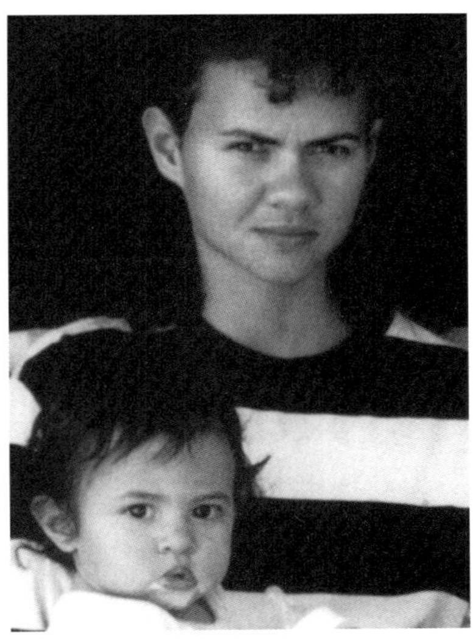

Samantha Meeks

THE OLD TIMES - DORMITORY TIMES

Samantha is about to embark on a journey back to her Yarrabah family. Yarrabah, a coastal community about an hours drive from Cairns is home to many of her family. Both of her grandparents lived under the dormitory system in the Anglican run mission of Yarrabah. Her grandfather, William Frank Meeks, is from the Kuku Djungan tribe of the Atherton Tablelands, near Mount Mulligan. Her grandmother, Audrey Sands, is from the Kuku Yalanji tribe from the Cooktown/Laura area. The influence of the missionary system, which suppressed the practice of traditional culture, has left Samantha with a desire to rediscover her culture through her art. She completed an Associate Diploma (Aboriginal and Torres Strait Islander) at the Cairns TAFE in 1992, and went on to complete a Bachelor of Visual Art in Fine Arts in Brisbane in 1996. Her Art skills include print-making, installation art, painting, illustration and public art. Samantha has been involved in numerous exhibitions, worked as a part-time teacher at Griffith University in Brisbane and undertaken many commissions.

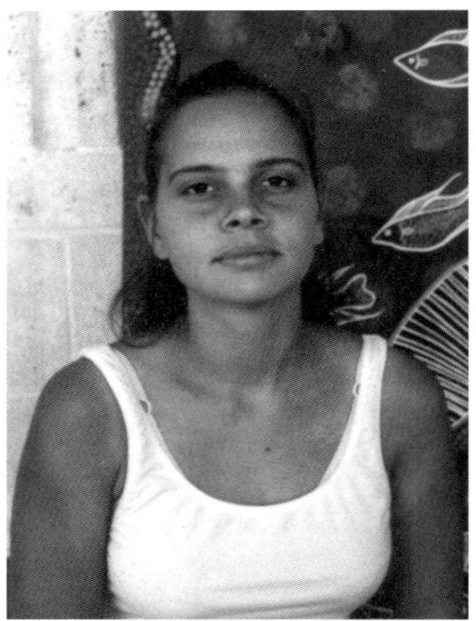

Lisa Michl
EELS
Lisa was born in 1977 to the Kokoberrin Kokonar Language group of Inkerman station, situated between the Staaten and Nassua Rivers on the West Coast Cape York Peninsula. She began a certificate in ATSI Arts at the Banggu Minjaany Arts and Cultural Centre at Cairns TAFE before graduating with an Associate Diploma in 1997. She enjoys painting, silk painting, and experimenting with other art mediums and techniques. At present, Lisa has her own studio and is concentrating on further promoting her art works.

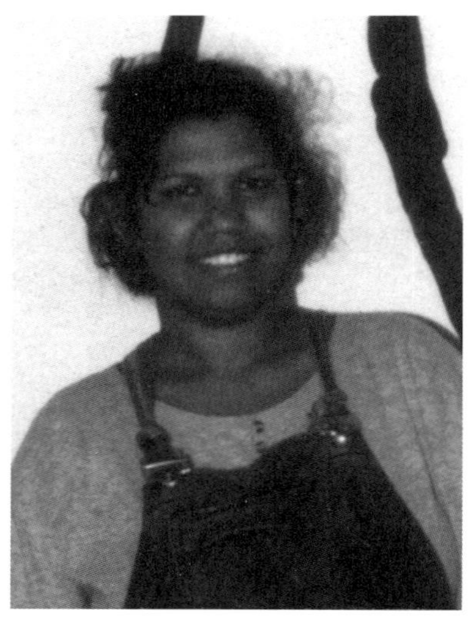

Patty Morris
DANCING BROLGA
A mother of two, Patty became deaf at the age of two. At the age of four she was sent to Cairns to attend the Cairns West Preschool for the Deaf, where she would later meet her foster parents Beverly and Percy Trezise. She credits Percy with introducing her to art. Watching him draw and paint led her to try it herself, and to develop her own individual style. Patty lost her blood father in 1990, an event that led her to turn to an innerworld. As opposed to drawing the things she sees outside of herself, she prefers to draw what she describes as the "deep dreams about Aboriginal life in Australia, the imaginings of people not only here and now, but in the past as well". As an artist, Patty has been most successful. In 1995 her entry in the Bold Type Touring Exhibition featuring poster designs concerning racism in the workplace was acknowledged by the Qld Branch of the Australian Council of Trade Unions, giving her the confidence to have her own exhibition in 1996 at the Sheraton Mirage in Port Douglas. In 1998 she received a grant to exhibit paintings in Cairns, Brisbane and Sydney.

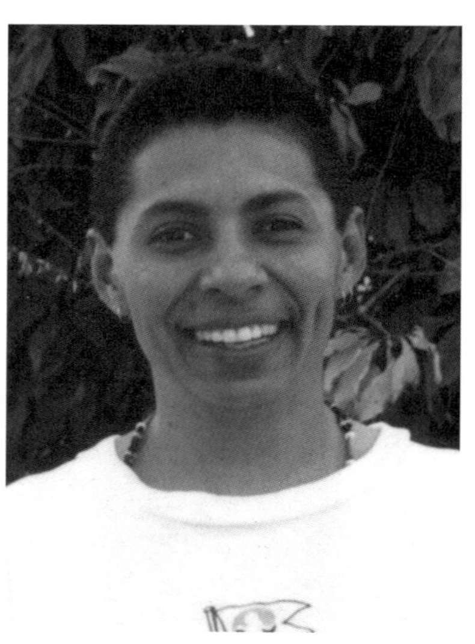

Shelley Monkland
THE SEVEN SISTERS
Shelley's heritage lies in both the Bunjalung and Gubbi Gubbi people's traditions. Her Aboriginal name Djarainj (meaning rainbow) comes from her mother's Bunjalung language. It is an appropriate name for this mother of four daughters, as her preferred artistic medium is colourful textile design. Shelley was not exposed to television until she was twelve years old, and as a result she had time to learn tapestry, crochet, knitting and sewing. After school she completed a Certificate for Fashion Design, and spent the next few years studying towards an BA in Aboriginal Affairs during which time she also started acting and performing in the South Australian schools and theatres. However, art, particularly textile design, was her passion. Shelley originally completed a Certificate in Textiles at Nungalinga College in Darwin, and managed her own business in Brisbane for several years before deciding to do the Advanced Diploma in Visual Arts at the Tropical North Queensland Institute of TAFE in 1997.

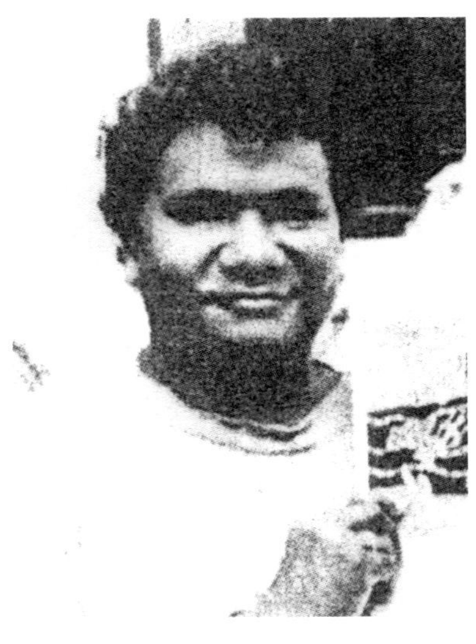

Joseph McIvor

Searching For Food

Joseph is an artist with a strong indigenous background. His heritage is from the Guugu Yimithirr Tribe. He is a story- teller, teacher, and keeper of tribal law and custom. He possesses a deep sense of mythological expression and an ability to capture the spirituality which fills everyday life. Joseph has held a number of solo exhibitions in Far North Queensland and has been included in group exhibitions, including Ageless Art at the Queensland Museum in 1988. His work was included in the 1992 Californian Calendar 'Aboriginality" and in 1994 he won an Arts Queensland grant.

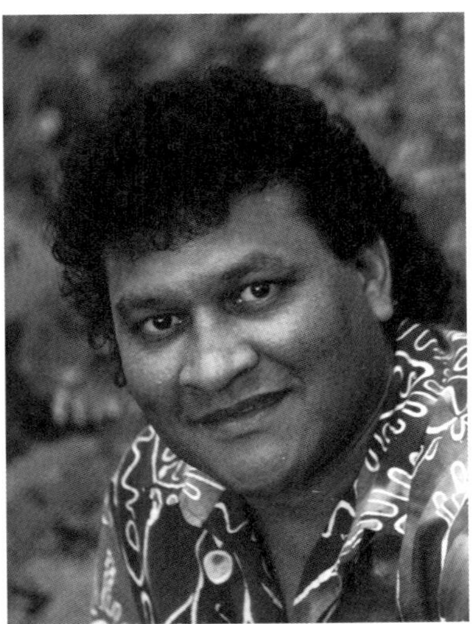

Munganbana (Norman Miller)

Mangrove Mudflats

Munganbana means "Mountain Water" in Jirrbal. The Jirrbal tribe originates from the lands that cover the Atherton Tablelands and Upper Tully area in Far North Queensland. Munganbana specialises in limited edition lino prints, acrylic on canvas paintings, greeting cards with Aboriginal art on the cover, batik and silk wall hangings, silk scarves, batik dress lengths and T-shirts. Seascapes, riverscapes, the rainforest and wildlife feature strongly in all of his work. Married with one son, Munganbana is a graduate of the Associate Diploma of Art (ATSI) Course at Cairns TAFE. He works from his own studio in his Cairns home, and also teaches art classes. Munganbana's work has been exhibited at various local and international shows, and the Queensland Museum has recently purchased a series of twelve limited edition prints featuring traditional shield designs based on Jirrbal tribal culture. The Queensland University of Technology bought one of the shield prints for its 'Oodgeroo' Collection which toured in 1999.

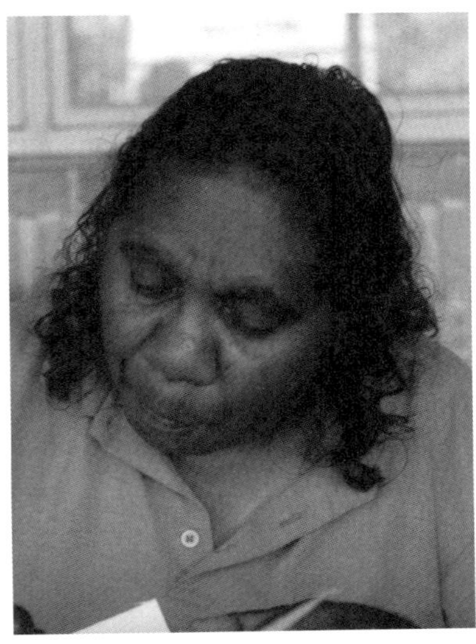

Linda Kamara Myers

Women's Dreaming Place

Linda was born of the Aranda tribe at the 'Caterpillar Dreaming Place' in Alice Springs. Her language is eastern Arrenta. She grew up in an urban, non-traditional environment, and was discouraged from expressing the culture and art she had learnt in her childhood; however, in recent years she has been able to rediscover those early influences. Linda's art work consists of animals, plants, and dreaming places from the Alice Springs area. Although mainly working in batik and fabric screen printing , Linda also utilises canvas, acrylic painting, ceramics and other print making mediums. She loves to use earthy colours, and the traditional symbols of her tribe such as circles, dots and lines, which signify dreaming places, animals, plants and other sacred objects of the Aranda people. During her eighteen years of working in the Education Department, Linda studied a number of courses including: Preliminary Course in General Studies for Aborigines at Darwin TAFE; the Advanced Diploma of Art Course ATSI and Survival Skills in Visual Art, both at Cairns TAFE.

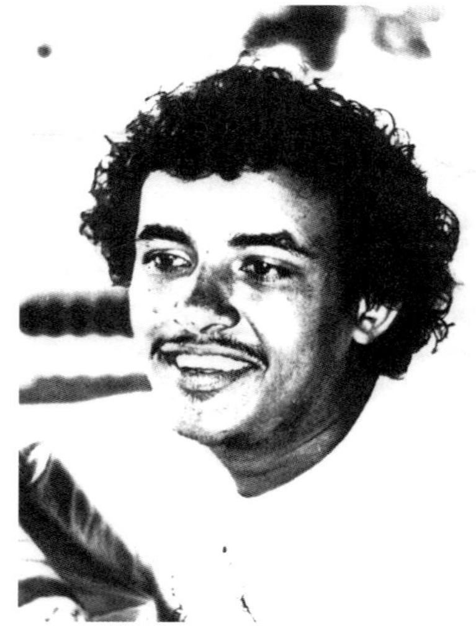

Dennis Nona
MAL LAG AR DAPPARR- AW WHURAL AR IDAL
SEA, LAND AND AIR CREATURES.
Dennis was born on Thursday Island in January 1973 and soon moved to Badu Island. His great grandfather was from Western Samoa, and his great grandmother was from Niuguini. They settled on Badu Island to participate in the pearling industry. At that time there were over one hundred pearling luggers working in the waters of the Torres Strait. Dennis spends much of his time on his uncle's lugger 'Yancy Taum' crayfishing, and diving for trochus and pearlshell. Much of Dennis's art circles around the themes of the sea and its creatures. They are heavily influenced by coastal Papuan art such as masks and trading items like drums carved with traditional designs. Dennis feels that art is the best way for him to preserve his culture for those in the future.

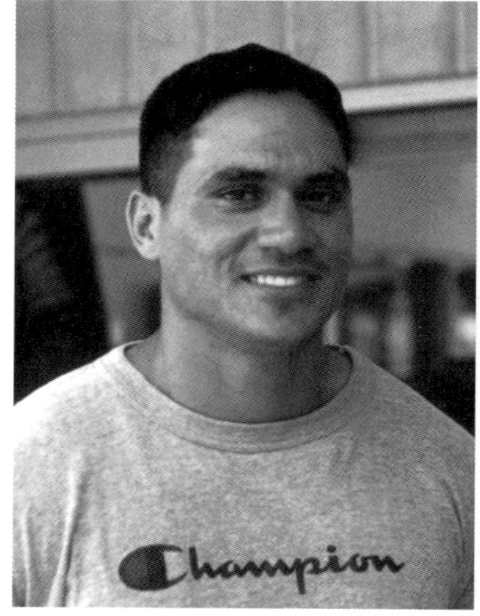

Laurie Nona
LAGAU DUNALAIG (ISLAND LIFESTYLE)
Laurie was born on Thursday Island in the Torres Strait, but his heritage is of the Island of Badu. His early childhood was spent in traditional cultural surroundings on Badu Island before moving to Thursday Island for his secondary schooling and later to Cairns for his senior schooling at Saint Augustine's College. He is currently employed as a Police Liaison Officer in Cairns, and in his spare time studies visual arts with the Faculty for Aboriginal and Torres Strait Islander Studies at Cairns Institute of TAFE. All of his work is based on his cultural experiences and stories of his home on Badu Island. His greatest dream is to se the young people of his culture understand and value the history of the Kuikumabaigal (Council of Elders). His artwork Lagau Dunalaig shown in this book is being purchased for the National Print Collection in Canberra.

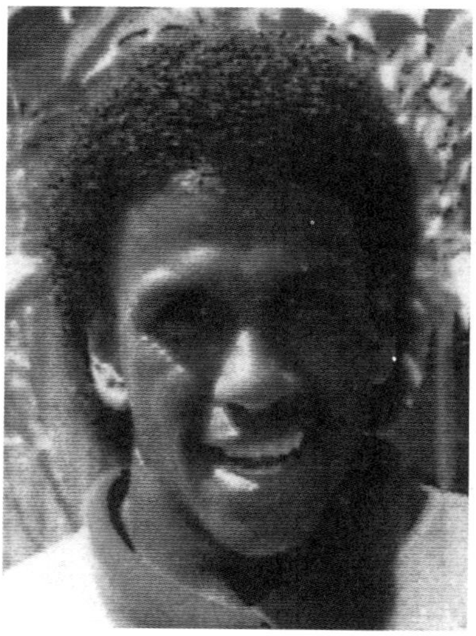

Harry Nona
FISH POT
Harry comes from Badu Island in the Western Torres Strait. He was born on Thursday Island in 1971, Thursday Island having the only hospital in the island group. Harry completed the Associate Diploma in Visual (Aboriginal and Torres Strait Islander) Arts in 1993 at the Cairns TAFE. Images from his island home inspired his art- images developed from island dancing, cultural artefacts, and legends handed down from the elders. There was no lack of subject matter to be explored by Harry and the other young artists who made up the early student groups from the Torres Strait. Harry's two and three dimensional artworks feature many of the sea creatures of the tropical seas that surround his home on Badu Island.

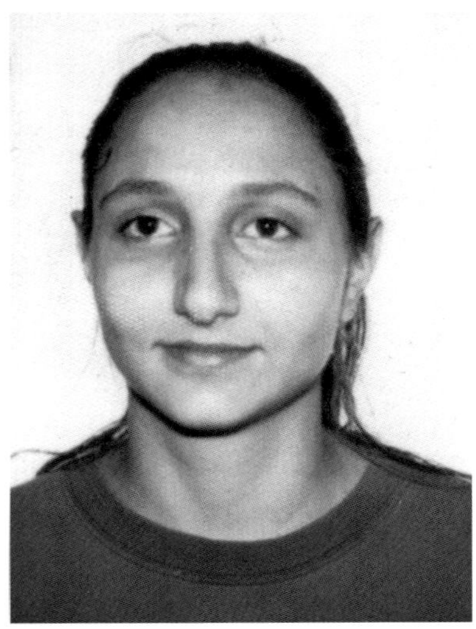

Kathryn Norris
The Coming of the Light
Kathryn was born in 1977 in Brisbane, Queensland. She has recently commenced studies at James Cook University (Cairns Campus) undertaking a Bachelor of Education. She aims to be a secondary teacher by the year 2002, with art as her primary teaching area, and Japanese as her secondary area. She has been involved in the national travelling exhibition entitled Painting the Land Story, and has had her artwork The Coming of the Light purchased by the National Museum of Australia in Canberra from the Guddhabungan Exhibition.

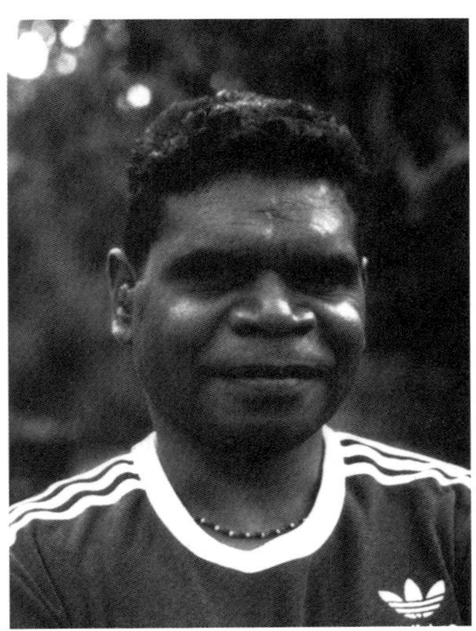

Allan Palm Island
Two Lobsters
After completing the Associate Diploma in Visual Arts (Aboriginal and Torres Strait Islander) at the Cairns TAFE campus in 1993, Allan moved to Darwin and gained a Diploma in Fine Art at the Northern Territory University. In 1998 he was the Artist in Residence at the Royal Melbourne Institute of Technology in Victoria and presented a solo exhibition at the University Gallery. After gaining a scholarship he is now studying for a Bachelor of Art (Fine Arts) at RMIT. This is all a long way from home on Palm Island (off the coast from Townsville in North Queensland)., but in his paintings and prints he will always be expressing his cultural heritage through his images.

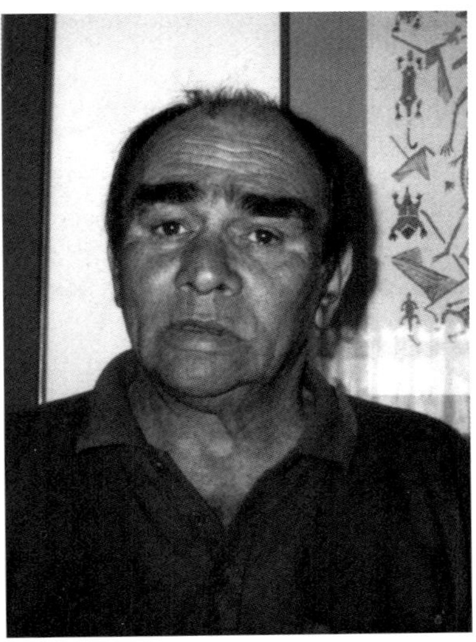

Pooaraar
Bevan Hayward
Tweret Spirits, Njoorlum Spirits, and Anthropomorphs of Aboriginal Life
Born at Gnowangerup, south of Perth in 1939, Pooaraar's childhood was spent at the United Aboriginal Mission. His later life was spent travelling extensively throughout Australia . Pooaraar returned to Perth in 1977, attending an Aboriginal Bridging Course at the Western Australia Institute of Technology in 1978. In 1986, he undertook the Aboriginal and Torres Strait Islander Arts and Crafts Course in Cairns, before moving to Canberra where he graduated from the Canberra School of Art in 1991. He produces linocuts, etchings, and lithographs. A prolific artist, Pooaraar's credits include: five solo exhibitions, twenty group exhibitions, eight International exhibitions, twelve collections represented, three public and school educational slideshows. He is represented in no fewer than eight books, various Art Journals, magazines and newspapers. During his career, he has won two prestigious awards: Mitchelton National Inaugural Print Award (June 1990), and Mawalan's Eldest Son's Award in Seventh National Aboriginal Art Award (1990).

Ceferino Garcia Sabatino
Sea God
Born on Thursday Island in 1975, Ceferino has spent most of his life on another Torres Strait Island, Hammond Island. After attending the Torres Strait campus of the Far North Queensland TAFE, and graduating in 1994 with an Associate Diploma of Arts (ATSI) from Cairns TAFE, he feels he now has a more confident approach to his artwork. His work relates to the island life surrounding his home, and to all those things that have been part of his heritage. He is particularly interested in the spiritual and cultural connection Torres Strait Islanders have with the sea and its creatures, and his people's traditions.

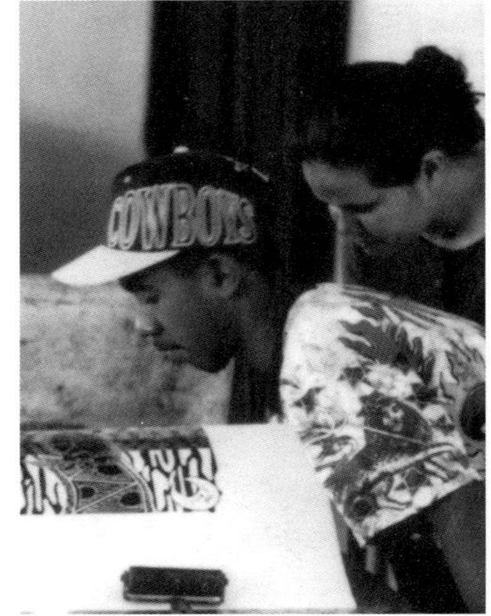

Ethel Sambo
Pink and Purple Water Lily Dreaming
Born in 1940, Ethel spent most of her childhood in Darwin , except when her family was evacuated to Adelaide during the second World War for a short period of time. A mother of seven children, grandmother of many, and great- grandmother of two, Ethel credits her grandmother (a child of the stolen generation) as a major influence in her life, particularly in relation to cultivating life skills and the sharing of Aboriginal culture. Ethel has spent much time seeking her true heritage, and her family has finally been accepted and recognised as belonging to the Mari-amor clan, coming from Rak-Chindi in the Daly River area. Ethel undertook an Access Course at Rockhampton College of TAFE, before working for the Department of Social Security until 1997. It was during this time Ethel felt a strong need to express her struggle to find her grandmother's heritage which was haunting her dreams. This led her to enrol in a Visual Arts Course, where she successfully painted what she had been seeing , ultimately satisfying her inner self.

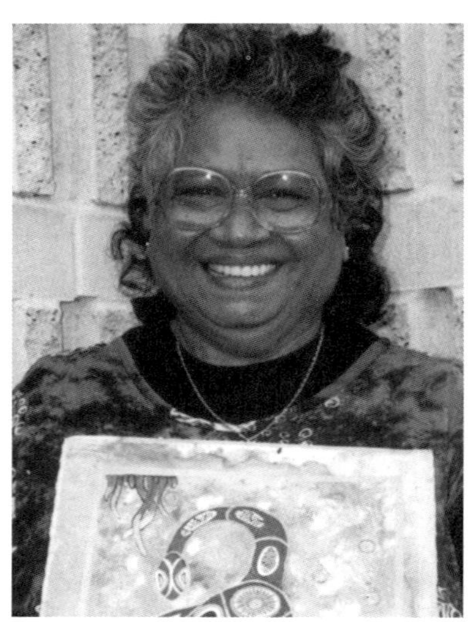

Zane Saunders
In Search of...
Although his mother's parents come from the Butchulla people of Fraser Island, Zane has lived all his life in Kuranda on the Tablelands above Cairns. He spent his childhood exploring the rainforest surrounding Kuranda, fishing, and swimming in the beautiful Barron River with his three brothers and two sisters. Zane's work recalls his memories of these childhood experiences, his mother's stories of Fraser Island, and his family's strong sense of tradition. He captures images which are individually strong, statements that encompass that which is totemically spiritual for his people. He has been involved in numerous group exhibitions in Australia, and overseas, and to date has held two solo exhibitions. His works are also represented in important national and private collections.

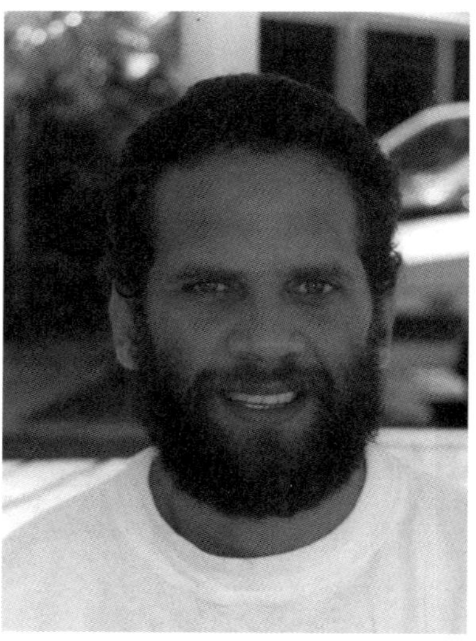

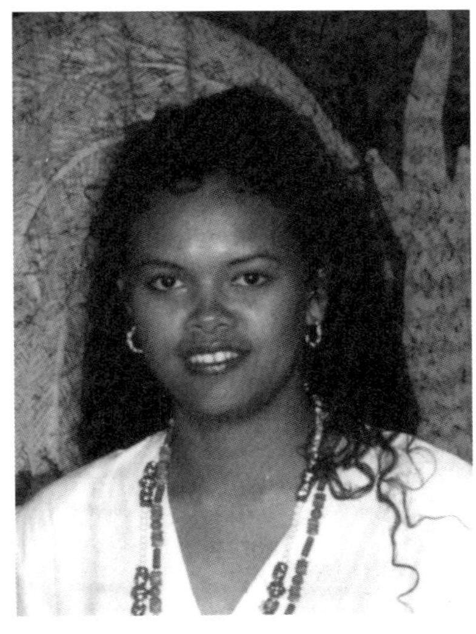

Priscilla Seden
Blue Shark
Although being born with a hearing impairment, Priscilla Seden has not allowed this to prevent her from achieving her goals. A young emerging Torres Strait Islander artist, Priscilla completed the Cairns TAFE Diploma of Arts in 1993 and is proud to say she learnt many new techniques and modes of communication through art and design. Living in Cairns, Queensland for most of her life, Priscilla is inspired by her memories of Thursday Island and the beauty of the island's sealife - colourful fish, coral, stingrays, crabs, crayfish and turtles.

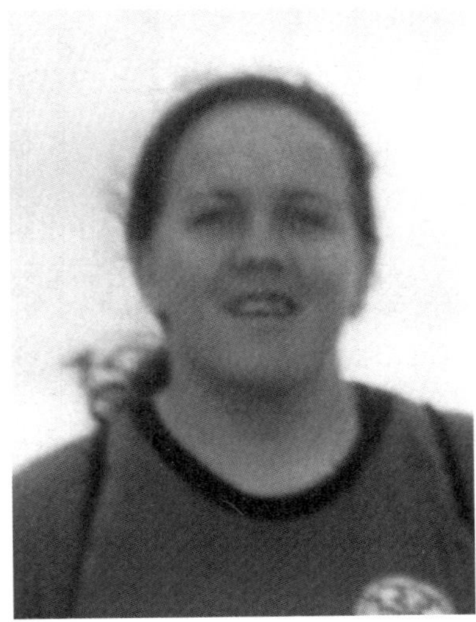

Shannon Shaw
The Women's Shield
Shannon, whose father is from the Yirrganydji Tribe, enjoys painting the legends, animals and stories of her Aboriginal heritage. She has lived in Cairns all of her life. It is there she undertook the ATSI Visual Arts Course at TAFE in 1997. Her artwork mainly centres around animals, dots and lines, using earthy colours like black, red, white, red oxide and yellow oxide. She has painted a mural at the Cairns North State Primary School, and hopes in the future either to be working in a local Aboriginal shop or selling her artwork through shops or galleries.

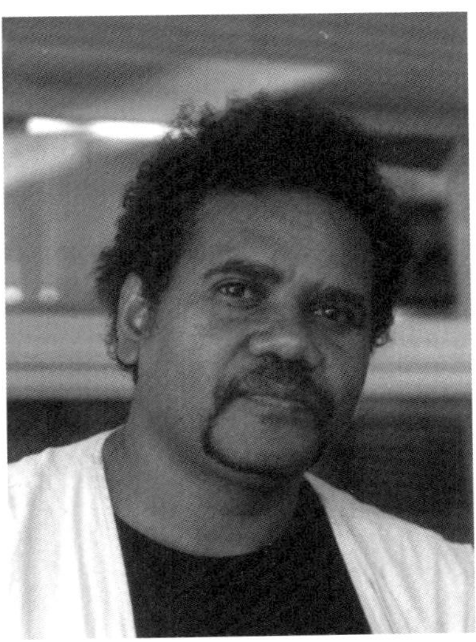

Glen Sheppard
Shark Head
Glen, who was born in 1961 has always lived in Kuranda, high on the Tablelands above Cairns in Queensland. His parents and grandparents grew up at Mona Mona Mission, situated Northwest of Kuranda. He is one of eight Aboriginal and Islander artists in a group called You P'la Me P'la (You & Me), who maintain their friendship and shared aspirations after graduating from the Associate Diploma of Art Course at the Cairns TAFE. His artwork was exhibited along with four of these artists at the Cairns Regional Gallery in 1995. He has also been involved in group exhibitions in Cairns and Brisbane, and is represented in private collections in Australia and overseas.

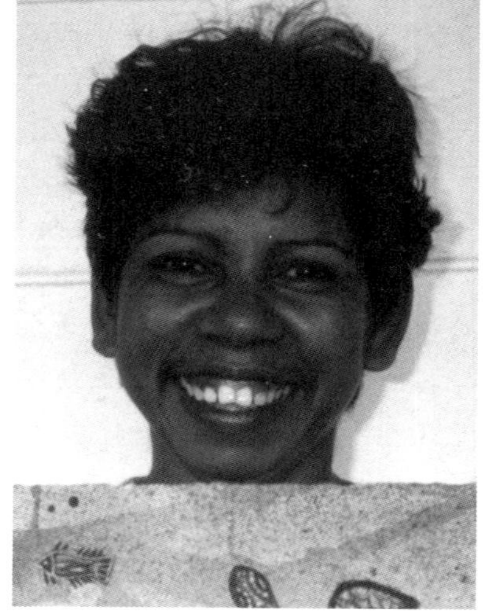

Patricia Singleton
Yirrganydji Dreaming
Patricia is a descendant of the Yirrganydji Tribe, whose traditional areas span from Cairns to Port Douglas in North Queensland. Born in 1959, she considers herself a contemporary artist, and is currently undertaking a small business course to help her maintain her career as an artist. Her preferred artistic medium is acrylic on paper, depicting rainforest and sea images, representing the traditional lifestyle of the Yirrganydji people. A commercially successful artist, Patricia has sold her work in various exhibitions in Cairns, Brisbane and Melbourne, and has to date sold various artworks to private collections and institutions both locally and overseas.

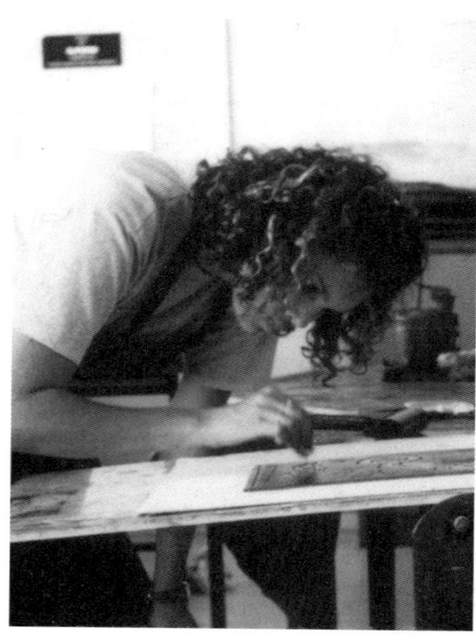

Jakki Skeen
Self Portrait
Jakki was born in Brisbane, Queensland in 1973, and lived there most of her life until moving to Cairns in 1994 to study at the ATSI Art Centre. She started painting at an early age, and has always loved expressing herself as a woman artist. Jakki learnt much from her father and credits him for his wisdom, strength, and hard work. Jakki's ancestry stems from two tribes. Her grandfather's tribe is the Birri-Gubba, and her grandmother's tribe is the Kuku Yalanji which originates from Laura /Cooktown. Jakki recently visited the Laura country and was amazed by the old ways, and the cave paintings. She feels they had a strong influence on her, making it easier for her now to express herself more freely through her art. Jakki writes: "My art comes from within my soul, so when I am painting and drawing it is either about my culture, my clan or myself."

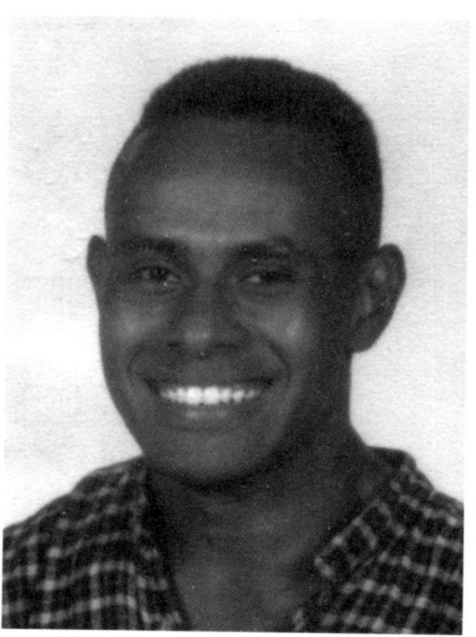

Ken Thaiday
Coming of the Light
Ken was born 1971, in the town of Gordonvale, situated near Cairns, North Queensland. Although Ken did not grow up on the islands, he grew up with the values of Christianity and traditional Torres Strait culture, which he says he learnt mostly from his Father, He is the son of Ken Thaiday Snr, who is well known for his imaginative headdresses, artefacts and Torres Strait Islander dancing. Ken graduated with a Diploma of Aboriginal and Torres Strait Islander Art from the Cairns TAFE in 1993, and following a short stint at a Brisbane College, then returned to work with his father. In 1996 Ken participated in a Kick Arts Inc. project called Linkage/Leakage with six other contemporary artists. Based at the Tanks Art Centre, the project enabled Ken to develop his own style of modern artefacts, sculpture, designs and lino prints. He now plans to concentrate on drawings to translate to larger paintings for an exhibition. Ken says " I want people to look at my artwork and see it's unique and explains Torres Strait Islander culture and Christianity".

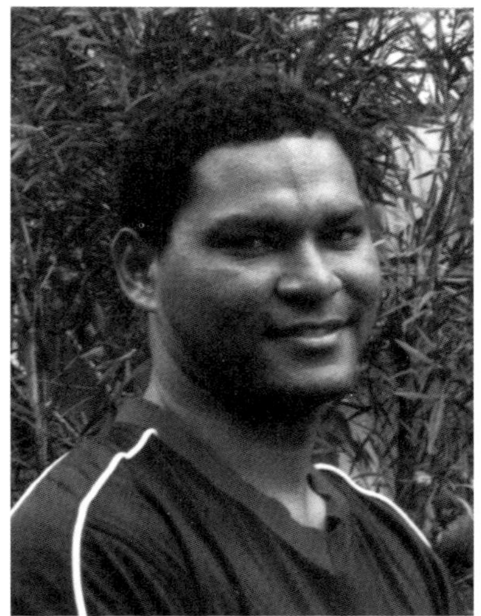

Alick Seriba Tipoti
MURA URUIAU DANAKA
Alick's mother is from Saibai Island , and his father comes from Badu Island. The talented Alick speaks four different languages : Kala Kawaw Ya (Mother's language), Kala Lagaw Ya (Father's language), Creole or Torres Strait Pidgin, Papua New Guinea Pidgin (Pislama), and English. Alick has always been very proud of his culture, and has dedicated his art to help the recognition of Torres Strait culture. He credits his father with his knowledge of the past, and uses his art to tell and illustrate the stories of his father and other Torres Strait elders. Alick says "The one thing I will never do is let my forefathers' words be lost." Alick specialises in printmaking and linocutting as he feels they are the best techniques to achieve traditional works. He has studied art in Cairns and Canberra, and has also illustrated a book called Kuiyu Mabaigal. The book is based on a story told to him by Mr. Aidan Laza of Badu Island. It is published by Magabala Books.

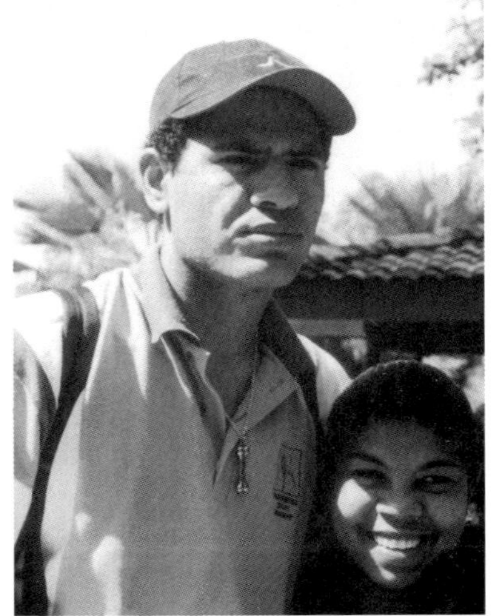

Matatia Warrior
THE ZUGUTIAM-THE SHARK OF ZUGU
Born on Thursday Island, Matatia is of Torres Strait Islander parentage. Matatia was inspired to undertake the Diploma in Visual Arts Course at the Cairns TAFE by his friend, the well known young artist Alick Tipoti. He plans to undertake university studies after completion of his diploma.

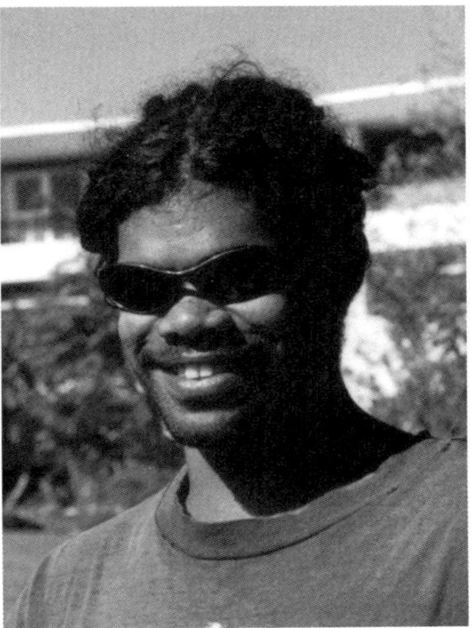

Sam Wason
PLATYPUS
Young artist Sam Wason has lived in Kuranda, a small village on the tablelands above Cairns all of his life. It is there, in the abundant surrounding rainforests and rivers, he discovered his love of animals, and the inspiration to paint and draw them. He has always had a special love for art. This interest was further developed by Sam completing a Visual Arts Course at the Cairns TAFE college.

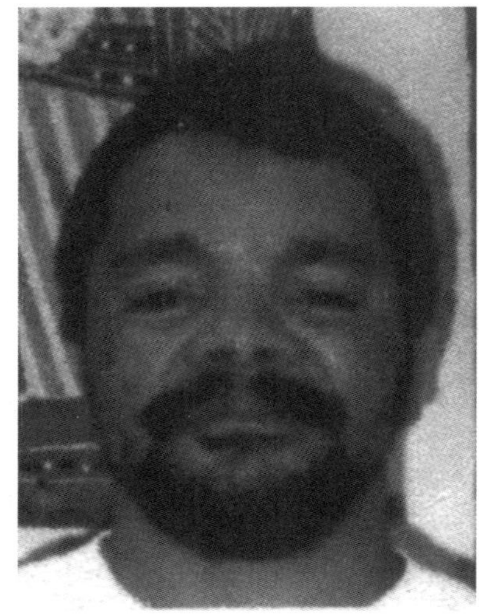

Colin Wightman
Creation Painting
Colin comes from a small Aboriginal community called Toomelah, situated on the border of Queensland and New South Wales. Toomelah means Aboriginal moving from place to place. He claims his ancestry from the Goomeroy Tribe of Northern NSW and uses many of the images of the flora and fauna of NSW in his paintings. In 1991 Colin enrolled in the Aboriginal and Torres Strait Islander Arts Associate Diploma Course at the Cairns College of TAFE, and graduated in 1992. He continued to paint and study, and in 1994 graduated from the TAFE with a certificate in Survival Skills for Artists, plus an Associate Diploma in Visual Arts. His artistic endeavours have included screen printing, painting two murals for the Jack Martin Centre for Aboriginal Sports at Toowoomba, held exhibitions in Cairns, Canberra, Brisbane, the Sydney museum, and continues to achieve his artistic and professional goals today.

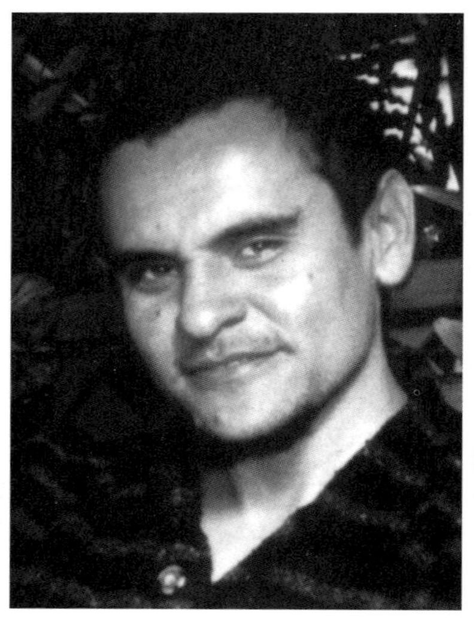

Andrew Williams
On the Lugger
Born in Cairns in 1970, Andrew has enjoyed an urban lifestyle surrounded by the tropical atmosphere of North Queensland. He credits his family for having shown him the respect and discipline needed to pursue his ambitions and goals throughout his life. Andrew regards himself as an urban artist, as he is not familiar with the real traditions and laws of his cultural heritage. He does however, feel a deep pride that he is able to draw on what he does know of his culture in his art. After completing high school Andrew undertook an Associate Diploma of Aboriginal and Torres Strait Islander Art at the Cairns TAFE. Following this, he later achieved a BA of Visual Art in Fine Art at the Queensland College of Art in Brisbane in 1993. Andrew has various teaching experience, is a member of three working committees, has been involved in twenty-seven exhibitions, undertaken fifteen commissions to date, and has had his art purchased for many private Australian and overseas collections. His artworks are also part of the Queensland Art Gallery collection, and the art collection of the Sydney Maritime Museum.

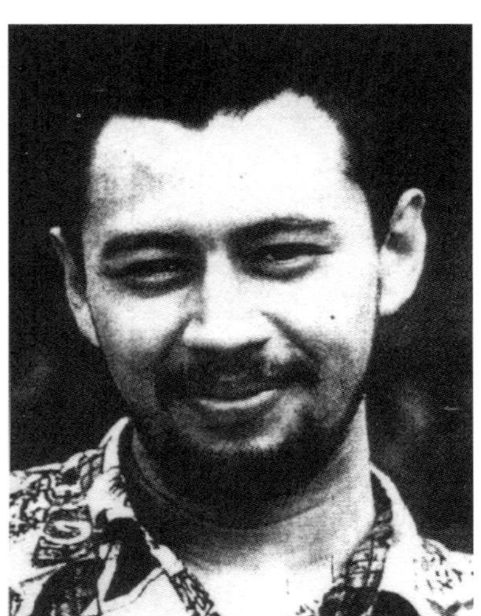

Brian Robinson

The Sea Gods have Awoken

Brian was born in 1973 and grew up in the idyllic tropical surroundings of the Torres Strait Islands. During this time he gained valuable knowledge and appreciation of the culture of his people, and was particularly influenced by the myths and legends of the Torres Strait and the traditional motifs and natural carving ability of the islanders. He is a multi-skilled contemporary artist whose practice includes painting, printmaking, ceramics, sculpture and design. His artwork is found in major Australian and international collections including the National Gallery of Victoria, the Queensland Art Gallery, Queensland Museum, the Jean-Marie Tjibaou Cultural Centre, New Caledonia, the Australian Embassy in the Philippines as well as a number of regional galleries and private collections. Brian's current work position is the first full-time Indigenous Curator with the Cairns Regional Gallery. In 1997-1998 Brian worked as co-curator with Tom Mosby to develop and present the Illan Pasin:Torres Strait Art (This is our way) touring exhibition. Since 1998 Brian has been a member of the Community Advisory Board of the Faculty of Aboriginal and Torres Strait Islander Studies at Cairns TAFE . He is a member of the Cairns City Council's Indigenous Reference Group, and his most significant appointment in 1999 as the youngest and first Torres Strait Islander was to the governing body of Queensland's Premier Visual Arts Organisation.

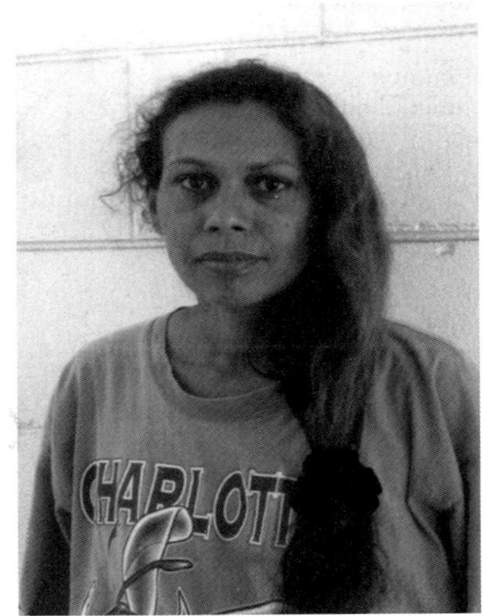

Wanjidari (Leanne Reid)

Hunting Dugong

Wanjidari is her tribal name and means 'White Flower'. Her father is from Lockhart River on Cape York and her mother is from Woorabinda in Central Queensland. A lot of her childhood was spent in both communities and the very different environments - coast and inland- have influenced the subjects she paints today. When she was 17, Wanjidari and a friend were on the way to Darwin when they heard about the art course that had just started at the Cairns TAFE. They decided to apply and were accepted for study the next year, 1985, and as Wanjidari says, she "has been painting ever since". Wanjidari possesses a highly distinctive and figurative style highlighted by a broad range of colour, unusual texture and form , and has developed a much sought after reputation with both private and public collectors. She has been involved in eight exhibitions and her work is featured in five public collections as well as numerous local and overseas private collections. Using traditional imagery, combined with contemporary mediums, Wanjidari's paintings capture in fine detail the culture and lifestyle of her ancestors. Often these works incorporate such themes as hunting and gathering of marine and bush foods, mens' corroborees and womens' ceremonies.